AF806404

International Law and the Global South

Perspectives from the Rest of the World

Series Editor

Leïla Choukroune, International Law and University Research, Portsmouth University, University House, Winston Churchill Ave, Portsmouth, UK

Editorial Board

Balveer Arora, Centre for Multilevel Federalism (CMF), Institute of Social Sciences, Delhi, India

Eros Roberto Grau, Faculty of Law, Universidade de São Paulo, São Paulo, Brazil

Denise Prevost, Department of International & European Law, Maastricht University, Maastricht, The Netherlands

Carlos Miguel Herrera, CY Cergy Paris University, CERGY, France

This book series aims to promote a complex vision of contemporary legal developments from the perspective of emerging or developing countries and/or authors integrating these elements into their approach. While focusing on today's law and international economic law in particular, it brings together contributions from, or influenced by, other social sciences disciplines. Written in both technical and non-technical language and addressing topics of contemporary importance to a general audience, the series will be of interest to legal researchers as well as non-lawyers. In referring to the "rest of the world", the book series puts forward new and alternative visions of today's law not only from emerging and developing countries, but also from authors who deliberately integrate this perspective into their thinking. The series approach is not only comparative, post-colonial or critical, but also truly universal in the sense that it places a plurality of well-informed visions at its center.

The Series

- Provides a truly global coverage of the world in reflecting cutting-edge developments and thinking in law and international law
- Focuses on the transformations of international and comparative law with an emphasis on international economic law (investment, trade and development)
- Welcomes contributions on comparative and/or domestic legal evolutions

Tonny Raymond Kirabira

Transnational Networks and Justice in the Global South

Comparative Examination of African and Asian Contexts

Springer

Tonny Raymond Kirabira
Department of Law, Justice and Policing,
Royal Docks School of Business and Law
University of East London
London, UK

ISSN 2510-1420 ISSN 2510-1439 (electronic)
International Law and the Global South
ISBN 978-981-95-3136-3 ISBN 978-981-95-3137-0 (eBook)
https://doi.org/10.1007/978-981-95-3137-0

© The Editor(s) (if applicable) and The Author(s), under exclusive license to Springer Nature Singapore Pte Ltd. 2025

This work is subject to copyright. All rights are solely and exclusively licensed by the Publisher, whether the whole or part of the material is concerned, specifically the rights of translation, reprinting, reuse of illustrations, recitation, broadcasting, reproduction on microfilms or in any other physical way, and transmission or information storage and retrieval, electronic adaptation, computer software, or by similar or dissimilar methodology now known or hereafter developed.
The use of general descriptive names, registered names, trademarks, service marks, etc. in this publication does not imply, even in the absence of a specific statement, that such names are exempt from the relevant protective laws and regulations and therefore free for general use.
The publisher, the authors and the editors are safe to assume that the advice and information in this book are believed to be true and accurate at the date of publication. Neither the publisher nor the authors or the editors give a warranty, expressed or implied, with respect to the material contained herein or for any errors or omissions that may have been made. The publisher remains neutral with regard to jurisdictional claims in published maps and institutional affiliations.

This Springer imprint is published by the registered company Springer Nature Singapore Pte Ltd.
The registered company address is: 152 Beach Road, #21-01/04 Gateway East, Singapore 189721, Singapore

If disposing of this product, please recycle the paper.

Foreword

Contemporary developments in international law and relations continue to elicit concerns about the relevance and legitimacy of global justice especially within an increasingly polarised global order. Perspectives from emerging or developing countries are easily dwarfed by stronger voices from powerful States in the Global North, but also organisations. This book uniquely explores the impact of transnational networks and justice in the Global South.

The author's wide professional and academic experiences in Uganda, United States and Europe add interesting dimensions to the book's findings on the impact of transnational networks and NGOs on the work of institutions like the International Criminal Court. The in-depth comparative examination of transitional justice in Uganda and Myanmar shows the variance of global justice strategies and outcomes within States in the Global South. Ultimately, there are new insights into the construction and implementation of global justice across nuanced contexts.

The book's analysis and findings mirror my own work over the past four decades across the spaces of global justice. Between 1995 and 2002, I actively participated in sessions of the Preparatory Commission for the International Criminal Court and the Rome Diplomatic Conference on the Establishment of the International Court. I participated as an expert in the NGO Coalition for the International Criminal Court. I can testify without fear of contradiction that to a great measure the Court owes much of its existence and effectiveness to the indefatigable efforts of the Coalition and of its numerous members, national and international. Indeed, some innovative provisions of the Rome Statute, such as those relating to gender justice and to victim participation trace their provenance from the NGOs. In this regard, it is noteworthy that the Rules of Procedure and Evidence of the International Criminal Tribunal for the former Yugoslavia (ICTY) were largely based on the draft of the Lawyers' Committee for Human Rights, an NGO. Back to the ICC, its Statute came in force much earlier than anticipated, again, thanks to the world-wide ratification campaign by the NGOs.

As judge of the ICC and of the Special Tribunal for Lebanon (STL), I witnessed firsthand the value of the NGOs' contribution to their investigative and trial processes, including the NGOs' *amicus curiae* submissions. Again, working as a trial observer on Amnesty International's missions in several countries, I had the opportunity to observe the catalytic role of transnational networks in ensuring justice. Equally important, because of the limited financial and human resources available for global justice institutions, NGOs have stepped in and filled the gap, especially in relation to community outreach and victims' support. All this and more, lend credence to the book's thrust on the immense contribution of transnational networks to Justice in the Global South.

The book paves ways for actors in international law to make transitional justice more localised and targeted for the relevant contexts in a manner that dominates the traditional hegemonic structures of global governance. It stimulates illuminating conversation for students, academics, NGOs and practitioners in a range of areas like international law, human rights, transitional justice, sociology and political affairs.

Maryland, USA Professor Daniel David Ntanda Nsereko

Acknowledgements

My intellectual work on the design, shaping and writing of this project have been greatly driven by the support I have received from academic colleagues, esteemed academics, practitioners and civil society. I am immensely grateful to Prof. Leïla Choukroune for offering her diligent attention and support towards this project and Dr. Panos Kapotas for the much-needed support and advice, even before I started my doctoral research at the University of Portsmouth.

Special thanks to Dr. Line Engbo Gissel for the great advice on the theoretical aspects of the project and also performing the time-consuming tasks of reviewing my ethics process and reading drafts of the work. Thanks also to Prof. Pádraig McAuliffe, Sir Howard Morrison KC and Prof Belen Olmos Giupponi for the comments and suggestions on this work. Tremendous thanks to Prof. Mikkel Jarle Christensen for the useful comments on portions of the work and hosting me at iCourts-The Danish National Research Foundation's Centre of Excellence for International Courts and Governance.

This research would not be possible without the generosity of my interviewees spread out across 4 continents. I am grateful to Jessica Olney and Lucy Okwera for the assistance with the interviews.

In the course of my research, I have been fortunate to participate in a host of both local and international seminars and conferences, where I received immeasurable feedback on the project. These include the University of Portsmouth Business and Law School Research & Innovation conference 2020; the International Criminal Justice–A Counter Hegemonic Project? workshop 2021 organised by Humboldt University in Berlin, Freie University in Berlin and the Berlin University Alliance; the Narrating Transitional Justice: History, Memory, Poetics and Politics international conference organised by McMaster University, Canada; the Transforming Evidence and Proof in International Criminal Trials conference at University of Copenhagen, Denmark, 2021; the International Conference on Religion and Culture in Conflict and Peace 2022 at University of Winchester; the EuPRA Conference 2022 at Tampere University, Finland; the 2022 Global Meeting on Law & Society Annual Conference in Lisbon, Portugal; the Research Writing Workshop organised by the Raoul Wallenberg Institute of Human Rights and Humanitarian Law in Nairobi, Kenya in

2022; and the Socio-Legal Studies Association (SLSA) Annual Conference 2024 conference in Portsmouth.

Finally, the emotional support and encouragement from my family pushed me to pursue this research but has also kept me going. My mother, Gertrude Nyanzi has always encouraged and supported me throughout my academic and professional journey, knowing the value of hard work, determination, excellence and above all—the faith in our God.

Contents

Introduction

1 Introduction

Experiencing first-hand how law works in action—specifically how formal ideas and practices of law collide with more traditional ideas of justice—is a key motivation for writing this book. I look back to my experiences and practical insights in Uganda that preceded my legal and academic career. As a final year law student at Uganda Christian University, I experienced the difficulty of implementing formal laws within pluralist societies. During the Clinical Legal Education field work, I worked under the auspices of International Justice Mission (IJM), an international non-governmental organisation (NGO) with offices in Uganda. I spent a week training local leaders on issues related to access to justice for women and children affected by violence. Whilst our work focused on promoting justice through criminal justice and formal judicial avenues, the language of alternative dispute resolution and reconciliation featured prominently in the discussions with the local leaders. As such, the most common understanding of justice at the local level was non-retributive, facilitated by the local leaders and elders within the communities.

The understanding of justice at these local levels, as I noted, was also based on wider factors such as social inequalities and armed conflicts within the societies. The fact that the societies had experienced war in recent years contributed to the leaders' reconciliatory approaches to formal disputes. As such, I developed an interest in examining the justice-making processes in post-conflict contexts. More importantly, experiencing the tension between the formal judicial and traditional reconciliation processes provided the impetus for me to think about the production and delivery of justice within post-war contexts, and the work of NGOs in this regard. From my experiences, a clear understanding of such overlaps and tensions between law-on-the-books and law-in-action requires empirical inquiries in specific post-war or mass atrocity contexts. Overall, my experiences in Uganda demonstrate that solving

This chapter has some overlaps with my doctoral thesis.

© The Author(s), under exclusive license to Springer Nature Singapore Pte Ltd. 2025

T. R. Kirabira, *Transnational Networks and Justice in the Global South*, International Law and the Global South, https://doi.org/10.1007/978-981-95-3137-0_1

complex legal problems within specific contexts requires looking beyond the formal legal rules, to the social relationships surrounding the affected people and disputes. This view is certainly not novel, but rather an accentuation of sociological jurisprudence and approaches from criminology, sociology and anthropology.[1] Secondly, the experience of working with IJM ignited a keen interest in the work of NGOs, in the field of justice. NGO work has a strong impact on law-in-action and shapes the way in which laws are implemented and understood at the local levels.

This book contributes new insights into the construction and implementation of global justice across different constituencies. In particular, it investigates the impact of transnational networks and NGOs on redress mechanisms for mass atrocities and violence, using the scholarly field of transitional justice. By utilising this scholarly lens, the book is able to draw into a wide range of discussions and mechanisms aimed at addressing mass violence and armed conflict in the Global South. Whilst the book is broadly framed within the scholarly field of transitional justice, it draws on two branches of international law—International Human Rights Law (IHRL) and International Criminal Law (ICL). It also benefits from scholarship in the field of international relations to explicate the legitimacy and institutional power of NGOs and international courts. These disciplines are converged through the literature review and analysis.

2 Why Explore Transnational Networks and Justice in the Global South?

The aim of this book is to explore how transnational networks influence justice in the Global South, particularly their impact on transitional justice in the different contexts. There is no standard definition of transnational networks, as the term may be interpreted differently depending on the scholarly background or research focus. The seminal work by Margaret Keck and Kathryn Sikkink is quite elaborate—defining transnational advocacy networks to include 'those actors working internationally on an issue, who are bound together by shared values, a common discourse, and dense exchanges of information and services'.[2] In looking at the ways in which transnational networks impact on the practice and implementation of Global Justice, it is vital that we explore how they link with each other. The most practical way to draw these linkages is using the 'boomerang' pattern of influence to understand how Global Justice spaces are promoted and implemented, especially in countries where the domestic state actors are unable or unwilling to act.[3] Transnational networks are big spheres of influence among NGOs and state actors at local, domestic, regional and

[1] For further considerations, see generally Ehrlich (1916), Hunt (1978), Christensen and Levi (2018), and Clarke (2019).

[2] Keck and Sikkink (1998, p. 23; 1999, p. 89).

[3] Keck and Sikkink (1999, pp. 1–38).

international levels. The mode of influence by transnational networks is summarised by Margaret Keck and Kathryn Sikkink:

1. issue creation and attention/agenda setting;
2. influence on discursive positions of states and regional and international organisations;
3. influence on institutional procedures;
4. influence on policy change in 'target actors' which may be states, international or regional organisations, or private actors like the Nestle' corporation;
5. influence on state behaviour.[4]

Ultimately, under the boomerang pattern or model, domestic NGO actors interact with international actors through the transnational networks in a way that affects state behaviour on Justice and also influences the work of Global Justice institutions like the ICC. One may wonder whether transnational networks are not vehicles or enablers of dominant norms from the Global North. Indeed, looking broadly within the paradigm of global governance, it is important to be mindful about the power balances between Global South-based NGOs and transnational actors in the Global North, if one is to comprehensively assess the legitimacy of Global Justice institutions.[5] The last chapter of the book will address these pertinent issues and engage in deeper reflections on the nuances of Global Justice making in general.

Transitional justice in this context relates to a range of redress mechanisms to address gross violations of human rights following periods of authoritarian rule or armed conflict. The framework of transitional justice and larger debates on elements of accountability are discussed in detail in chapter "Navigating Justice, Transitional Justice and Global North–South Dimensions". As will be discussed, the existing theoretical and empirical research on transitional justice offers useful insights on local perceptions of globalised justice institutions like the International Criminal Court (ICC). However, the literature lacks a comprehensive and rigorous assessment of the role of transnational networks and NGOs within these often-contested forms and sites of justice. Specifically, the literature lacks a satisfactory explanation of why and how NGOs engage in transitional justice processes within specific contexts. The book utilises two country case studies as examples to illustrate how NGOs contribute to the legitimisation of both domestic and international transitional justice mechanisms.

The extant literature on NGOs and transitional justice is discussed in detail in chapter "Navigating Justice, Transitional Justice and Global North–South Dimensions", specifically Sect. 7. By exploring the work of NGOs in transitional justice, the book will confront the practical challenges of implementing globalised justice, for example, through the ICC. More generally, political scientists view the interventions of institutions like the ICC with skepticism. Tim Murithi, a transitional justice scholar from the Global South argues that international criminal justice is

---

[4] Keck and Sikkink (1999, p. 98).

[5] See Kennedy (1997, pp. 551–552) on comparative law and international governance. The later entails aspects of norm generation and enforcement.

deployed by powerful Western countries to subjugate those in the Global South in what he terms 'judicial imperialism'.[6] Third World Approaches to International Law illuminate ways in which globalised justice is subservient to Western countries.[7] The predominant geographic focus of international justice interventions on situations in the Global South permeates power imbalances, or as some critics suggest, racialised justice.[8] Whilst international law primarily deals with States, it is important not to lose sight of non-State actors working through transnational networks and NGOs.

There is a need for systematic explanation on how NGOs impact the work of transitional justice institutions. I will show that even though scholars have examined the effectiveness and legitimacy of such institutions, relatively little attention has been given to how NGOs impact their work, within the framework of transitional justice. This book makes a robust examination on transnational networks with new empirical data in respect to two case studies. The thrust of the argument is that transnational networks and NGOs either enhance or reduce the legitimacy of transitional justice mechanisms.

The concept of legitimacy will be used to analyse the way in which transitional justice is implemented, with a detailed discussion in chapter "Navigating Justice, Transitional Justice and Global North–South Dimensions" of the book, where Sect. 7 will show the link between transitional justice and legitimacy. These discussions are in line with the central question of how transnational networks impact justice in the Global South, and the legitimacy of transitional justice processes. This question triggers a robust exploration of the work of NGOs, leading to an evaluation of their work in transitional justice. More precisely, it allows the use of empirical methods to analyse the impact of transitional justice across different sites of justice. This book thus examines the question analytically and empirically, using the theory of legitimacy, as one of the ways in which to explain the power dynamics of global justice and institutions. The book will offer significant contributions to the existing literature on Global Justice and legitimacy in transitional justice, with country case specific examples of Uganda and Myanmar.

3 Doctrinal, Socio-Legal Legal Research and Comparative Legal Methodologies

This book combines doctrinal and socio-legal empirical research, in order to explore how transnational networks influence justice in the Global South, particularly their impact on transitional justice in the different contexts. Doctrine is defined to mean 'a synthesis of rules, principles, norms, interpretative guidelines and values, which explains, makes coherent or justifies a segment of the law as part of a larger system

[6] Murithi (2020, pp. 1–240).

[7] See for instance Viljoen et al. (2022, pp. 1–358) on important contributions and approaches by African States to international law.

[8] See for instance López (2023, pp. 211–228).

of law'.[9] On the other hand, socio-legal research relates to 'the examination of how law, legal phenomena and/or phenomena affected by law and the legal system occur in the world, interact with each other and impact upon those who are touched by them'.[10] As will be discussed in this chapter, transitional justice is not simply about the normative work of judicial institutions. It is more about practices, discourses and interactions within the communities that these institutions serve. It is important to set out that my personal research position is inclined towards a social-legal approach to legal research, as law should seek to serve the society where it operates. Against the backdrop of this method, the book gains from interdisciplinary contributions, using qualitative methods to answer the defined set of aims.

The book thus strives to contribute to the evolving shift from traditional international legal scholarship towards the empirical study of international law. A common aspect of socio-legal studies is the use of Empirical Legal Research (ELR), which involves the systematic application of qualitative methods. Critiques of ELR argue that it is reductive and conservative.[11] Nonetheless, it is vital to step out of the traditional doctrinal research approach, in order to understand how the law affects society, but also how NGOs affect law and policy implementation. Social-legal scholarship enables legal researchers to benefit from approaches associated with other disciplines, whilst engaging with their empirical aspects.[12]

As a lawyer, the use of ELR made it necessary for me to consider theoretical and methodological approaches from other disciplines. This is vital in examining the normative aspects of transitional justice and the impacts they create within the communities. This method is particularly useful in analysing the role of international law in global governance.[13] As Shaffer and Ginsburg argue, 'Empirical scholarship provides a set of tools to refine understandings of institutional design and practice so as to enhance international legal institutions' effectiveness'.[14] Whereas doctrinal research uses legal doctrine to ask what the law is on a particular issue, ELR addresses developments in the 'real (social) world' or law in action.[15] This research project is perfectly suited for ELR as the primary unit of analysis pertains to the work of NGOs. This resonates with the conceptualisation of ELR as a critical methodology for examining the work of institutions in the legal field, inquiring 'What they do, how they do it, what the consequences are of their work'.[16] The emphasis of the book remains the influence of transnational networks on justice in the Global South, under the remit of transitional justice.

An explanation on the need for comparative studies within the context of Transitional justice and NGO work is necessary. There have been extensive studies on the

[9] Leeuw and Schmeet (2016, p. 3).

[10] For a more detailed analysis see Webley (2019, p. 58).

[11] See generally Shaffer and Ginsburg (2012).

[12] Siems and Mac Síthigh (2012, pp. 651–655).

[13] Shaffer and Ginsburg (2012, p. 5).

[14] Shaffer and Ginsburg (2012, p. 5).

[15] Leeuw and Schmeet (2016, p. 3).

[16] Leeuw and Schmeet (2016, p. 3).

impact of NGOs on Transitional Justice within particular Global South contexts—from the Khulumani Support Group in South Africa to Mothers of Plaza de Mayo (*Madres de Plaza de Mayo*) in Argentina.[17] For a more comprehensive analysis of their impact in the Global South, this book takes the approach of Comparative Legal Methodology and study entailing 'the construction of a realistic research design based on empirical research questions about human rights events or performances, and where observation of a relationship between dependent and independent variables can be analyzed and inferences drawn'.[18]

The comparative approach is used to examine the variation and similarities in the work of transnational NGO networks, and their impact on transitional justice. Within human rights research, the application of comparative study approaches regarding State or non-State behaviour necessitates the use of socio-legal methods.[19] This methodology is an appropriate design for this book, since the objects of analysis are NGOs that are assessed and compared across different sites of justice in order to answer the research questions. As such, comparing and contrasting transitional justice processes in more than one case study allows an in-depth examination of transnational networks in the Global Justice spaces, particularly how NGOs (de)ligitimatise transitional justice.

There is a growing interest in the use of comparative legal methods in legal scholarship.[20] This line of research is also attributed to the cosmopolitan nature of contemporary legal research, in an increasingly globalised legal environment.[21] Comparative legal studies allow for the investigation of legal phenomena across geographical levels—local and global—making distinctions between legal traditions and cultures to inform global perspectives.[22] Comparative legal methodology is therefore well-suited to explore the impact of NGO actors in transitional justice.

Similarly, a comparison of empirical evidence is possible, following a set of questions that were carefully designed for participants across the case studies.[23] More specifically, the book searches for comparative sequences (processes and patterns) within the work of transnational networks and NGOs: how do they (de)ligitimatise transitional justice? The search for sequences within the field of transitional justice

---

[17] For detailed analysis see Stan and Nedelsky (2013, pp. 281–285) and Brankovic et al. (2020).

[18] Andreassen (2017, p. 225).

[19] Andreassen (2017, p. 225).

[20] Prominent law journals include the International and Comparative Law Quarterly, American Journal of Comparative Law, and Maastricht Journal of European and Comparative Law. Similarly, legal scholars encourage comparative legal research, for example, the Society of Legal Scholars (SLS). Similar attributes can be seen from the work of research institutions like the Max Plank Institute for Comparative Public Law and International Law.

[21] Paris (2016, p. 40).

[22] Twining (1999, p. 242).

[23] Andreassen (2017, pp. 232–236).

calls for comparative analysis.[24] Hence, as argued by Andreassen, a study that examines the interaction between domestic and international actors necessitates the application of theoretical perspectives to comparative empirical studies.[25] In line with Andreassen's recommendations, a comparative methodology adds great value to this book, if we are to understand and examine the strategies of NGO actors.[26]

A qualitative comparison of NGO strategies for transitional justice in Uganda and Myanmar is well-suited to closing the gaps within the scholarship that focuse on single case studies. Besides exploring the linkages in Global Justice spaces and transitional justice across different contexts, the design also allows the book to contribute to the emerging comparative studies on the domestic impact of globalised judicial institutions.[27] Moreover, comparative examination between the two case studies will help policy makers when implementing similar approaches across cases—for example, global justice interventions. In other words, the book also tests the validity of globalised forms of justice across different contexts, examining whether global justice institutions fulfil the expectations of their key constituents, in this case, local NGOs and victims' representatives.

It is important to explain the rationale for the two case studies, Myanmar and Uganda. The book uses the case studies of Uganda and Myanmar as prisms through which to explore the influence of transnational NGO networks on Global Justice, particularly the role of NGOs in transitional justice. A theoretically informed sampling technique was utilised to select the case of Myanmar, in addition to that of Uganda. This technique involves the identification of key traits that influence the research phenomenon, for example, level of economic development, geographical location, legal tradition and customs.[28] Therefore, both theoretical and practical considerations informed the choices of Uganda and Myanmar. Theoretically, the two countries, as former British colonies, share common traits in respect to the colonial history and development of the legal systems. Besides the predominant common law legal systems, the countries are situated in two regions of the Global South—Asia and Africa. As such, the book is able to make a claim for the reconceptualisation of transitional justice in the Global South, based on the outcomes of the two cases. Comparing the two cases helps to illustrate that transitional justice is not a monolith, as it is open to new interpretations, but also contestations across specific contexts in the Global South.

Regarding the practical considerations, my experience as a lawyer in Uganda provides a good knowledge base about the country's transitional justice process. Similarly, I was able to map out the relevant NGO actors involved in the different transitional justice initiatives at both domestic and international levels. Secondly, the start of this research at the end of 2019 coincided with the ICC and ICJ interventions in Myanmar. My work as a Visiting Professional at the ICC in 2020 provided

[24] Andreassen (2017, pp. 232–236).

[25] Andreassen (2017, p. 229).

[26] Andreassen (2017, p. 223).

[27] See generally Mieth (2018), Horovitz (2013) and De Vos (2020).

[28] See Linos et al. (2018, p. 42) and Linos (2015, pp. 479–480).

another layer to understanding how the Hague-based justice institutions and NGOs might contribute towards justice for the Rohingya in Myanmar. More importantly, the new international interventions for the Rohingya situation in Myanmar meant that I could closely follow the proceedings in The Hague, specifically, the interventions of NGOs. Succinctly, my own experience and the contemporary developments offered a reflective environment for me to think about these specific case studies.

The two case studies vary somewhat, in terms of the nature of atrocities and democratisation. The Ugandan case is focused on redress mechanisms for victims of the two-decade war in Northern Uganda, as will be discussed in detail in chapter "The Case of Uganda: A Fusion of Domestic Transitional Justice and International Criminal Law". The Myanmar case rotates largely on the situation of the Rohingya in Northern Rakhine. Comparing these two cases adds an important layer to the discussions on transnational networks, NGOs and legitimacy of transitional justice within nuanced contexts. The discussions will illustrate that the concept of transitional justice might not seem a concept directly applicable to Myanmar, except in the limited sense of potential. Nonetheless, the findings will reveal the vital role of transnational networks and NGOs in promoting awareness of the need for and securing justice for atrocities committed against the Rohingya in general.

The bulk of the scholarly literature in this area focuses on single case studies, where countries are transitioning from armed conflict to peace. Therefore, focusing on these two case studies in Africa and Asia allows me to deeply explore how transnational networks influence justice in the Global South, adding a key contribution to the debates on how transitional justice is framed. It also enables the use of the analytical framework of legitimacy, across two different case studies in different continents. It is important to note that the basic unit of examination and analysis in the two countries is NGOs. As such, Uganda and Myanmar are ideal contexts for examining the work of transnational NGO networks in transitional justice, given the interventions from the international community.

3.1 Data Collection and Analysis Approaches

In terms of data collection, the book utilised two methods: document review and qualitative interviews. The major source of data in this book is information from secondary sources. Primary stakeholder interviews are also used as a supplementary source of data to validate the secondary information. Besides academic literature, secondary data was obtained from Court documents, websites, NGO reports and media organisations. In order to validate the secondary information and gather additional data, I had planned to conduct study trips to Uganda, Myanmar and Bangladesh. Unfortunately, this was not possible due to the COVID-19 disruptions in 2021. Similarly, it was not possible to conduct structured and comprehensive interviews in these locations due to political instability. Due to these potential risks in conducting this research, an alternative method was adopted: elite interviewing.

The participants were elites on account of their connection with and knowledge on transitional justice-related aspects, for example, NGO advocates, lawyers and independent researchers. Elite interviewing, a methodology derived from political science, generally targets individuals with privileged positions in society, with more influence on outcomes than the general public.[29] A lot of work has already been done in international law and the scholarly field of transitional justice, in respect to elite interviewing, but also their impact on global justice.[30] Besides helping in interpreting documents and reports, elite interviewing was useful in explaining the outcome of decisions on aspects of justice. Contacts with particular individuals also provided access to a wide range of networks within the context of transitional justice, for example, lawyers and judges.

Semi-structured interviews were carried out, using technological means of Skype and Zoom. Salmon's Qualitative e-Research framework was used as a tool for organising and designing the interviews.[31] My positionality as a Ugandan with a legal background helped in shaping the interview questions and in identification of the participants. However, it also raised a risk of bias in relation to the Myanmar case study. An awareness of the risk of bias was important from the start, since this book makes a comparative analysis of transnational networks and NGO actors in two case studies—Uganda and Myanmar. To minimise the risk of bias towards the Ugandan case, the interviews were based on pre-designed interview guides.

The selected participants represented NGOs that were directly involved with transitional justice in the case studies. Whilst a few identified their work as primarily transitional justice, many had elements of transitional justice within their work. The lawyers, ICC officials, victims' representatives, academics, human rights activists and journalists were directly involved with Uganda's and Myanmar's transitional justice. In addition to these key informants, additional elite actors were referred to me by other interviewees. These included judges, academics and individuals working with the United Nations and Government agencies. It was important to distinguish the nature of information required from the elite actors—those speaking in their official capacities; and those interviewed as primary participants based on their practice and expertise.

Semi-structured interviewing helped to ensure consistency in approach and issues covered. I asked open-ended questions whilst probing the respondents for clarity. Aware of the limitations of this approach and the different levels of individual confidence and articulation, I was flexible and altered the sequence of questions.[32] Flexibility is a cardinal element in elite interviewing.[33] As such, the questions differed slightly depending on the participant's institutional category and interaction with the transitional justice processes. Each elite interview with an NGO representative began with the following question: 'Can you tell me about your organisation and its

[29] Richards (1996, p. 199).

[30] See for example, McEvoy (2006), Burgis-Kasthala (2019) and McAuliffe (2019).

[31] See Salmons (2016).

[32] For more details, see Arthur and Nazroo (2003, p. 111).

[33] Richards (1996, p. 202).

justice activities?' The respondents were able to elucidate on the goals and strategies of their organisations.

Research ethics also informed the way I conducted the elite interviews. Whilst the method of doctrinal legal analysis does not pose risks of harm to the participants, the ELR raises critical issues regarding ethics. Therefore, ethics was an integral aspect of this research. As observed by human rights scholars, researchers should be cautious when dealing with participants in respect to situations of armed conflict or authoritarian rule, in order to avoid indirect harm.[34] Based on ethical considerations, I maintained confidentiality and anonymity as the standard approaches, with very few exceptions. In terms of duration, the interviews lasted thirty to forty-five minutes. They were all conducted in English, as all the elite participants were conversant with the language. Hand notes were taken during the interviews and later transcribed.

The data analysis was approached in a structured manner, with the book employing process tracing techniques—an approach widely used by qualitative and interdisciplinary researchers to document sequences and processes.[35] In theory, the technique 'involves looking at evidence within an individual case, or a temporally and spatially bound instance of a specified phenomenon, to derive and/or test alternative explanations of that case'.[36] The technique is useful when identifying causal mechanisms and outcomes following the implementation of international norms of human rights at domestic levels.[37] With respect to this book, process tracing involved looking at the empirical evidence for each of the case studies, to explore the influence of transnational networks on Global Justice, explaining the choice and acceptance of transitional justice approaches among different NGOs. In relation to legitimacy, process tracing enabled me to analyse how such NGO work (de)legitimises transitional justice, based on their engagements with institutions like the ICC. Process tracing is thus a useful methodological approach to understanding the relationship between NGOs and global justice institutions across local, domestic and global levels.

Two modes of analysis are used in this book: Grounded theory and Critical discourse analysis (CDA). Grounded theory entails the 'developing of theory as the research proceeds, rather than testing a hypothesis posited in advance'.[38] After the data collection, the NGOs were differentiated and classified within two categories: (1) judicially oriented NGOs that focus on court mechanisms, including providing advice and assistance to victims, and (2) research and advocacy-oriented NGOs.[39] CDA is an analytical mindset that uses language as a social phenomenon, to analyse ideologies and power asymmetries of institutions,[40] mostly by scholars in ICL, International Relations and Linguistics. In the scholarly field of international

[34] Ulrich (2017, p. 199).

[35] For details see Davidson (2021) and Gissel (2015, p. 431).

[36] Bennett (2008, p. 704).

[37] Andreassen (2017, p. 236).

[38] For more details see Webley (2010, p. 941).

[39] Haddad (2012, p. 132). Haddad draws a clear framework for assessing NGO participation at international courts.

[40] Potts and Kjær (2016, p. 528).

criminal justice, CDA is useful when investigating the impact of power, ideology and discursive practices of key actors, and how they operate to theorise and conceptualise objects, for example, victims.[41] CDA is also ideal for exploring the legitimacy of international criminal justice, revealing how notions of justice and accountability are constructed during the course of international criminal prosecutions.[42] As such, CDA is considered as a useful method when examining the impact of NGOs in transitional justice, and how they (de)legitimise its institutions.[43]

In this book, the focus was on the discourse on Global Justice and transitional justice approaches and their implementation in general. The approach was guided by the question of how transitional justice mechanisms are discursively constructed and manifested in the work of NGOs. Empirical legal scholars view discourse as 'socially constructed and as a way in which the speaker or writer can establish a particular version of the world'.[44] In this vein, the method of discourse analysis was close textual analysis of NGO reports and transcripts from interviews. The primary and secondary data were critically analysed to identify relevant recurrent themes. The themes related to (1) beliefs about the current international justice interventions, and (2) beliefs about what is needed to provide justice for the victims. The aim was to reveal how their ideas of transitional justice shape the current processes. This approach also helped to locate shifts in transnational networks and NGO framing of different interventions, creating an understanding of the power dynamics that transitional justice produces.

3.2 Outline of the Book

This book is structured in eight chapters. This chapter which is the introduction has highlighted the reasons that motivated my research, explaining the aims and objectives of this book. It started by setting out my positionality, which explains the book's aims and objectives. It also explained the choice of methodology, design and data collection process, demonstrating how they informed the creation of this research project. It briefly touched on the theory of legitimacy, which will be utilised to analyse the role of NGOs in transitional justice.

Chapter "Navigating Justice, Transitional Justice and Global North–South Dimensions" explores the conceptual framework of the book under the scholarly field of transitional justice. It starts with preliminary discussions on legal theories of justice that underpin the normative foundation of transitional justice, as a starting point for analysing the contemporary critique of elements like punitive justice and liberalism. More broadly, the chapter explores critical discourse and practice within

41 See for example Fletcher (2015, pp. 306–307).

42 See Glasius and Meijers (2012, p. 233).

43 Palmer et al. (2013, p. 13).

44 Webley (2019, p. 940).

transitional justice, highlighting a gap between Global North and Global South understandings of aspects like retribution. It also discusses the normative boundaries of ICL, making a case for examining transnational networks and NGO engagement with global mechanisms like the ICC. More importantly, the chapter introduces the analytical framework of the book—the theory of legitimacy—in order to explore how transnational networks and NGOs (de)legitimise transitional justice.

Chapter "The Case of Uganda: A Fusion of Domestic Transitional Justice and International Criminal Law" begins the shift from doctrine to practice, introducing the first country case study: Uganda. The aim is to explore the state of transitional justice in Uganda. It starts with a historical analysis of the Northern Uganda situation, to set the stage for analysing the various transitional justice mechanisms: amnesty, traditional justice and formal criminal accountability. In doing so, it highlights the tensions surrounding the application of traditional justice mechanisms and formal justice mechanisms like the ICC intervention and prosecution. In tracing the cultural and social narratives around justice and reconciliation, the chapter highlights the difficulties faced in relying on formal judicial mechanisms. The central subjects of the discussions are the victims of the war in Northern Uganda. Based on the existing laws, policies and contemporary discussions, I argue that Uganda is still a State under transition. As the title of the chapter indicates, the case of Uganda reflects a unique fusion of domestic transitional justice and ICL.

Chapter "Actor-Oriented Analysis of Accountability Mechanisms in Uganda" builds on the analysis in the preceding chapter in order to examine how transnational networks and NGOs (de)legitimise transitional justice. It begins with a historical analysis of the Ugandan case at the ICC, highlighting the salient role of different actors and how they relate with the victims. The chapter maps out the roles of different actors in the establishment and functioning of the domestic war crimes prosecution and trial. The core of the analysis is based on empirical data on the practice and discourse of NGOs, revealing their impact in the contested transitional justice processes. More specifically, I reveal key dimensions of NGO work and engagement with international criminal justice through their victim-oriented work, and technical and capacity-building initiatives around the Courts. Based on the analysis, I argue that NGOs greatly enhanced the legitimacy of the ICC and the domestic war crimes tribunal in Uganda.

Chapter "Achieving Transitional Justice in Myanmar: Between Accountability and National Reconciliation" turns to the other country case study: Myanmar. It starts with an exploration of the ethno-political history and process of democratisation, in order to understand the nature of democratic transition in Myanmar. Central to these discussions are the contemporary issues surrounding race and identity in Myanmar. The chapter will not set out to show Myanmar as a country under a definite form of transitional justice. Rather, it will aim to set the stage for exploring the prospects of transitional justice, in line with the country's history and contemporary developments. In analysing the dynamics of Myanmar's transition to democracy, I show that the high level of militarisation in the country is a critical barrier towards meaningful transition, be it from authoritarianism to democracy, or armed conflict to peace. The core of the chapter is on the Rohingya Question. A range of transitional justice mechanisms aimed at providing justice for the Rohingya will be explored, showing the gaps in implementation and challenges for non-State actors involved in such processes. The discussions on the process of democratisation in Myanmar, as will be shown, have direct repercussions concerning redress mechanisms for the Rohingya, within the context of transitional justice. As the title of the chapter indicates, transitional justice in Myanmar entails a compromise between accountability and national reconciliation. The chapter will pave way for a more comprehensive examination of the different transitional justice mechanisms at the international level.

Chapter "Mapping NGO Work in Myanmar: Impact of Transnational NGO Networks" is hinged on these questions: What is the role of transnational networks in achieving transitional justice for the Rohingya? How do NGOs impact on the legitimacy of the existing justice mechanisms? The chapter provides a comprehensive and critical examination of NGO engagement with transitional justice within the context of the Rohingya. It also opens the empirical part of the Myanmar case study, mapping a transnational network of international NGOs and Rohingya in the diaspora. More specifically, it critically analyses the different NGO actors involved in the Rohingya cases—the ICC Investigation into the Bangladesh/Myanmar situation, the International Court of Justice case and the universal jurisdiction case in Argentina. I show that whilst the cases in The Hague are considered as vital in the quest for accountability and respect for rights in Myanmar, they are not in themselves the only viable alternatives for transitional justice, as illuminated in NGO practice and discourse. Crucially, I argue that transnational NGO networks have enhanced the interventions of The Hague-based institutions, before the Rohingya victims. In doing so, I will pave the way for analysing how such global mechanisms could influence hegemonic structures of global governance under the purview of transitional justice.

Chapter "Comparing Uganda and Myanmar Contexts: Challenges in Localising Transitional Justice" synthesises the findings from both case studies under two paradigms. Firstly, it makes a comparative analysis of the nature of transitions in both countries and the impact they have on transitional justice. Secondly, it also makes important distinctions between the two case studies in respect to the nature of the ICC intervention and proceedings. The analysis is particularly relevant when examining transitional justice within the context of mass displacement. For instance, I show how transitional justice actors could contribute to the resettlement of conflict-affected communities, based on the findings in the two case studies. I also discuss how the experiences of displaced victims could inform their perceptions on transitional justice, depending on how they interact with the key actors. In line with the question on how transnational networks and NGOs (de)legitimise transitional justice, I show the similarities and divergences within the NGO work in both contexts. I use the empirical data from both case studies to show the common themes in the discourses and practices on transitional justice. I also show the challenges of implementing bottom-up approaches in transitional justice.

Finally, in chapter "Concluding Remarks", I revisit the overall aims of the book, before making concluding remarks. I will connect transitional justice and the work of NGOs to the wider context of global governance, whilst making deeper reflections on the nuances of Global Justice making in general. I will draw attention to the dual dimension of NGO work across global spaces—the legitimation of transitional justice and enhancing of global governance. I propose ways of diffusing the hegemonic forms of global justice, through the exploration of emerging regional and sub-regional avenues for accountability. In doing so, I also pave the way for more research on how actors could counter-hegemonic structures of global governance under the purview of transitional justice. The closing discussions in the book also benefit from my previous scholarship, to inform future interactions between transitional justice and global governance. Parts of this chapter have been published in a conference paper and journal article.[45] A key contribution of the book to the literature on transitional justice and ICL is its use of a sociological lens of legitimacy to assess the impact of transnational networks and NGOs on the field, using personal and empirical insights from two case studies.

References

Arthur S, Nazroo J (2003). Designing fieldwork strategies and materials. In: Ritchie J, Lewis, J (eds) Qualitative research practice: a guide for social science students and researchers. Sage, pp 109–137

Andreassen BA (2017) Comparative analyses of human rights performance. In: Andreassen BA, Sano H-O, McInerney-Lankford S (eds) Research methods in human rights: a handbook. Edward Elgar Publishing, pp 222–252

Bennett A (2008) Process tracing: a Bayesian perspective. In: Box-Steffensmeier J, Brady H, Collier D (eds) The Oxford handbook of political methodology. OUP, Oxford, pp 702–719

Brankovic J et al (2020) Violence, inequality, and transformation: apartheid survivors on South Africa's ongoing transition. DSI-NRF Centre of Excellence in Human Development, Johannesburg

Burgis-Kasthala M (2019) Entrepreneurial justice: Syria, the Commission for International Justice and Accountability and the renewal of international criminal justice. Eur J Int L 30:1165–1185

Christensen M, Levi R (eds) (2018) International practices of criminal justice: social and legal perspectives, 1st edn. Routledge, Abingdon

Clarke K (2019) Affective justice: the racialized imaginaries of international justice. Polit Leg Anthropol Rev 42:244–267

Davidson N (2021) Process-tracing the meaning of international human rights law. In: Deplano R, Tsagourias N (eds) Handbook on research methods in international law. Edward Elgar Publishing, Cheltenham, pp 228–243

De Vos C (2020) The ICC in Uganda, Kenya and the Democratic Republic of Congo. In: De Vos C (ed) Complementarity, catalysts, compliance: the International Criminal Court in Uganda, Kenya, and the Democratic Republic of Congo. CUP, Cambridge, pp 147–194

Ehrlich E (1916) Montesquieu and sociological jurisprudence. Harvard L Rev 21:582–600

Fletcher L (2015) Refracted justice: the imagined victim and the International Criminal Court. In: De Vos C, Kendall S, Stahn C (eds) Contested Justice: The politics and practice of International Criminal Court interventions. CUP, Cambridge, pp 302–325

Glasius M, Meijers T (2012) Constructions of legitimacy: the Charles Taylor Trial. Int J of Transit Justice 6:229–252

Gissel L (2015) Justice tides: how and when levels of ICC involvement affect peace processes. Int J Transit Justice 9:428–448

[45] Tonny R Kirabira (2021).

Haddad H (2012) Judicial institution builders: NGOs and International Human Rights Courts. J Hum Rights 11:126–149
Horovitz S (2013) How international courts shape domestic justice: lessons from Rwanda and Sierra Leone. Israel L Rev 46:339–367
Hunt A (1978) The sociological movement in law, 1st edn. Palgrave Macmillan, London
Keck M, Sikkink K (1998) Activists beyond borders: advocacy networks in international politics. Cornell University Press, Ithaca, pp 1–228
Keck M, Sikkink K (1999) Transnational advocacy networks in international and regional politics. Int Soc Sci J 51:89–101
Kennedy D (1997) New approaches to comparative law: comparativism and international governance. Utah L Rev 545:1–637
Kirabira T (2021) NGO influence in global governance: achieving transitional justice in Uganda and beyond. Camb Int L J 10:280–299
Linos K (2015) How to select and develop international law case studies: lessons from comparative law and comparative politics. Am J Int L 109:475–485
Linos K (2018) Methodological guidance: how to select and develop comparative international law case studies. In: Roberts A et al (eds) Comparative international law. OUP, Oxford, pp 35–52
López R (2023) Black Guilt, White Guilt at the International Criminal Court. In: Sirleaf M (ed) Race and national security. OUP, New York, pp 211–228
Leeuw F, Schmeet H (2016) Empirical legal research: a guidance book for lawyers, legislators and regulators. Edward Elgar Publishing, Cheltenham
Mieth F (2018) Transitional justice and social transformation: reflections from Sierra Leone and South Africa. Swisspeace, pp 18–27
McAuliffe P (2019) The problem of elites. In: M Evans (ed.) Transitional and transformative justice, 1st edn. Routledge, Abingdon
McEvoy J (2006) Elite interviewing in a divided society: lessons from Northern Ireland. Politics 26:184–191
Murithi T (2020) Judicial imperialism: politicisation of the International Criminal Justice in Africa. Fanele, Johannesburg, pp 1–240
Palmer N et al (2013) Transitional justice methods manual: an exchange on researching and assessing transitional justice. Swisspeace, p 15
Paris M (2016) The comparative method in legal research: the art of justifying choices. In: Cahillane L, Schweppe J (eds) Legal research methods: principles and practicalities. Clarus Press, Dublin, pp 39–55
Potts A, Kjær A (2016) Constructing achievement in the International Criminal Tribunal for the Former Yugoslavia (ICTY): a corpus-based critical discourse analysis. Int J Semiot L 29:525–555
Richards D (1996) Elite interviewing: approaches and pitfalls. Politics 16:99–204
Salmons J (2016) Doing qualitative research online. Sage, Thousand Oaks
Shaffer G, Ginsburg T (2012) The empirical turn in international legal scholarship. Am J Int L 106:1–46
Siems M, Síthigh D (2012) Mapping legal research. Camb L J 71:651–676
Stan L, Nedelsky N (eds) (2013) Mothers of the Plaza de Mayo/Asociacion Madres de Plaza de Mayo (Argentina). In: Encyclopedia of transitional justice. CUP, Cambridge, pp 281–285
Twining W (1999) Globalization and comparative law. Maastricht J Eur Compar L 6:217–243
Ulrich G (2017) Research ethics for human rights research. In: Andreassen B, Hans-Otto Sano, McInerney-Lankford S (eds) Research methods in human rights: a handbook. Edward Elgar Publishing, Cheltenham
Viljoen F, Sipalla H, Adegalu F (eds) (2022) Exploring African approaches to international law: Essays in honour of Kéba Mbaye. Pretoria University Law Press, Pretoria, pp 1–358
Webley L (2010) Qualitative approaches to empirical legal research. In: Cane P, Kritzer H (eds) The Oxford handbook of empirical legal research. OUP, Oxford, pp 926–948

Webley L (2019) The why and how to of conducting a socio-legal empirical research project. In: Creutzfeldt N, Mason M, McConnachie K (eds) Routledge handbook of socio-legal theory and methods, 1st edn. Routledge, Abingdon, pp 58–69

Navigating Justice, Transitional Justice and Global North–South Dimensions

1 Conception of 'Gross' Human Rights Violations and Accountability

A starting point for the theoretical discussions is a clarification on key terminologies and concepts that are often used in Global Justice- gross human rights violations and accountability. Theoretical conceptions under IHRL and IHL have expanded over the past decades, and developed notions of 'gross and systematic human rights violations'[1] The notions of gross human rights violations and accountability were utilised in detail by UN Human rights bodies, and further influenced by the increasing links between IHRL, IHL and ICL.[2] The notion of crimes against humanity is particularly stressed, in this juxtaposition.[3] Ironically, ICL differs from the other two strands, regarding the apportion of responsibility, as it emphasises individual culpability. By contrast, both IHRL and IHL usually seek to establish state responsibility, whilst relegating the identity and culpability of perpetrators.[4]

When gross human rights violations occur and are documented, the notion of accountability demands that the relevant States provide redress to victims, including individual accountability under criminal law. According to the former UN High Commissioner for Human Rights, accountability 'reinstates public trust in justice and security institutions to rebuild the rule of law and sustainable peace'.[5] Scholars make strong legal arguments for accountability as an emerging principle in international law, with State obligations to overcome impunity for crimes like extrajudicial

[1] For a more elaborate explanation, see Karimova (2014, p. 10).

[2] Karimova (2014, p. 10).

[3] Karimova (2014, p. 10).

[4] Karimova (2014, p. 10).

[5] See Pillay (2012).

This chapter has some overlaps with my doctoral thesis.

© The Author(s), under exclusive license to Springer Nature Singapore Pte Ltd. 2025

T. R. Kirabira, *Transnational Networks and Justice in the Global South*, International Law and the Global South, https://doi.org/10.1007/978-981-95-3137-0_2

execution, torture, disappearances and prolonged arbitrary arrests.[6] Generally, States are obliged under four obligations and correlative rights; to investigate, prosecute and punish perpetrators; to disclose to the victims and their families the truth about the events; to offer the victims adequate reparations; and to separate perpetrators from law enforcement and positions of authority.[7]

Traditionally, atrocities like genocide and disappearances have emerged out of authoritarian societies, and thus the emerging use of the notion of accountability as a measure of transitional justice. The emphasis on 'successor governments', assumes that states have affirmative obligations to investigate state-directed atrocities.[8] Aside from contexts such as paradigmatic transitions to democracy, accountability is vital during conflicts and humanitarian situations. As Juan Mendez suggests, accountability is also relevant in order to seek solutions to armed conflicts.[9]

A clear manifestation of the accountability debate is inherent in discussions about genocide. The UN Convention on the Prevention and Punishment of the Crime of Genocide (Genocide Convention) requires State parties to 'prevent and punish' genocide.[10] Article V requires States to enact the necessary legislation to effectuate the Genocide Convention, and to provide effective penalties for persons found guilty of genocidal acts.[11] Apart from crimes against humanity, genocide and war crimes are regarded as gross violations of human rights.[12] Moreover, the Genocide Convention is interpreted as having explicit obligations requiring State parties to prosecute perpetuators of genocide.[13] Ultimately, the notion of accountability for gross human rights violations is firmly established within the scholarly discourse. The next section will review the legal philosophy on human rights and justice, as a foundation for transitional justice theory.

2 Legal Philosophy on Justice: The Relevance of Legal Theory

This sub-section considers theories of justice, that underline the normative nature of transitional justice. It revisits four major currents of thought within legal theory: natural law, legal positivism, legal realism and liberalism.

There is no definitive definition for legal theory or jurisprudence. However, for the purpose of this book, we could consider the expansive definition derived

[6] See generally Méndez (1997) and Leyh (2021).

[7] Méndez (1997).

[8] Roht-Arriaza (1990, p. 458).

[9] Méndez (1997, p. 257).

[10] See Convention on the Prevention and Punishment of the Crime of Genocide, adopted 09 December 1948, entered into force 12 January 1951) 660 UNTS 195, Art. I.

[11] See Convention on the Prevention and Punishment of the Crime of Genocide, Art. V.

[12] Pillay (2012).

[13] Orentlicher (1991, p. 100).

from Devlin's scholarship. He perceives legal theory and jurisprudence as 'a multi-dimensional and multi-tiered interrogative process in the pursuit of a greater understanding of the nature and functions of law, which itself must be understood as a complex, controversial and problematic phenomenon'.[14] This 'interrogative dimension' is further demonstrated through theoretical questions about the perspectives of law in society and how it informs legal institutions.[15]

Legal researchers build on the 'interrogative dimension' of legal theory to examine the relevance of legal institutions in broader societies.[16] In line with the book, legal theory is also relevant in determining the role of transitional justice institutions in developing social attitudes like reconciliation and peacebuilding. In the context of criminal justice, it is also important for judges to understand the evolving societies. This is augmented by scholarly support of legal jurisprudence as a 'direct instrumental value' to judges and lawyers.[17] In the specific context of human rights, legal theory was a key influence on the global human rights regime as codified under the Universal Declaration of Human Rights (UDHR).[18]

2.1 *Old Theory: Natural Law, Positivism and Realism*

The existence of 'natural rights' has been the subject of numerous legal and philosophical debates. Substantive law is derived from moral principles that are specific to human nature, reason and conscience.[19] Despite criticism against natural law theorists that present God as the supreme authority and good in moral arguments, theism is recognised as playing a key role in perceptions of moral life.[20]

In addition to human nature and reason, John Finnis argues that principles of natural law are also understood from 'political philosophy and jurisprudence, in political action, adjudication, and the life of the citizen'.[21] In a related manner, jurists such as Kelsen, Hart and Raz illuminate competing and divergent perceptions about the idea of natural law theory, across natural and positivist literature. To HLA Hart, natural law theory relates to human being's common pursuit of knowledge and justice, a position which is regarded as a fallacy by classical natural law theorist, Finnis.[22]

How should we view the aspect of morality within international law, as a background for discussions on transitional justice? The most prominent among the

[14] Devlin (1997, p. 23).
[15] Devlin (1997, p. 24).
[16] Devlin (2001, p. 165).
[17] Devlin (2001, p. 167).
[18] McCrudden (2008, p. 678).
[19] Zuber (2019, p. 18).
[20] Taliaferro (2001, p. 284).
[21] Finnis, Natural Law and Natural Rights (2011b, p. 23).
[22] Finnis, Natural Law and Natural Rights (2011b, p. 29).

contemporary natural law theorists is Ronald Dworkin. Taking into consideration the direct and intimate connection between law and morals, Dworkin's theory rejects utilitarianism, based on the principle that people should be treated as equals.[23] More importantly, scholars working in the field of natural law defend and apply moral imperatives in legal discourse. They thus identify principles of justice for human rights violations, based on natural law theory.[24] Finnis follows Aristotle's conception, in describing justice through categories of 'distributive' and 'commutative' justice.[25] New natural law theory stresses the relationship between principles of justice and the international common good. Finnis makes an essential connection between human rights and basic human goods,[26] suggesting that the requirements of justice are explained 'by referring to the needs of the common good at its various levels'.[27]

A direct link is created with International Human Rights Law (IHRL), through the fundamental human values, of common significance to all persons in the universal community. This is implicitly outlined under the UDHR, where: 'Everyone is entitled to a social and international order in which the rights and freedoms set forth in this Declaration can be fully realized'.[28] Immanuel Kant's philosophy provided a major ground for human rights, through the perception of human rights as based on individual autonomy and human dignity.[29] This philosophy influenced contemporary understanding of the intersection between human rights across different levels. Carozza emphasises the relevance of human dignity, from a universal perspective, as 'a basic ground of commonality'.[30] Little wonder, individual autonomy and dignity are central themes in the UDHR, due to the influence of Aquinas and natural law scholars.[31] The preamble to the UDHR provides: 'Whereas recognition of the inherent dignity and of the equal and inalienable rights of all members of the human family is the foundation of freedom, justice and peace in the world...'[32] These concepts could also be potential critical points for the critique of transitional justice, where global justice institutions are perceived as legitimate forms of justice across nuanced contexts.

New natural law principles of practical reasonableness bare close relationship with non-derogable rights discourse.[33] This argument is well formulated in Finnis's discussions on natural law.[34] This makes a good argument for accountability for

---

[23] Guest (2012, p. 208).

[24] Finnis, Natural Law and Natural Rights (2011b, pp. 161–163).

[25] Ibid. 166–167.

[26] Finnis, Collected Essays: Volume III. Human Rights and Common Good (2011a, pp. 4–5).

[27] Finnis, Collected Essays: Volume III. Human Rights and Common Good (2011a, p. 210).

[28] Universal Declaration of Human Rights, 10 December 1948, 217 A (III), Art. 28.

[29] Bayefsky (2013, p. 811).

[30] Carozza (2008, p. 931).

[31] McCrudden (2008, p. 665).

[32] Universal Declaration of Human Rights, 10 December 1948, 217 A (III).

[33] Universal Declaration of Human Rights, 10 December 1948, 217 A (III) Art. 4.

[34] Finnis, Natural Law and Natural Rights (2011b, pp. 111–112, 117, 121–122).

gross human rights violations like genocide and war crimes, from a natural law perspective. Besides Finnis's work, Buchanan presents a justice-based theory of international law, perceiving justice as a morally obligatory goal for International Law.[35] His work further draws a comprehensive normative theory of international law and justice, emphasising a 'Natural Duty of Justice'.[36] Similarly, Grotius's theory of natural justice presented a novel humanitarian intervention to justice, advocating for a natural right to punish violators of the law of nature.[37]

The developments of ad hoc tribunals, the ICC and the prosecution of war crimes and other crimes against humanity can be viewed as a moral progress, away from the traditional State-centred international law.[38] However, this could raise fundamental issues of legitimacy of transitional justice mechanisms at the global level. For example, legal critics of the present International Criminal Tribunals (ICTs) argue that they operate under the 'claims of a 'universalized moral theory', taking 'humanity' as 'a banner and institutionalizing themselves by decontextualizing and individualizing State violence'.[39] In light of these concerns, it is relevant to examine the second legal theory: legal positivism. Applying both natural and positivist law ideas to transitional justice enables us to have a good understanding of legal obligations and outcomes.

The second legal theory is that of positivism. There is no general definition of positivism in legal philosophy. However, for the purpose of this book, Hart's three theses on the nature of law offer a comprehensive understanding of legal positivism. Firstly, he views it as a conceptual separation of law and morality.[40] His second positivist thesis concerns the social sources of the law. He argues that:

> the existence of law requires some form of social practice that includes judges and ordinary citizens, and this social practice determines, in any given legal system, the ultimate sources of the law, or the ultimate criteria or ultimate tests for legal validity.[41]

Hart's third positivist thesis concerns judicial discretion, due to his argument that the law is incomplete.[42] Legal positivism focuses on the form, in order to determine the validity of the norms, unlike natural law which is mainly concerned with the moral context of law.[43] The first renowned proponents of positivist thought such as John Austin and Jeremy Bentham made these daring views against natural law.[44] One of the fundamental postulates of legal positivism is the separation between law

---

35 Buchanan (2004, pp. 191–193).

36 Buchanan (2004, p. 73).

37 Kingsbury and Straumann (2010, p. 43).

38 Buchanan (2010, p. 95).

39 See for instance Carlson (2017, p. 4). Based on their foundations in Natural Law, there is a doubt about the capacity of International Criminal Tribunals to perform the socially constructed paradigms that underpin transitional justice.

40 HLA Hart (2016, p. 460).

41 HLA Hart (2016, p. 460).

42 HLA Hart (2016, p. 460).

43 HLA Hart (1958, p. 621).

44 HLA Hart (1958, p. 599).

and morality, drawing on John Austin's and Hans Kelsen's theories.[45] In this respect, legal scholars apply the Kelsen theory that:

> Pure theory of law is a theory of positive law. As far as theory ... it seeks to answer the following question: 'What is law and what is law like?' It is not interested in posing the question around how it should be, according to what criterion must be constructed. It is legal science, not politics of law.[46]

Such understandings also contribute to legal reasoning and perceptions of justice. Aparisi Miralles attempts to reconcile legal reasoning through her perception of justice as 'what is just, legal, and natural … making sure that each one receives what they are due, what corresponds to them by virtue of their nature, the law, or a pact or convention'.[47]

Fagan makes a distinction between positivist and natural law perceptions about human rights and justice. Whilst natural law posits the existence of human rights and justice as existing independently of political or legal institutions, positivists view human rights as a product of law, that require legal recognition and codification.[48] As such, legal positivism has a strong influence within ICL work, through the inherent goal of retribution. Despite acknowledging the 'moral truth' element, Luban views 'norm projection' as a key justification for International Criminal Tribunals.[49] A clear example of legal positivism will be highlighted in chapters three and four of the book. Specifically, in the foundational positivist v realist debates on transitional justice when the ICC was first seized of the Uganda situation. The two chapters will highlight interesting discourses among key actors, between international or retributive justice, and traditional or restorative justice. Back to the philosophy, legal scholars note a jurisprudential gap created by the positivist neglect of international law, due to its primary focus on specific domestic legal systems.[50] This observation mirrors Hartian arguments about the absence of an international legislature.[51]

Legal realism relates to the interpretation of the law according to the real-world experiences, as opposed to mere descriptive and normative approaches.[52] This can be attributed to jurisprudential thinking about the role of courts and decision-making by American legal scholars, in what is referred to as American Legal Realism (ALR). Jurist Oliver Wendell Holmes Jr. influenced philosophical development through his book, *The Common Law*. He asserted that:

> The actual life of the law has not been logic: it has been experience. The felt necessities of the times, the prevalent moral and political theories, institutions of public policy, avowed or unconscious, even the prejudices which judges share with their fellow-men, have had a

[45] Miralles (2008, p. 381).

[46] Miralles (2008, p. 381).

[47] Miralles (2008, p. 390).

[48] Fagan (2009, p. 32).

[49] Luban (2010, p. 577).

[50] Ammann (2019, p. 387).

[51] Ammann (2019, p. 391).

[52] Quinn (2012, p. 35).

> good deal more to do than the syllogism in determining the rules by which men should be governed.[53]

In addition, legal realism highlights a movement for sociological jurisprudence, through the works of Roscoe Pound, who observed that:

> The attitude of the sociological jurist is essentially functional ... He rather looks upon the law as a social institution which may be consciously bettered by deliberate effort whether through a process of making law or finding it. The sociological jurist affirms the efficacy of effort. He finds the sanction of law not in the force of Austin or the custom of Carter but in the social ends which law is designed to serve. From this it follows that the sociological jurist has no essential preference for any one type of legal precept (e.g., statute or custom) except as one particular type of precept may more effectively serve as a means to secure the desirable end in a particular situation.[54]

A more nuanced strand of realism has also emerged in feminist legal scholarship.[55] Perhaps, this could account for the evolution of feminist debates within transitional justice literature. More importantly, the emphasis on 'social-scientific methods in the application of legal rules and assessment of legal processes' is vital in transitional justice.[56] A-M Slaughter identifies three characteristics of realism in international relations: first, the emphasis on States as role-players in international society; second, the centrality of self-survival; and third, the right to exercise self-help due to the inherent possibility of war.[57] Away from the ALR, theorists have constructed a New Legal Realism discourse (NLR) based on European philosophy. Inevitably, we see differences between ALR and NLR. For example, European realists Max Weber and Alf Ross are considered as seeking a 'different epistemological ambition than American realism's pragmatist approach'.[58]

One key element within realist legal theory relates to the philosophy of legal decisions and judicial reasoning. In describing the realist legal doctrine, Danish legal realist Alf Ross uses the term 'the judge ideology' and argues that it is a 'process determined by attitudes and concepts, a common normative ideology, present and active in the minds of judges when they act in their capacity as judges'.[59] In contrast, legal doctrinal theorists with a Kelsen and Hart philosophy, treat the 'validity of law as an inter-normative relation between norms established through chains of deontic reasoning'.[60] This contrasting engagement of law forms a basis for legal research and transitional justice, specifically with regard to how norms of ICL are understood and diffused across different sites of justice. Holtermann and Madsen summarise the philosophy of NLR under two claims: firstly, 'the negative claim that traditional doctrinal approaches to law fail to provide sound epistemological justifications for

---

[53] Holmes is quoted in Burrus (1962, p. 37).

[54] Burrus (1962, p. 38).

[55] Quinn (2012, p. 18).

[56] Quinn (2012, p. 42).

[57] Slaughter (1995, p. 507).

[58] Holtermann and Madsen (2015, p. 221).

[59] Holtermann and Madsen (2015, p. 215).

[60] Holtermann and Madsen (2016, p. 24).

their operations and thus cannot be upheld as a basic scientific position'; and secondly, 'the positive or constructive claim that the possibility of a basic science of law can be developed by replacing traditional doctrinal approaches with an empirical study of law and its institutions'.[61] These perceptions provide support for the methodological approach of this book which combines doctrinal and ELR methodologies. As already pointed out in the introduction, this line of inquiry is relevant in order to understand how transnational networks impact justice in the Global South, and the legitimacy of transitional justice processes.

2.2 *Contemporary Theory: Liberalism as a Basis for Justice*

The conception of justice, largely in times of political transitions, leads to our thinking about liberal narratives in human rights and international relations, especially when applied in the Global South. Beyond international law, liberalism has a key influence in international relations. Anne-Marie Slaughter attempts to make a distinction between realism and liberalism. In contrast to realists who focus on 'states as monolithic entities in their interaction with other States within an anarchic international system, liberals focus primarily on state society relations'.[62] Besides its roots in political theories of democracy, liberalism 'denotes a family of positive theories about how states do behave rather than how they should behave'.[63] It can therefore be argued that the international relations theory influences transitional justice, through the interaction of liberal states. In addition, the limitation of State power serves as a good ground to limit impunity.

Proponents of positive law and liberalism view the right to personal liberty as a core right, from which other rights are derived.[64] Whilst several liberal theorists base their major arguments on rejection of utilitarian and state interventions, Joseph Raz views utilitarianism is an abstract moral theory which may lead to controversies within the liberal discourse.[65] Scholars with a natural law philosophy view liberalism as 'more than a set of discrete beliefs about rights to personal freedom, or to the treatment of people as equals, or to the unhampered exercise of one's personal morality'.[66] In a more subjective manner, Guest argues that true liberal individuals should be tolerant to what other people do.[67]

The concept of human dignity has had a prominent effect on liberalism. Jean-Jacques Rousseau, one of the key contributors to the development of liberalism, associates human dignity to communitarianism within republics, to justify human

[61] Holtermann and Madsen (2016, p. 23).

[62] Slaughter (1995, p. 508).

[63] Slaughter (1995, p. 508).

[64] Raz (1988, p. 169).

[65] Raz (1988, p. 169).

[66] Guest (2012, p. 209).

[67] Guest (2012, p. 208).

rights.[68] Theorist John Rawls is strongly associated with a new egalitarian liberal theory.[69] Even though Rawls explicitly endorses the theory of equality, his definition of justice presents a broader understanding of the role of States in the protection of human rights. Rawls holds justice as 'the first virtue of social institutions', with the 'priority of the right to the good'.[70] He identifies two principles of justice. Firstly, the equal right to 'basic liberty' like freedom of expression, and secondly, limited state intervention through 'fair equality of opportunity'.[71] Michael Zuckert draws a distinction between classical liberalism and contemporary liberalism, contending that the latter is more egalitarian through positive legal obligations of the state.[72] This distinction poses an interesting perception of the role of States in the protection of human rights, within the ambit of achieving transitional justice following gross human rights violations.

Liberalism is also part of the design of ICL. To begin with, the work of ICTs like the ICC reflects a shift from a state-centric system to one where individual interests are recognised too.[73] This is reflected in the application of the maxim of Roman law *hominum causa omne jus constitutum est* (all law is created for the benefit of human beings).[74] This is well articulated in the Concurring Separate Opinion of Judge Eboe-Osuji in the appeal judgement of Jean-Pierre Bemba Gombo, where he held that: 'The interests of international human rights law in protecting the individual are not to play second fiddle to the interests of States in conducting warfare to the complete submission of 'the enemy'.[75] Secondly, liberalism is part of the ICL design, through the application of fundamental principles. As scholars have observed, the principles of personal culpability and legality (*nullum crimen sine lege*) are core commitments of the liberal criminal justice system.[76]

Legal theories of liberalism and philosophical arguments are well represented in empirical studies. Albert Nell adopted a systematic content analysis (SCA), to identify philosophical justificatory arguments in a selection of ICL pronouncements.[77] Through a coding system, he observes a tension between 'criminal law liberalism' and 'HR liberalism'.[78] Critics of the present ICL structure observe gaps created by the contextualisation of criminal law practice. To Kerstin Carlson: 'International

[68] For a more detailed understanding see McCrudden (2008, p. 660).

[69] Zuckert (2001, p. 49).

[70] Zuckert (2001, p. 51).

[71] Zuckert (2001, p. 52).

[72] Zuckert (2001, p. 50).

[73] See generally Fletcher and Ohlin (2005).

[74] See *Prosecutor v Tadić,* ICTY Appeals Chamber, Decision on the Defence Motion for Interlocutory Appeal on Jurisdiction) IT-94-1, 2 October 1995, para 97.

[75] *Prosecutor v Jean-Pierre Bemba Gombo* (Judgment on the appeal of Mr Jean-Pierre Bemba Gombo against Trial Chamber III's "Judgment pursuant to Article 74 of the Statute") ICC-01/05-01/08 A (8 June 2018) Concurring Separate Opinion of Judge Eboe-Osuji para 359.

[76] See for example, Robinson (2013, p. 133).

[77] See Nell (2018, p. 219).

[78] Nell (2018, p. 219).

criminal law, constructed in the shadow of this liberal outcome, has thus far neglected to engage in liberalism's practices'.[79] In their analysis of the criteria of culpability, George Fletcher and Jens Ohlin argue that customary international law has no role in ICL.[80] Others are critical of the replication of the principle of individual culpability due to the collective nature of crimes of war.[81] These concerns suggest a need for empirical studies regarding the effectiveness of ICL as form of transitional justice in local contexts.

Transitional justice has been conceptualised as part of a global set of liberal and neoliberal human rights norms, with a link to liberal democracy.[82] This is reflected in the ongoing tension in transitional justice practice between global liberal discourse and what is revealed by empirical study.[83] A notable example is the South African transitional justice process which exemplifies a compromise between liberal understanding of justice on one hand and specific local context on the other. South Africa's Truth and Reconciliation Commission (TRC) accorded widespread amnesty to perpetrators of gross human rights violations.[84] It is hard to argue that TRCs are not liberal institutions, as they are normally considered as a core aspect of the liberal transitional justice toolbox.

In addition, because basic human rights norms arise out of liberal thought, legal scholars are critical about the process of standard setting at the international level, as observed from vigorous disagreements and attempts to build a consensus.[85] In particular, Makau mentions John Locke's idea of individual autonomy and political democracy as a normative foundation for international human rights.[86] Because of a 'new moral vacuum', he proposes a 'cultural reimagination of the human rights project'.[87] This reflects the need to find a balance between liberal accounts of justice and specific contexts. A review of the literature indicates that the dominant human rights jurisprudential discourses relate to the liberal theory of individual liberty. The next section reviews the theoretical framework of transitional justice and its criticisms.

---

79 Carlson (2017, p. 41).

80 Fletcher and Ohlin (2005, p. 559).

81 Robinson (2013, p. 134).

82 Gready and Robins (2014, p. 341).

83 Gready and Robins (2014, pp. 343–349).

84 Dyzenhaus (2003, p. 167).

85 Makau (2016, p. 24).

86 Makau (2016, p. 169).

87 Makau (2016, p. 178).

3 Dialogues of Transitional Justice

The foregoing account of different legal philosophical conceptions of justice and human rights lays the groundwork for articulating principles of transitional justice. The discussion below builds on these theories to expound on the evolving concepts of transitional justice, that are relevant in different interdisciplinary studies, beyond the field of international law.

In recent decades, the conception of transitional justice has expanded to encompass local understandings of democracy and legitimacy. And yet, the traditional understanding of the notion was perceived from a universal human rights discourse. Following the end of the Cold War, there was an increase in the global management of conflict resolution, as observed by Ruti Teitel.[88] This created a conflation of IHRL, ICL and IHL discourses in the hope of averting future conflict, whilst holding perpetuators accountable. As seen in the previous section, the notion of accountability creates a demand for justice.

In response to genocidal conflicts in Rwanda and the Balkans, the IHL regime was expanded to include the creation of ad hoc International Criminal Tribunals.[89] Further development was done, through the creation of the ICC,[90] which expanded the ICL regime. To Teitel, this was a sign of normalisation of transitional justice jurisprudence.[91] The dominant discourse is on post-conflict law, as the global rule of law for transitional justice.

A similar narrative is adopted within socio-legal perspectives, concerning law and development. Scholars in the area of peace studies emphasise reconciliation in post-conflict contexts. In her examination of dialogue processes in complex political contexts, and their usefulness in advancing reconciliation and transitional justice, Gita Sabharwal draws on the case of Sri Lanka, on the basis of a recent political transition.[92] As a result, she develops the idea of national dialogue in order to secure both long-term political solutions, whilst dealing with past grievances.[93]

Besides Sri Lanka, transitional justice studies in other contexts highlight nuances of ICL and retributive justice in general, from a range of disciplines. In doing so, critical reflections can be made on how to further assess the development and impact of ICL in such contexts. Political scientist Jo-Marie Burt raises critical arguments in favour of more qualitative studies as opposed to quantitative literature, in order to

---

[88] See generally Teitel (2002).

[89] Statute of the International Tribunal for the Prosecution of Persons Responsible for Serious Violations of International Humanitarian Law Committed in the Territory of the Former Yugoslavia since 1991, U.N. Doc. S/25704 at 36, Annex (1993) and S/25704/Add.1 (1993), Adopted by Security Council on 25 May 1993, U.N. Doc. S/RES/827 (1993).) amended by Security Council resolutions 1166 (1998) of 13 May 1998, 1329 (2000) of 30 November 2000, 1411 (2002) of 17 May 2002 and 1431 (2002) of 14 August 2002.

[90] Rome Statute of the International Criminal Court, U.N. Doc. No. A/ CONF.183/9 (1998).

[91] Teitel (2002, pp. 902–903).

[92] See Sabharwal (2017, pp. 1–4).

[93] Sabharwal (2017, pp. 1–4).

understand the politics of transitional justice.[94] Based on her extensive field research in Latin America, particularly in deeply divided societies such as Peru and Guatemala, Burt argues that large macro studies and quantitative literature cannot explore the unique historical narratives and the 'politics of trials—who supports them, who challenges them, what trials mean to victims, how they are viewed by the broader society'.[95] From the discipline of ICL, there are important conceptual and normative developments—for example in the prosecution of sexual violence and related crimes—that have historically been marginalised.[96]

Another contribution of the ICL discipline to transitional justice is reflected through the work of the Extraordinary Chambers in the Courts of Cambodia (ECCC), a hybrid court where local prosecution and context are supplemented with international participation and international standards. The ECCC facilitates transitional justice through accountability for gross human rights violations, as discussed in the first sub-section of this chapter.[97] As scholars have equally noted, the unique mechanism generated the momentum for a broader societal debate.[98] The ECCC is particularly important for analysing how ICL is translated at the domestic and local levels, in a polarised social and political environment. One pertinent aspect relates to the mode and scope of victims' participation in these transitional justice initiatives, which also invite transnational networks and NGO participation.

In terms of context, this interdisciplinary intersection enables the use of socio-legal methods to analyse the work of NGOs in contexts like Uganda and Myanmar. Burt also agrees that this kind of contextual analysis is very useful, especially when researching about the politics and processes of enacting transitional justice mechanisms.[99] A new paradigm dominates the literature on transitional justice, which is the underlying idea of 'transitional justice from below', emphasising justice ideas of affected communities.[100] Against this backdrop, it is important to examine how transitional justice is accepted or diffused within specific contexts like Uganda and Myanmar.

A more elaborate understanding of the key elements of transitional justice is relevant. In practice, what is transitional justice all about? What is the relationship between judicial and non-judicial forms of justice? Moving from the theoretical discussions in the preceding paragraphs, transitional justice entails a broad spectrum of avenues for justice in practice—both judicial and non-judicial processes. This sub-section discusses the four elements of transitional justice: truth commissions, criminal prosecutions, reparations programmes and institutional reforms. More

---

94 Fletcher and Weinstein (2018, p. 250).

95 Fletcher and Weinstein (2018, p. 252).

96 Clark (2018b, pp. 509–537).

97 For a more elaborate analysis, see the website of the Court: https://www.eccc.gov.kh/en/introduction-eccc.

98 Kirsten (2014, p. 134).

99 Fletcher and Weinstein (2018, p. 251).

100 For a more elaborate analysis see Ullrich (2016, pp. 543–568).

importantly, the discussions help to situate the practice of ICL within the parameters of transitional justice.

3.1 *Truth Commissions*

Truth Commissions are a popular dimension in transitional justice. From a normative perspective, we can view Truth Commissions under the purview of the right of individuals to know the truth. This right is supported by several treaty bodies, regional courts and international tribunals. For example, in the case of enforced disappearances, it is construed as the right of relatives of the missing or disappeared, to learn the fate and whereabouts of their loved ones.[101] As transitional justice emanates from international norms, States are encouraged to comply with their obligations in line with international standards.[102]

In theory, a literature review points towards a recognition of the need to establish a historical record, whilst implementing other remedial approaches. Scholars draw a connection between truth and transitional justice. As noted by Pablo de Greiff, the first UN Special Rapporteur on the Promotion of Truth, Justice, Reparation and Guarantees of Non-recurrence, truth is fundamental in all discussions about proper responses to atrocities.[103]

In terms of context, there are interesting developments that link truth to victims explicitly. It is closely linked with other rights, and construed from both individual and societal dimensions.[104] The report of the UN Secretary-General on the rule of law and transitional justice in conflict and post-conflict societies is particularly important, as it highlights the concept of a 'victim-centered approach'.[105] This supports the earlier theoretical framework, that 'victims and their families have the imprescriptible right to know the truth about the circumstances in which human rights violations took place'.[106]

---

[101] Convention for the Protection of All Persons from Enforced Disappearance (20 December 2006) E/CN.4/2005/WG.22/WP.1/Rev.4, Entered into Force 23 December 2010.

[102] UN Commission on Human Rights, Study on the Right to the Truth, Report of the Office of the United Nations High Commissioner for Human Rights, (2006), E/CN.4/2006/91, at p. 1.

[103] De Greiff (2016).

[104] UN Commission on Human Rights, Study on the Right to the Truth, Report of the Office of the United Nations High Commissioner for Human Rights, (2006), E/CN.4/2006/91, 2006).

[105] UN, Report of the Secretary-General, The Rule of Law and Transitional Justice in Conflict and Post-Conflict Societies (2004), S/2004/616, at p. 1.

[106] See UN Commission on Human Rights, Report of the Independent Expert Diane Orentlicher, "Updated Set of Principles for the Protection and Promotion of Human Rights through Action to Combat Impunity" (2005), E/CN.4/2005/102/Add.1 [Hereinafter UN Updated Set of Principles], Principle 4.

In practice, some States have adopted the right to truth, either through explicit constitutional recognition or the formation of Truth Commissions.[107] The efficiency of Truth Commissions in transitional justice is still a subject of scholarly debate. The roles of the commissions are generally ambiguous in contemporary transitional justice studies. In this regard, some scholars argue that truth commissions acknowledge the truth, rather than find the truth.[108] In this regard, it is important to explore additional elements like reparations. In the two case studies of this book, the centre of the discussions and analysis will be on ICL. As much as Truth Commissions are not the focus of this book, this discussion is relevant to show the broad transitional justice toolbox that is available, specifically for the Myanmar case study.

3.2 *Victims' Reparations*

As indicated in the previous sub-section, the focus of this book is not on Truth Commissions or reparations per se. However, the discussions on these elements are included to show the broad transitional justice toolbox that is available.

The second element towards a state's duty of accountability in transitional justice relates to the provision of reparations to victims. This duty was affirmed by the UN General Assembly under its Basic Principles of 2005, where Basic Principle IX requires States to 'provide reparation to victims for acts or omissions which can be attributed to the State and constitute gross violations of international human rights law or serious violations of international humanitarian law'.[109]

The Permanent Court of International Justice expounded on this notion by holding that 'reparation must, as far as possible, wipe out all the consequences of the illegal act and re-establish the situation which would, in all probability, have existed if that act had not been committed'.[110] In this regard, the States are obliged to make reparations as elaborated by the International Law Commission under article 34 of the Draft Articles on Responsibility of States for Internationally Wrongful Acts (ILO draft articles) which may take the form of restitution, compensation and satisfaction.[111]

---

[107] For a good example and elaborate explanation, see Constitutional Court of South Africa *The Citizen 1978 (Pty) Ltd and others v McBride Case CCT 23/10*, 2011, ZACC 11, 8 April 2011, para11.

[108] Chapman and Ball (2001, p. 3).

[109] See 'Basic Principles and Guidelines on the Right to a Remedy and Reparation for Victims of Gross Violations of International Human Rights Law and Serious Violations of International Humanitarian Law' (2005), A/RES/60/147.[hereinafter UN Basic Principles 2005].

[110] *Factory at Chorzow (Germ v Pol)* (1928) P.C.I.J (ser. A) No. 17, Judgement (13 September 1928).

[111] International Law Commission, 'Draft Articles on Responsibility of States for Internationally Wrongful Acts' (2001) Supplement No. 10 (A/56/10).

Restitution as a form of reparation means the State's obligation to re-establish the situation that existed before the wrongful acts were committed.[112] This principle is thus a core remedy for the human rights violations in the context of mass displacement, like that of the Rohingya. Similarly, it would be important to explore the reparative processes in the case study of Uganda, following the successful implementation of ICL.

IHL and IHRL recognise a long-standing duty for States to offer compensation as a form of accountability. This was reiterated during an international inquiry on Darfur region where Sudan was obliged to pay compensation for all the crimes perpetrated in Darfur by its agents and officials. In its report, the Commission maintained that:

> whenever a gross breach of human rights is committed which also amounts to an international crime, customary international law not only provides for the criminal liability of the individuals who have committed that breach, but also imposes an obligation on States of which the perpetrators are nationals, or for which they acted as *de jure* or *de facto* organs, to make reparation (including compensation) for the damage made.[113]

Another form of victim reparation takes the form of rehabilitation, which is vital as it enables the realisation of other forms of accountability. Thomas Antkowiak advocates for this measure based on the traumatic suffering of victims, suggesting that all litigation and negotiation procedures adopted must be sensitive to that reality.[114] In the context of genocide and forced displacement, the States' obligation would relate to providing rehabilitative and physiological care for victims of sexual assault. From a sociological perspective, victims' health is associated with the suffering around them. In a study done in 2016 about social determinants of immigrant womens' mental health, researchers identified three significant determinants of mental health: social connectedness, freedom from discrimination and violence, and economic participation.[115] These aspects highlight the need for both short- and long-term strategies for transitional justice.

Despite the notable positive interventions, taking a victimological approach towards transitional justice invites critical concerns about reparations, specifically regarding the legitimacy of the strategies. Helen Chang Mack, a victim in Guatemala, advocates for collective reparations, arguing that individual reparations delegitimise the victims.[116] Generally, there are scholarly arguments for both individual and collective reparations in transitional justice.[117] In the context of displacement, reparation programmes are criticised for the failure to satisfy progressive rights of victims, as noted in the Colombian context as observed by Luis Murcia.[118] The scholarly

---

[112] International Law Commission, 'Draft Articles on Responsibility of States for Internationally Wrongful Acts' (2001) Supplement No. 10 (A/56/10), Art. 35.

[113] See Report of the International Commission of Inquiry on Darfur to the United Nations Secretary-General pursuant to Security Council Resolution 1564 of 18, (2004), para 598.

[114] Antkowiak (2008, p. 404).

[115] See detailed study and analysis in Delara (2016).

[116] Fletcher and Weinstein (2018, p. 234).

[117] For detailed explanation see Robins et al. (2022).

[118] Murcia (2013, pp. 191–206).

attention should then be on the designing and implementation of effective reputation measures, especially for victims of mass displacement.

3.3 *Other Measures to Prevent Repetition*

Designing and implementing transitional justice mechanisms would be incomplete without concrete measures to ensure that there is no future occurrence of the gross human rights violations and crimes. From a normative perspective, international law encompasses a State duty to provide guarantees of non-repetition as a way of combating impunity.[119] Thomas Antkowiak expounds on this principle of guarantees of non-repetition as being 'equally diverse, including, inter alia, the establishment of effective civilian control over State security forces and human rights educational and training programs'.[120]

Social reforms and acknowledgement are emphasised by scholars, as important elements in transitional justice. In regard to accountability, the concerned States are required to publicly acknowledge their actions. The holding of public ceremonies is regarded as a good way to commemorate the victims, but also prevent the repetition of past atrocities.[121] In addition to the acknowledgement, there is a growing emphasis on the adoption of social and political reforms, in order to prevent repetition of the violations in contexts like Myanmar.[122] Faruk Teksen examines the relationship between various transitional justice mechanisms established in the aftermath of the Bosnian War from 1992 to 1995, and recent reflections on political and social instability in Bosnia and Herzegovina.[123] He attributes the partial success of transitional justice initiatives to among others, the absence of thinking at the national level.[124]

Yet, from a victimological perspective, Helen Chang Mack notes important challenges associated with donors and national policies which do not resonate with the specific needs of victims.[125] It will therefore be interesting to see if similar challenges manifest within the two case studies of this book. Viewed from a sociological perspective, Ron Dudai relates transitional justice to retroactive social control.[126] He advocates for the recognition of social celebrations and roles of both victims and rescuers, whilst critiquing the view of transitional justice through the prism of accountability.[127] Both Teksen's and Dudais' arguments are based on post-conflict processes. There is a gap within socio-legal literature on the application of such social

[119] For a more elaborate analysis see UN Basic Principles 2005, Principle IX (18).

[120] Antkowiak (2008, p. 362).

[121] Antkowiak (2008, p. 381).

[122] For more details see Simpson et al. (2017).

[123] Teksen (2019, pp. 199–215).

[124] Teksen (2019, p. 212).

[125] Fletcher and Weinstein (2018, p. 234).

[126] Dudai (2018, pp. 691–711).

[127] Dudai (2018, pp. 691–711).

reparations during ongoing conflicts, like the case of the Rohingya. Arguments for institutional reform in countries like Myanmar and Uganda would require in-depth studies, specifically, the discourses and practices of transnational networks and NGO actors.

3.4 *Criminal Prosecutions: (I)llegitimate Forms of Transitional Justice?*

Finally, the element of criminal justice in transitional justice is highly relevant, in line with the principle of accountability, as discussed in Sect. 1 of this chapter. This book places an emphasis on criminal justice in the form of international trials or prosecution based on international crimes. Inevitably, such crimes, e.g. genocide, war crimes, etc., involve the violation of international human rights.

IHRL places a duty on States to investigate violations of gross human rights in an effective, prompt, thorough and impartial manner. The UN Basic Principles provide an additional State duty to submit to prosecution perpetuators of human rights violations.[128] Moreover, in these cases, States are obliged, in accordance with international law, to cooperate with one another and assist internationally.[129]

The Genocide Convention and the Convention on the Elimination of All Forms of Racial Discrimination (CERD) give rise to the duty to prosecute those acts that are categorised as grave breaches.[130] In addition to this, there is a duty to guarantee competent national tribunals.[131] In applying these concepts, some scholars regard the duty to prosecute as the most complete and satisfactory method of accomplishing other obligations of accountability.[132] Therefore, in theory, the lack of State investigations and prosecutions against perpetrators of human rights violations represents a violation of a State's duty to provide accountability.

A good example to show the impact of criminal justice within transitional justice is highlighted by Stephan Parmentier and Elmar Weitekamp, who examine the dominant role of criminal prosecutions within the context of past violations in the former Yugoslavia. They reveal a complex reality within the local populations, with mixed reactions about the legitimacy of the formal courts of justice and small community

---

[128] See UN Basic Principles 2005 (n 146) Principle III (4).

[129] UN Basic Principles 2005 (n 146) Principle III (4).

[130] Convention on the Prevention and Punishment of the Crime of Genocide approved and proposed for signature and ratification or accession by General Assembly resolution 260 A (III) of 9 December 1948 Entry into force: 12 January 1951.

[131] Convention on the Elimination of All Forms of Racial Discrimination adopted and opened for signature and ratification by General Assembly resolution 2106 (XX) of 21 December 1965 entry into force 4 January 1969, in accordance with Article 19.

[132] See for example Méndez and Bariffi (2012).

groups across the diverse ethnic groups—Bosniaks and Serbs, Croats and Albanians.[133] Key questions could be: what form of justice would transnational networks and NGOs promote, and how would their work impact on the legitimacy of the formal judicial institutions?

Researchers acknowledge the relevance of criminal trials, especially the effect they create on victims. Literature suggests that trials have an important symbolic value for the victims.[134] It is argued that there is an 'implicit contract established in the giving and receiving of testimonies'.[135] This suggests that truth, as a theory, is considered essential for criminal justice systems. In fact, a number of Truth Commissions have attempted to solve this hypothesis, but scholars still grapple with related questions.

An important question to ascertain, is whether the act of testifying is a healing action per se.[136] Truth-telling exercises, for example, may help to overcome group divisions and create a sense of shared destiny within a society.[137] As the Chilean case demonstrates, other measures like reparations are also relevant.[138] From a political perspective, a number of studies observe a lack of legitimacy of international criminal justice. Scholars allude to this problem whilst examining the operation of international criminal justice through formal institutions such as the ICC, noting a politicisation of the field.[139] This observation generally resonates with the arguments for victim-centred propositions.[140]

How, then, should we understand the 'criminal justice approach', as undertaken by both domestic bodies and international mechanisms like the ICC? There is a need to explore the ICC's alignment to justice practice through an exploration of the participation of victims within its legal proceedings. More specifically, it is important to examine how transnational networks and NGOs engage with victims' work in respect to the ICC interventions in the two case studies.

4 International Criminal Law: Moving Beyond the Transitional Justice Borders

As a rather popular measure of transitional justice, ICL is often used to prosecute and punish crimes at the international level. This individual criminal responsibility developed radically after the First World War. It is justified by different theories,

---

[133] For a more detailed analysis see Parmentier and Weitekamp (2013, pp. 43–62).

[134] Wemmers and Manirabona (2014, pp. 101–109).

[135] Laplante and Theidon (2007, pp. 228–250).

[136] Laplante and Theidon (2007, pp. 228–250).

[137] Duthie and Seils(2017, p. 151).

[138] Laplante and Theidon stress the importance of reparations in post-conflict settings. Laplante and Theidon (2007, pp. 228–250).

[139] Findlay (2013, p. 148).

[140] Findlay (2013, p. 149).

which are similar to those existing in domestic criminal law systems.[141] Rowen argues that there is no clear difference between transitional justice and international criminal justice.[142] Moreover, empirical research credits ICTs for their legal and judicial developments in target countries like Rwanda.[143]

From a normative perspective, international criminal prosecutions are criticised as not being relevant when applied during the course of active human rights violations or armed conflict. With the reliance on customary law, Archibugi and Pease wonder whether such norms will ever be universally acceptable.[144] The other point of criticism against the use of ICL is that it is based on a liberal model of Western justice.[145] Besides this normative theory, procedure under ICL is regarded as selective, and there are several factors outside the traditional legal arguments, that determine who is prosecuted.[146] In addition, there are still scholarly debates about the procedural flaws. For example, critics of the Nuremburg Tribunal argue that all components of a fair hearing were lacking.[147] However, that was not the case with mechanisms since the ICTY and ICTR (and later the ICC and hybrid tribunals).

Similarly, the use of ICL as a deterrent measure is criticised by some scholars. Archibugi and Pease pose an important question: Whether the fifty-five sentences delivered by the ad hoc tribunal for Rwanda can be considered sufficient punishment for the 800,000 deaths?[148] Yet, within 'ethno-social' contexts, different dimensions affect the discourse on ICL. An important dimension to think about relates to feminist approaches towards crimes in the context of mass violence.

The treatment of women in the criminal justice system remains tenuous. Feminist approaches tend to formulate a narrow understanding of female participation in atrocities. For example, scholarly discussions about rape in genocide tend to focus on the experience of women victims.[149] In her exploration on how law limits the ways women are able to express themselves, Sheri Labenski notes the 'lack of visibility of female defendants in Western feminist dialogues and international criminal law'.[150] The feminist approach and its construction is very visible in the Rwandan genocide trials on Sexual and Gender Based Violence.[151]

---

[141] Case law provides additional clarity, for instance *Prosecutor v Zlatko Aleksovski*, Judgement, Case No IT-95-14/1-A (24 March 2000), para 185. It was emphasized that sentences of International Tribunals 'should make plain the condemnation of the international community of the behaviour in question and show that the international community was not ready to tolerate serious violations of international humanitarian law and human rights'.

[142] Rowen (2018, p. 51).

[143] For instance, see Horovitz (2018).

[144] Archibugi and Pease (2018, p. 36).

[145] Archibugi and Pease (2018, p. 61).

[146] Archibugi and Pease (2018, p. 37).

[147] Archibugi and Pease (2018, p. 13).

[148] Archibugi and Pease (2018, p. 49).

[149] Von Joeden-Forgey (2017, p. 301).

[150] Labenski (2017, p. 56).

[151] Kaitesi (2013, p. 43).

However, as A.L. Smeulers observes, women play supportive and administrative roles during periods of mass violence.[152] Noting the example of the Rwanda genocide, she notes that less than ten per cent of the close to two million suspects who were tried in the Gacaca courts were female.[153] Sheri Labenski draws a more elaborate understanding of womens' ability to perpetrate violence.[154] Yet, according to Linton, there is no informed view of the kinds of crimes, or the mode of female participation in ICL.[155]

The lack of conceptual clarity about the aims of ICL is acknowledged by scholars.[156]Moreover, beyond the traditional aims of international criminal justice, scholars acknowledge the role of ICL in peace-building, like the case of Northern Uganda.[157] Against this background, the next sub-section will discuss the different international criminal justice theories, showing criticism and gaps in the existing literature, which are all essential when analysing the implementation of transitional justice.

4.1 Rehabilitative Justice

One particular theory that requires further study within comparative transitional justice contexts is that of rehabilitation. It is not defined in any of the rules governing the functioning of the major International Criminal Tribunals (ICTs). Nonetheless, theorists draw an emphasis on rehabilitation, as a means of reintegrating offenders back into society, with interventions during and after their incarceration.[158] In this respect, there is particular attention towards prisoners and family relations.[159] One would pose a question, whether such a form of justice would be appropriate within deeply diverse and divided societies, especially those still dealing with the legacy of genocide.

With a close review of current literature, one would argue that the different transitional justice goals are competing with each other. Whilst some scholars often disregard rehabilitation, others argue that the retributive function of ICL has no bearing on crimes, in the real world.[160] However, Jens David Ohlin argues that without retribution, victims lose confidence in the ICL system.[161] Other theorists juxtapose these

152 Smeulers (2015, pp. 207–253).
153 Smeulers (2015, pp. 207–253).
154 Labenski (2017).
155 Linton (2016, p. 162).
156 Archibugi and Pease (2018, p. 41).
157 Knoops (2014, p. 313).
158 For example, see Kelder, Holá and van Wijk (2014, pp. 1177–1188).
159 Kelder, Holá and van Wijk (2014, p. 1188).
160 Archibugi and Pease (2018, p. 49).
161 Ohlin (2009, pp. 373–404).

theories with processes of procedure and outcome. For example, in his legal discussion on the objectives of deterrence and retribution, Payam Akhavan views reconciliation as an incidental outcome, and not the purpose of ICL,[162] whilst criminologist Kathleen Daly argues that restorative justice is not a type of justice.[163] In a related manner, there are feminist critiques of restorative justice, arguing that it is inappropriate within the context of partner, sexual and family violence.[164] These different scholarly perceptions point towards a potential gap between expectations and reality under ICL. This is further acknowledged in arguments against the retributive function of ICL.[165]

Beyond this discourse, victims, especially survivors of war rape and sexual violence, suffer psychological harm that requires long-term solutions.[166]This kind of harm would certainly require the use of rehabilitative approaches. Since rehabilitation is a subject of contest and critique, this mode of justice requires deeper theoretical and empirical inquiry.

4.2 Retributive Justice

Another theory worth noting is that of retribution, and its influence on ICL. This theory is likely to influence the use of proportionality in the imposition of sentences. One could ask the question: How do transnational networks and NGOs engage with retributive approaches within legally pluralistic environments? In response to this question, it is important to examine both ICL materials and literature in the disciplines of sociology and criminology. The jurisprudence of the decisions of the ICTs suggests in some ways that retribution is associated with the concept of 'just deserts', as highlighted in the Kordic Appeal.[167] Scholars use a common conception of 'vengeful desert', arguing that punishments should correspond to the harm or suffering caused to victims.[168] The criminal law element of proportionality is also applied, when determining whether a sentence is retributive.[169] Both case law and literature suggest a duality of retribution and rehabilitation. Retributive justice is exemplified in this book through the discussions and analysis on international criminal justice and the work of institutions like the ICC.

---

[162] Akhavan (2013, pp. 527–536).

[163] Daly (2015, pp. 9–29).

[164] See generally Daly and Stubbs (2006, pp. 9–28).

[165] Archibugi and Pease (2018, p. 49).

[166] See generally Clark (2018a, pp. 1–288) and Clark (2018b, pp. 509–537).

[167] *Prosecutor v Kordic and Cerkez* (Appeal) IT-95-14/2-A (17 December 2004) para 1075.

[168] See Robinson (2008, pp. 144–147).

[169] For an explanation, see *Prosecutor v Simic* et al. (Judgment) IT-95-9-T (17 October 2003) para 1059.

4.3 Reparative and Restorative Justice

Moving beyond the duality of retributive/rehabilitative paradigms, the reparative justice theory is analysed as a victim-centred proposition. The term 'restorative justice' is contested among scholars. In addition, there is no universal definition of its practice under ICL or transitional justice. From a criminological perspective, there is a debate regarding its conception as a process or outcome.[170] From a sociological perspective, reparative justice is conceived as a 'response to the complex and shifting realities of societies torn apart by conflict, as well as the varied and often contradictory claims for justice that arise therein'.[171] For the purposes of this book, Albert Eglash's definition is utilised for its prioritisation of a conception of restorative justice as both a process and outcome, with the full participation of victims.[172] Proponents of international criminal justice argue that it promotes reconciliation. As Antonio Cassese notes, war crimes promote reconciliation by dissipating calls for revenge whilst establishing truth and individualising the guilt.[173]

Closely related to restoration is the theory of reparative justice. One can argue that reparations to victims are crucial, and this is equally highlighted within the Rome Statute.[174] Similarly, reparations are addressed in the ICC Rules of Procedure and Evidence.[175] It is important to note that these Rules are ambiguous on the mode of reparations, although they recognise the relevance of both individual and group reparations.[176] The scope of reparations is not clear in ICL, as evidenced by the evolving jurisprudence. The Appeals Chamber in Thomas Lubanga's case set out five basic principles:

> (1) it must be directed against the convicted person; (2) it must establish and inform the convicted person of his or her liability with respect to the reparations awarded in the order; (3) it must specify, and provide reasons for, the type of reparations ordered, either collective, individual or both, pursuant to rules 97 (1) and 98 of the Rules of Procedure and Evidence; (4) it must define the harm caused to direct and indirect victims as a result of the crimes for which the person was convicted, as well as identify the modalities of reparations that the Trial Chamber considers appropriate based on the circumstances of the specific case before it; and (5) it must identify the victims eligible to benefit from the awards for reparations or set out the criteria of eligibility based on the link between the harm suffered by the victims.[177]

---

[170] Daly (2015, p. 4).

[171] For sociological perspectives, see Mani (2005, pp. 511–526).

[172] Albert Eglash defines Restorative Justice as providing 'a deliberate opportunity for offender and victim to restore their relationship, along with a chance for the offender to come up with a means to repair the harm done to the victim'. See elaborate definition and analysis in Gavrielides (2012, pp. 3624–3643).

[173] See generally Cassese (1998).

[174] Rome Statute of the International Criminal Court, U.N. Doc. No. A/ CONF.183/9" (1998), n.d.).

[175] Rule 94 and 95 Rules of Procedure and Evidence.

[176] Rules of Procedure and Evidence, Rule 97(1).

[177] *Prosecutor v Thomas Lubanga Dyilo* (Appeals Chamber) ICC-01/04-01/06-3129 (A A2 A3) (3 March 2015) [hereinafter Lubanga Case] paras 32, 55.

From the above context, questions can arise regarding how to determine individual or collective reparations within ethnically diverse conflict communities. In addition, researchers would need to determine the extensiveness of reparation hearings and programmes for victims during active armed conflict.

An important issue that arises relates to the relevant forms of reparative and restorative justice for victims of sexual violence. Scholars note a historical practice regarding the use of rape as a weapon of war, which is further aggregated by social and religious contexts. Besides the feminist approaches highlighted in the earlier discussions, there is growing attention towards male survivors of rape and sexual violence.[178] Kelly Askin suggests that the impacts extend beyond communities and societies, especially those with deep gender stereotypes.[179]

As noted, sexual violence-related crime is often overlooked, but yet very prevalent during active conflicts as was observed in Bosnia-Herzegovina.[180] It is important to note that before 1998, ICTs neglected rape and sexual violence as grave offences during war.[181] Crucially, it is important to consider how best to provide reparations, and restore the victims to their normal situations, if possible. In addressing these concerns, scholars would be assessing the relevance of ICL as a redress mechanism and transitional justice model for victims of sexual violence in general.

5 Conceptualising Victims Within International Criminal Justice

5.1 *Social Context and Inequality: Barriers or Enhancers of Victims' Rights?*

The book examines how transnational networks impact justice in the Global South, and the legitimacy of transitional justice processes. NGOs certainly impact on the legitimacy of transitional justice within conflict-affected communities. Transitional justice mechanisms deal with an important category of actors, who are the victims of gross human rights violations and atrocities. As such, it is important to understand the position of victims within transitional justice, and how they relate with the international criminal justice systems. This background is useful to determine if transnational networks and NGOs effectively address the diversity and underlying vulnerabilities of victims when promoting or implementing transitional justice.

178 See generally Clark (2018a, pp. 1–288) and Clark (2018b, pp. 509–537).

179 Askin (2003, pp. 288–349).

180 See Clark (2018a, pp. 1–288) and Clark (2018b, pp. 509–537).

181 *Prosecutor v. Jean-Paul Akayesu* (Trial Judgement), ICTR-96-4-T, International Criminal Tribunal for Rwanda (ICTR) (2 September 1998) [hereinafter *Akayesu Case*]. For the first time, an international tribunal (the International Criminal Tribunal for Rwanda) considered rape as a grave offence, which constitutes a crime against humanity and an element of genocide.

As a starting point, the theoretical conceptualisation of victims (victimological approach) helps to understand and address their peculiar desires and remedies. Victims are defined to mean:

> persons who, individually or collectively, have suffered harm, including physical or mental injury, emotional suffering, economic loss or substantial impairment of their fundamental rights, through acts or omissions that are in violation of criminal laws operative within Member States, including those laws proscribing criminal abuse of power.[182]

Alongside the contemporary approach to ICL, a criminological approach better informs discourses on victims and international criminal justice. This is alluded to by different scholars who acknowledge the vital role of criminology in addressing the 'changing landscape of mass atrocity crimes and to study the mushrooming strategies and mechanisms of transitional justice',[183] given its multiple theoretical frameworks and extensive methodological toolboxes.

Victimology opens up for an expansive study of criminal justice and victims in mass conflicts and violence. Contemporary 'victimologists' use the term 'cultural victimology',[184] and Hall Matthew notes two significant aspects as being central to the 'cultural approach to victimization': firstly, the wider sharing and reflection of individual and collective victimisation experiences; and secondly, the mapping of those experiences through the criminal justice process.[185] This approach resonates with the idea of contextualising international criminal justice within a broader social context. This therefore creates a dilemma regarding the application and effectiveness of ICL among socially diverse victims. One would therefore be hard pressed to tell whether criminal justice is well-suited as a form of accountability for gross violation of human rights in such circumstances. A vital question could be whether a cultural understanding of victimisation points more towards restorative justice as a response to gross violation of human rights. As such, transitional justice studies and international criminal justice approaches might need to engage fully with culturally derived ideas of harm, especially within socially diverse communities and victims.

It is pertinent to consider how victims are perceived within transitional justice scholarship. Victimologists perceive 'the ideal victim' within contemporary criminal justice, as being the kind of victim in whose name victim services are typically justified.[186] Within the broader international criminal justice context, Christine Schwöbel-Patel argues that the victim is a 'Symbolic and Political Reference Point'.[187] This is mainly due to the previous trials of the ICTR and the ICTY, which did not explicitly provide for victim participation.[188]

---

[182] UN General Assembly, Declaration of Basic Principles of Justice for Victims of Crime and Abuse of Power: resolution/adopted by the General Assembly, 29 November 1985, A/RES/40/34, (Victims Declaration).

[183] Karstedt and Parmentier (2012, p. 467).

[184] Hall (2017, p. 4).

[185] Hall (2017, p. 4).

[186] See generally Spalek (2005).

[187] Schwöbel-Patel (2018, pp. 703–724).

[188] Schwöbel-Patel (2018, pp. 703–724).

Children are often victims of atrocities during armed conflicts, as they are mostly dependent on the survival of their guardians or even combatants. As a result, the vulnerability of children presents a legal dilemma, in distinguishing between child victims and child perpetrators in ICL. This is highlighted by Mark Drumbl in his observations on the trial of former Ugandan child soldier Dominic Ongwen before the ICC.[189] He is critical about the blurriness between the lines of victims and perpetrators and the faultless passive victim image of child soldiers.[190] With these gaps in victimological and legal discourses, it is thus vital to consider victims' justice needs and participation before the ICC, with a close focus on the social context.

As was noted in the previous section, different scholars closely affiliate with the recognition of wrongs committed by, and punishment of, the offenders.[191] This theoretical definition raises a question: whether accountability is a process or the outcome? Taking an example of criminal justice, would the outcomes of courts and tribunals be secondary to the processes of investigation and prosecution? In answering these questions, the central subject of the debate is the victims of these gross violations of human rights, who engage closely with NGOs.

Whereas some victims might be interested in the outcomes such as punishment and reparation, others might focus majorly on the criminal justice process itself. In fact, available literature suggests that victims do not necessarily equate punishment with accountability, but require other forms of justice like recognition and reparations.[192] The case study of the former Yugoslavia is a perfect example of the limitations of ICL within diverse ethnicities within the context of transitional justice.[193] The fact that the atrocities in the former Yugoslavia were propagated along ethnic grounds means that there is little or no possibility for all the conflict-affected communities to consider the international trials as legitimate. In essence, legitimacy of the mechanisms would depend on who is prosecuted, and their ethnic background.

Nonetheless, researchers acknowledge the relevance of criminal trials, especially the effect they have on victims. Literature suggests that trials have an important symbolic value for the victims.[194] It is argued that there is an 'implicit contract established in the giving and receiving of testimonies'.[195] As such, truth as a theory is considered essential for criminal justice systems. Nonetheless, scholars still grapple with the practical relevance of truth commissions to victims. A critical question that can be raised from the scholarship, is whether the act of testifying is a healing action per se?[196] Truth-telling exercises, for example, may help to overcome group divisions and create a sense of shared destiny within a society.[197] As the Chilean case

[189] Drumbl (2016, pp. 217–246).

[190] Drumbl (2012).

[191] Prominent among them are Wemmers and Manirabona (2014, pp. 101–109).

[192] See for instance Parmentier and Weitekamp (2013, pp. 43–62).

[193] Parmentier and Weitekamp (2013, pp. 43–62).

[194] See for instance Wemmers and Manirabona (2014, p. 106).

[195] Laplante and Theidon (2007, p. 229).

[196] Laplante and Theidon (2007, p. 229).

[197] Duthie and Seils (2017, p. 155).

demonstrates, other measures like reparation are also relevant.[198] Truth-telling can help overcome divisions when the different conflict-affected communities acknowledge the causes of the conflicts and can also apportion blame and apologise. In a similar way, in the wake of authoritarian rule, reparations-restitution, compensation, rehabilitation and satisfaction—allow for broader participation of conflict-affected communities in the transitional justice processes.

Concerning the theory of 'guarantees of non-recurrence', it is important to consider the unique conceptual issues of victims in a diverse society. There is a need to further investigate an important conceptual question posed by the Special Rapporteur, on the 'subject', or who the beneficiaries of the guarantees are supposed to be, i.e. the victims, a wider group of 'potential' victims, or society at large.[199] Underlying social contexts often constitute inequality, marginalisation and discrimination. Researchers conclude that this facilitates gross violation of human rights and drives conflict.[200]In line with these concerns, the book will explore the justice approaches of different victims' representatives to show how they (de)legitimise the transitional justice mechanisms.

Criminal justice, as typically designed, may also be poorly suited to meet the needs of diverse societies. Structural inequality has been identified as an important cause of conflict and gross violations of human rights. Lars Waldorf points out prominent problems associated with the term 'transition', arguing that 'the remedying of socio-economic injustices is a long-term political project'.[201] In a related context, surveys from DRC and Rwanda suggest that 'everyday injustices rooted in historical inequalities may be as important for many survivors than the extraordinary injustices of gross human rights abuses'.[202]

In addition to inequalities, there is a need to examine the influence of collective societies on the commission of crimes. Individual responsibility is reflected in the adoption of the positive law concepts of the *actus reus* and *mens rea* principles, under most domestic jurisdictions and the Rome Statute.[203] The theories of collective responsibility and individual responsibility would need to be examined from a transitional justice perspective. Most of the scholarship, however, ignores the coexistence of these theories, because of the institutional framework of criminal justice. Moreover, we cannot ignore the crimes committed by State actors within this evolving international law landscape.[204]

Therefore, it is important to critically investigate and contextualise social dimensions in conflicts and transitional justice. In doing so, important questions remain,

---

[198] Laplante and Theidon (2007, p. 229).

[199] See Report of the Special Rapporteur on the Promotion of Truth, Justice, Reparation and Guarantees of Non-Recurrence,' UN Docs. A/HRC/30/42 (2015), 6, and A/HRC/36/50 (2017).

[200] See for instance Duthie and Seils (2017, p. 12).

[201] Lars (2012, pp. 171–186).

[202] Lars (2012, pp. 171–186).

[203] Articles 6 and 7 of the Rome Statute set out the *actus reus* of the offences. Article 25 sets out the concept of individual criminal responsibility.

[204] For a more detailed analysis see Cassese (2008, pp. 404–415).

such as: How, then, should we understand the 'criminal justice approach' undertaken by both domestic bodies and international mechanisms like the ICC? There is a need to explore the ICC's alignment to justice practice through an exploration of the work of NGOs. How would NGOs navigate the different perceptions and expectations on transitional justice within diverse conflict-affected communities?

5.2 The International Criminal Court and Victims: Key Strengths and Limitations

The ICC has been most active in the Global South over the past decade, with interventions in African situations. Like I have argued elsewhere, the way in which the Court engages with the victims (not just States) can either enhance or reduce its legitimacy in the region.[205] Thus in order to explore how transnational networks and NGOs impact on the work of the ICC within the context of transitional justice, it is important to understand the Court's practice and how it operationalises and measures its theories for both perpetrators and victims of international crimes. The ICC is regarded as the most influential institution of individual criminal accountability, with broad avenues for victims' engagement and justice.[206]
From a theoretical perspective, the ICC scope somewhat differs from the definition of victims provided under the Declaration of Basic Principles of Justice for Victims of Crime and Abuse of Power (Victims Declaration):

> Victims' means persons who, individually or collectively, have suffered harm, including physical or mental injury, emotional suffering, economic loss or substantial impairment of their fundamental rights, through acts or omissions that are in violation of criminal laws operative within Member States.[207]

According to the ICC Rules of Procedure, the definition of victims may include organisations or institutions.[208] But more broadly, the conceptualisation of victims includes not only those who are participating in ongoing proceedings, but also, those who applied for participation in proceedings.[209] As noted in the introduction, the ICC cannot assert territorial jurisdiction over the crimes against the Rohingya because Myanmar is not a party to the ICC. There are also doubts whether the UN Security

---

[205] I use case studies of Sudan and Kenya to offer insights on the Court's legitimacy and demonstrate new perspectives on the ICC in Africa in Kirabira (2021, pp. 23–32).

[206] See Schwöbel-Patel (2018, p. 708), Hoyle and Ullrich (2014, pp. 681–704).

[207] See UN General Assembly, Declaration of Basic Principles of Justice for Victims of Crime and Abuse of Power: resolution/adopted by the General Assembly, 29 November 1985, A/RES/40/34, (Victims Declaration). Arts. 1 and 2.

[208] See Rule 85 of the ICC Rules of Procedure and Evidence.

[209] See ICC, Representing Victims before the International Criminal Court: A Manual for Legal Representatives (2018).

Council (UNSC) could refer the case to the ICC, owing to China and Russia's veto and relations with Myanmar.[210]

Despite these legal impediments, it is important to examine the framework within which the ICC would operate in contexts like Myanmar. The ICC, for example, operates under the complementarity principle,[211] which means that it investigates violations of international law—namely war crimes, crimes against humanity, and genocide—only when domestic judicial systems prove unwilling or unable to do so themselves. More importantly, the ICC framework is envisaged as a springboard for States' compliance with the Rome Statute—enabling States where it has intervened to equally develop their domestic capacity to address core international crimes.[212]

The approach of universal jurisdiction is highly relevant for this book and arguments regarding the use of ICL as a form of transitional justice. Universal jurisdiction creates an avenue for the international community, through the prosecution of penetrators of gross violations of human rights within foreign courts, when the domestic courts are unable or unwilling to prosecute them.[213] Against this backdrop, there is a need to explore how transnational networks and NGOs engage with universal jurisdiction within the context of transitional justice. This examination needs to take into consideration the dangers of transitional justice processes driven primarily by external interests and perceptions.[214]Where this happens, transitional justice will likely fail to meet the needs of victims and the broader community affected by violence.

Victim participation is a crucial dimension of transitional justice, which is also reflected in the ICC legal framework and practice. The ICC has an independent unit, the Office of Public Counsel for Victims (OPCV), established in September 2005.[215] This could be construed as an effective step in strengthening the legal representation of victims in proceedings before the ICC. In order to achieve this, there is a need to consider the realities of each specific country, as noted by the OPCV.[216]

In addition to legal representation, the administrative support to victims is offered by the Victims Participation and Reparations Section (VPRS), another unit within the Registry. It is responsible for assisting victims in the process of submitting representations. It is largely considered as the ICC's general programme of outreach and communications,[217] and undertakes field missions to situation countries. Although not expressly authorised to make submissions on behalf of victims, the VPRS has

[210] See for instance Higgins (2019, p. 119).

[211] Preamble to the Rome Statute of the International Criminal Court, para 10.

[212] See Uche (2024) on ways to implement the ICC's Policy on Complementarity and Cooperation, highlighting contexts in the Global South. See also Lugano (2023, pp. 46–78) for detailed examination of African States' Cooperation and Complementarity under the Rome Statute.

[213] For a detailed exploration on how NGOs supported victims of mass atrocity using Universal jurisdiction, see Bekou (2015, p. 223).

[214] See generally McAuliffe (2019).

[215] See ICC, Regulations of the Court, ICC-BD/01-01-04, Regulation 81.

[216] See ICC, Office of Public Counsel for Victims Manual (2010).

[217] See ICC, Report on Participation of and Reparations to Victims, ICC-ASP/3/21 (25 August 2004).

previously communicated victims' representations, in the context of a request from the Prosecutor to open investigations.

Several factors have been raised among the challenges of victim participation. These include the limited contact with victims living in remote areas, whilst others relocate often, due to conflict.[218] Notably, the OPCV lacks a precise or clear role during trials involving multiple victims, and various Chambers take different approaches.[219] An important normative question that often arises is: Who speaks for the victims? There is a mixed but interesting scholarly debate about victims' representation before the ICC and its effectiveness. For example, whilst questioning the extent to which the ICC can be considered 'victim-centric', Rachel Killean and Luke Moffett are critical of the Courts approach of 'collectivizing victims' voices.[220] Representational practices through legal representative could as well represent diverging views among victims. Some theorists argue for a legal avenue for 'resisting representation as part of an abstract collectivity' and emphasise the need for individual victim representation.[221] In addition to these procedural gaps, legal scholars observe an overlap in the roles filled by the VPRS and the OPCV.[222] To this end, there is a need for a clear approach to common legal representation of different victims.[223]

Another challenge that could limit victims' participation before the ICC and other ICTs is the institutional bureaucracy. This is acknowledged by Jean Galbraith, in her analysis, noting that the average length of time between custody and the ultimate judgement was 5.9 years for the ICTR, and 4.7 years for the ICTY.[224] These delays affect tens of thousands of victims in a given context, whilst the fallibility of the ICC victims processes affects only the few going through its procedures. In general, the long timelines point to questions regarding the legitimacy of such mechanisms before the conflict-affected communities. Secondly, we could also think about the gender dimensions of victims' participation, specifically women, who often are limited by social responsibilities.[225] Thirdly, some religions might emphasise repentance and forgiveness, as opposed to retribution.[226] Finally, victims without legal capacity are unlikely to fully participate in these processes.

With the foregoing challenges, the strands of legal research in international criminal justice need to review victims' participation with comprehensive and effective approaches, based on local context. For example, in multi-ethnic, multicultural and

---

218 See ICC, Office of Public Counsel for Victims Manual (2010).

219 *Prosecutor v Jean-Pierre Bemba Gombo*, Decision on Victim Participation, ICC-01/05-01/08-103-para10, (Pre-Trial Chamber III, 12 September 2008). It was noted that 'Where no legal representative has been appointed by the victims', the OPCV would act as legal representative of the victims 'from the time they submit their applications for participation'.

220 Killean and Moffett (2017, pp. 733–734).

221 For more elaborate analysis see Kendall and Nouwen (2014, p. 76).

222 War Crimes Research Office (2011, p. 48).

223 War Crimes Research Office (2011, p. 1).

224 For a more detailed analysis see Galbraith (2009, p. 117).

225 Feminist scholars emphasise the distinct experiences and harm towards women in conflict situations that are often overlooked by international Courts. Grey and Chappell (2020).

226 See for example Stahn (2012, pp. 251–282).

multilingual societies, it might be of relevance to remove discriminatory provisions in domestic laws, in order to embrace all victims as participants in the justice mechanisms. One of the notable barriers is gender-based discrimination, which might limit the effectiveness of criminal justice mechanisms in criminal tribunals. As Kelly Askin observes, prosecution of gender crimes is 'typically fraught with inherent difficulties and gratuitous obstacles, and the crimes are usually investigated and indicted only after concerted pressure by women's rights organisations and feminist scholars to prosecute the crimes',[227] The next section will carry these discussions ahead, as part of the wider criticisms against ICL and the ICC within the practice of transitional justice.

6 Contemporary Criticisms of Transitional Justice: Pathways for Global South Engagement

It is important to explore the criticisms of transitional justice, in order to understand how best to respond to different post-war contexts or democratic transitions. The most prominent criticism of transitional justice arises from the interaction of the Global North and Global South discourses. The dominant post-conflict legalistic discourse is problematic. In the era of globalisation, Tietel attributes the challenges in the field to the interaction of transitional justice and globalisation.[228] In a related manner, Rowen proposes a shift in the scholarship in transitional justice, to mask the 'instrumentalization' and 'politicization' of the idea, where there is ongoing conflict.[229]

Academic scholars have sought to answer this question: Is there a North–South gap in understandings and beliefs about what transitional justice is and what it can do? Whereas Stephan Parmentier explicitly agrees that this gap exists,[230] Chris Dolan uses the terminology of 'North-based transitional justice operators'.[231] Dolan raises an interesting argument for 'South-based transitional justice', for example, the building of memorials in the conflict-affected societies, as opposed to State-controlled truth-telling and reconciliation.[232] Clark builds on and adds to this inclusivity critique, in the context of rape and social violence, arguing for 'bottom-up' approaches.[233]

Away from the North–South differences, the nature of transitional justice itself is also a point of contention. A starting point of concern is the dilemma relating

[227] For a more detailed review of Gender Based crimes within the context of war or mass violence, see Askin (2003, p. 317).

[228] Teitel (2002, p. 899).

[229] Rowen (2018, p. 60).

[230] Fletcher and Weinstein (2018, pp. 38–39).

[231] Fletcher and Weinstein (2018, pp. 228–230).

[232] Fletcher and Weinstein (2018, p. 229).

[233] Clark (2018a, p. 8).

to the stages and nature of transition: post-authoritarian, post-conflict or even non-transitions. Scholars grapple with the question; can transitional justice be achieved where there is no transition? According to Jamie Rowen, 'promoting Transitional Justice too soon can divert attention from more pressing concerns, such as stopping the violence'.[234]However, transitional justice is not always about redressing post-war situations or armed conflict, but can also be applied in contexts of transition from authoritarian rule to democracy. Nonetheless, reflecting on the concern about the stages of transition will be crucial in understanding how transnational networks and NGOs impact transitional justice in the two case studies of Uganda and Myanmar.

The second question relates to legitimacy, and the potential legitimisation of the status quo.[235]The case of Democratic Republic of the Congo (DRC) is highlighted an example of a context where transitional justice is weakly institutionalised, with a diversity of victims and perpetrators.[236] In Rwanda, the government was viewed as delegitimising the ITCR, because of political reasons, as the government's forces were equally implicated in the commission of crimes.[237]

The politiclisation of international tribunals links to the key questions about the nature of transitional justice. Over the last decade, scholars have concluded that transitional justice can be done without a democratic transition.[238] An important concern, however, is the limited scholarly focus on the promoters of transitional justice, a field associated with the idea of 'globalization'.[239] As such, the book will explore the work of transnational networks and NGOs as key actors within transitional justice, investigating how they (de)legitimise transitional justice mechanisms. Specifically, the criticisms against the politicisation of ICTs invite a closer assessment of the role of transnational networks and NGOs within the field.

Another criticism relates to the level of crimes prosecuted under retributive mechanisms. One popular argument for transitional justice is the accountability of high-level perpetrators, through criminal prosecution, in relation to crimes committed during conflict. According to Helen Chang Mack and Monica Segura Leonardo, this demonstrates the commitment to rule of law, whilst improving the public's faith in the criminal justice system.[240] However, the widespread crimes perpetuated by groups during armed conflicts are almost overwhelming for transitional justice mechanisms.

Scholars examining transitional justice in Guatemala, for example, argue that 'transitional justice models often fail to consider the meaning of crime in the daily experience of ordinary people'.[241] As a solution, they suggest that criminal justice mechanisms should address the social context in which it operates.[242] Scholars are

---

[234] Rowen (2018, p. 57).

[235] Fletcher and Weinstein (2018, p. 229).

[236] Fletcher and Weinstein (2018, p. 221).

[237] Horovitz (2018), Kendall and Nouwen (2016, p. 221).

[238] Fletcher and Weinstein (2018, p. 229).

[239] See generally Rowen (2018).

[240] Mack and Leonardo (2012, pp. 175–181).

[241] Mack and Leonardo (2012, pp. 175–181).

[242] Mack and Leonardo (2012, pp. 175–181).

skeptical about the ability of transitional justice in the transformation of institutions, culture and individual dispositions.[243] Besides institutional transformation, scholars suggest changes at the level of culture and personal dispositions.[244] The criticism is that transitional justice measures are in some instances questions of institutional change in reality.[245] One important aspect to draw from these suggestions is the crucial role of transnational networks and NGOs with sufficient power to complement the States.[246]

From a victimological perspective, there are concerns about the lack of contextual focus on victims. This arises mostly from the critics of the 'North-based Transitional Justice'. Pemberton, a professor of victimology, argues that this universal view of transitional justice ignores the local context.[247] From his perspective, the most important challenges of transitional justice need to be framed from the context of victims' priorities and justice.[248] Pablo de Greiff raises an important observation, about the diversity of types of victimhood, something that transitional justice proponents need to think about when intervening in different contexts,[249] not forgetting that NGO outreach plays a key role in localising the transitional justice concepts.[250]

Victims' narratives are not clear, regarding the two types of interventions: one regarding governance and rule of law initiatives, and the other criminal justice. Interesting insights are highlighted from localised context-specific contexts, but also from a macro-focused global point. For example, Helen Chang Mack, a victim in Guatemala, advocates for remediation and renunciation by government, as opposed to governance and rule of law.[251] In the context of sexual violence, Janine Clark observes a missing link between victims' contexts and transitional justice.[252] She develops the term 'social ecologies' arguing that context is particularly important in relation to storytelling involving sexual violence.[253] In the development of contemporary transitional justice, Teitel proposes further exploration of three dimensions relating to post-Cold War, globalisation and security state politics.[254] However, in addition to these theoretical approaches, there is a need for more contextualised and case specific studies in transitional justice. The book will explore in more detail how transnational networks and NGOs impact on the strategies adopted by ICTs.

---

243 Fletcher and Weinstein (2018, p. 369).

244 See generally Fletcher and Weinstein (2018).

245 Fletcher and Weinstein (2018, p. 36).

246 See Fletcher and Weinstein (2018, p. 37) for Pablo de Greiff's observations on the role of civil society organizations (CSOs) in transitional justice.

247 Fletcher and Weinstein (2018, p. 244).

248 Fletcher and Weinstein (2018, p. 221).

249 Fletcher and Weinstein (2018, p. 32).

250 Fletcher and Weinstein (2018, p. 236).

251 Fletcher and Weinstein (2018, p. 234).

252 Clark (2018a, pp. 1–288) and Clark (2018b, pp. 509–537).

253 Clark (2018b, pp. 509–537).

254 Teitel (2002, p. 906).

Finally, the use of customary practices as a means of transitional justice has attracted growing attention from scholars and policymakers as the standard forms of transitional justice have been criticised as too legalistic and Western. The emerging emphasis is on measures that resonate with communities.[255] As highlighted by Pablo de Greiff, the former UN Special Rapporteur on the promotion of truth, justice, reparation and guarantees of non-recurrence, there is need to give more attention to interventions in the cultural and the personal domains.[256] This suggests the need for more studies on the impact of actors like NGOs on the victims' perceptions on transitional justice.

What is clear from all the discussions is that transitional justice is an evolving field, with a lot of potential for transformation of its own norms and contextualization, in line with contemporary situations. In regard to a complex crisis like that of the Rohingya, there needs to be an exploration of how different NGOs navigate these social and cultural dimensions. The book therefore responds to calls for more comprehensive studies to understand how transitional justice works or would work across a range of paradigms.[257] As indicated in Chapter One, the book examines the impact of transnational networks and global justice institutions using the analytical framework of legitimacy, a concept discussed in more detail in the next sub-section.

7 Linking Legitimacy to the Work of Transnational Networks and International Criminal Law

This book highlights the productive power of transitional justice discourse, in a discursively constituted world of local and international actors. The previous sections have given a theoretical count of transitional justice, highlighting a lack of conceptual clarity regarding the adoption of certain initiatives like ICTs.[258] This section analyses the implementation and impact of transitional justice, using the theory of legitimacy, which is relevant to understand how transnational networks and NGOs (de)legitimise transitional justice. This link is particularly important, considering the proliferation of local and international NGOs in the field of transitional justice, over the past decades.[259] Against this backdrop, the next sub-section will discuss the concept of legitimacy as a crucial starting point for analysing the impact of transnational networks and NGOs on transitional justice.

---

[255] McAuliffe (2008, pp. 365–393). It is argued, 'Imposing norms from the outside or removing functions from the control or view of local people can conflict with the ideal of progressive self rule'.

[256] See Report of the Special Rapporteur on the Promotion of Truth, Justice, Reparation and Guarantees of Non-Recurrence, UN Docs. A/HRC/30/42 (2015), 6, and A/HRC/36/50 (2017, pp. 8–9).

[257] For detailed review on emerging transitional justice paradigms, see Sharp (2018).

[258] Linton (2016, p. 159).

[259] For an exploration of civil society roles in advocating for transitional justice in Africa, see Brankovic (2010).

7.1 *Legitimacy as a Conceptual Framework for Transitional Justice: Normative and Strategic Goals*

How do Transnational Networks and NGOs (de)legitimise transitional justice mechanisms? Answering this question requires an understanding of the theory of legitimacy, as a starting point. There is a growing justification for the use of legitimacy as an analytical angle in transitional justice.[260] Such analysis also touches on another important aspect, i.e. power. The concept of power offers a conceptual link between the theory of legitimacy and transitional justice, through the unique understanding of the discursive processes and practices of its actors. Scholars of international relations conceptualise power as ‘the production of effects that shape the capacities of actors to determine their circumstances’.[261] More specifically, the dimension of ‘productive power’ means the ‘Production of subjects through diffuse social relations’ and considers discourses as sites of social power.[262] These discursive processes produce social identities and give particular meaning to them.[263] This concept of power illustrates how actors, including international organisations, shape and set conditions.[264]

The concept of legitimacy is derived from the Latin word *legitimus*, meaning ‘lawful’, ‘appropriate’ or ‘just’.[265] It is a relevant element within the work and study of international organisations. It is particularly important within the context of transitional justice, due to often competing, yet legitimate approaches for criminal justice vis-a-vis peace or reconciliation.[266] There are distinctions between normative and empirical approaches to the theory of legitimacy. The normative dimension relates to an institution’s ‘right to rule’ whilst the sociological one relates to the widespread belief of the people that the institution has the right to rule.[267] Legitimacy is closely related with socially embedded beliefs like morality.[268] Besides morality, the concepts of legality and constitutionality play a key role in shaping legitimacy.[269] Within the context of international organisations, legitimacy matters because it is regarded as a source of compliance, but also gives an insight into their challenges.[270]

In terms of analysis, it is important to specify which approach to adopt, between normative and empirical legitimacy. Due to the emergence of international justice

---

[260] For an elaborate examination on legitimacy of transitional justice mechanisms in Cambodia and Sierra Leone, see Stensrud (2015).

[261] Barnett and Duvall (2005, p. 42).

[262] Barnett and Duvall (2005, p. 55).

[263] Barnett and Duvall (2005, p. 56).

[264] Barnett and Duvall (2005, p. 60).

[265] See Tankebe and Liebling (2013, p. 1).

[266] See Dempster (2020, p. 249).

[267] Buchanan and Keohane (2006, pp. 405–437).

[268] For detailed understanding of legitimacy as a social concept, see generally Zaum (2016).

[269] Clark (2005, p. 19).

[270] See Zaum (2016).

institutions like the ICC, there is a growing emphasis on the empirical approach of legitimacy, that relates to the output of institutions in what is termed 'people centered approach' or 'grounded, bottom-up approach'.[271] It allows for the empirical examination of whether certain rules or justice mechanisms are justifiable in particular contexts.[272] According to Barbara Oomen, this is the only approach that can help assess the role of institutions in transitional justice.[273]

The analysis in this book is informed by Beetham's theory on the legitimation of power, which encompasses both normative and social aspects of legitimacy.[274] This is in line with research that acknowledges the limitations with the current focus on sociological legitimacy, where the vast of academic literature underexplores the aspect of legal validity of NGOs.[275] By emphasising this socio-legal understanding of legitimacy, we can analyse the work of not just transnational networks and NGOs, but also international courts as separate actors within transitional justice. A major unit of analysis in this book is the work of the ICC within the context of transitional justice.

Why does legitimacy matter for institutions like the ICC? Voeten conceptualises legitimacy within the rubric of public opinion, defining it as 'the beliefs among the mass public that an international court has the right to exercise authority in a certain domain'.[276] This definition is important in the analysis of the legitimacy discourse regarding the ICC and other ICTs that try cases of gross human rights violations.

Over the years, the ICC and other international tribunals have faced challenges to their legitimacy from various stakeholders, including State and non-State actors.[277] Due to the exercise of universal jurisdiction, the ICC has been criticised for being overly focused on Africa, thus straining its relationships with the African Union and some member states.[278] According to Follesdal, the normative aspect is the central concept of legitimacy for international courts, defining their legitimate authority as 'a matter of why and when their judgements or recommendations should count as defeasible reasons for other actors deciding what to do'.[279]

Besides the normative aspect, sociological legitimacy also matters for the institutions. This kind of legitimacy can also be defined to mean '"how actors" perceptions may legitimise courts or how such perceptions allow courts to justify their practices and power'[280] One of the underexplored, yet key factors in this regard relates to the truth-finding capacity of international courts.[281] This is recognised by Holtermann,

---

271 Oomen (2007, p. 143).
272 See Stensrud (2009, pp. 5–15).
273 Stensrud (2009, p. 148).
274 Beetham (2013, p. 25).
275 Thrandardottir and Keating (2018, p. 209).
276 Voeten (2013, p. 414).
277 Hillebrecht (2020, pp. 453–486).
278 Mennecke (2017, p. 37).
279 Follesdal (2019, p. 225).
280 Alter (2018, p. 28).
281 For a detailed analysis on International Courts see Holtermann (2017), Holtermann (2015, p. 7).

through his elucidation on ontological and epistemological assumptions underlying the intuitive idea of justice among different stakeholders.[282] The ability to prosecute cases with increased interests and participation of large numbers of victims is a measure of the courts' legitimacy, as observed in the ICTY and the ECCC.[283] Similarly, critical legal scholarship suggests that through this interaction, international courts use NGOS to promote their goals.[284]

The ICC, for example, uses NGOs as intermediaries with complementary capabilities to leverage on their expertise and access to victims, whilst defending its legitimacy.[285] Moreover, legal scholars have noted a heavy reliance by the OTP on indirect evidence gathered from NGO reports as secondary sources.[286] From a constructivist perspective, De Silva elucidates how that international courts apply strategies to 'socialize' NGOs into their norms.[287] This supports the legal arguments that a court's legitimacy increases the chances of compliance with its decisions.[288]

Another type of legitimacy is termed 'diffuse support', which relates to the acceptance of the court's judgements by the public.[289] This is useful in the analysis of the ICJ as a transitional justice institution. Dothan argues that the ICJ issues judgements that are a compromise between the interests of the two states, in order to show impartiality and gain legitimacy.[290] In general, he notes that 'legitimacy is a currency that a court can spend',[291] As such, legitimacy is not only important in international criminal justice but can also be used to analyse Courts working on transitional justice-related cases like genocide.

Similarly, scholars emphasise the role of the general public in ensuring State compliance with international court judgements.[292] Voeten provides empirical evidence with regard to the European courts (the CJEU and the ECtHR), the ICJ and the 'ICC (with an emphasis on Uganda)'.[293] He observes a correlation between public opinions of international courts and people's attitudes towards the international organisations closely associated with the courts.[294] He argues that instead of worrying about the general public perceptions, the courts should 'focus their legitimizing behavior on other compliance constituencies, such as elites and nongovernmental

282 Holtermann (2017, p. 21).

283 Wierda, Nassar and Maalouf (2007, p. 1072).

284 Dothan (2015, p. 636).

285 De Silva (2017, pp. 178–180).

286 SáCouto and Cleary (2012, p. 73).

287 De Silva (2018, pp. 300–303).

288 See Dothan (2013, p. 458).

289 Dothan (2013, p. 456).

290 Dothan (2013, p. 461).

291 Dothan (2013, p. 477).

292 See for example Voeten (2013).

293 Voeten (2013, p. 413).

294 Voeten (2013).

organizations (NGOs)'.[295] This evidence points towards the need to investigate the impact of international actors, specifically NGOs, in transitional justice.

The legal theorist Madsen presents an interesting research angle, in relation to how international courts develop means of legitimisation within their relations with democratic politics and society.[296] This is further recognised by Follesdal, who notes a complex interdependence of international courts with these actors.[297] Mégret also highlights another legitimisation angle, where international tribunals seek to get closer to the reality through '[h]ybridisation and regionalization'.[298] Mikael Madsen contends that since international courts are not autonomous legal institutions, it is vital to comprehend their legitimating strategies from the way they respond to law, politics and society.[299] In sum, it is important to keep in mind that the local acceptance of international criminal justice mechanisms is linked not just to the outcome of the judicial process, but also to the process itself and the work of the institutions.[300] It will thus be important to assess how NGOs impact on the legitimacy of transitional justice.

7.2 *Situating NGOs in Transitional Justice: Legitimation of Power*

Having explored the key scholarly concerns within the field, it is important to understand how transitional justice relates to the central subjects of this book—transnational networks and NGOs. This sub-section discusses theoretical aspects of NGO work, showing the relationships between domestic and international NGOs. It also highlights how these connections map onto their work and ultimately the (de)legitimation of mechanisms. By using this analytical framework, the book responds to scholarly calls for a more comprehensive conceptualisation of the role of NGOs in transitional justice.[301] In addition to these discussions, the sub-section ends with an appraisal of the key scholarship on NGOs and their impact on international criminal justice.

There is no definite definition of the term NGO. In the context of international politics, it refers to: '(a) organisations whose purpose is for the public good, but not governmental or profitable in nature and (b) that these organisations fulfil the

295 Voeten (2013, p. 416).

296 Madsen (2012, p. 23).

297 Follesdal (2020, p. 480).

298 Mégret (2016, p. 209).

299 Madsen (2012, p. 26).

300 Buckley-Zistel, Mieth, and Papa (2016, p. 1).

301 See for more details Boesenecker and Vinjamuri (2011), Eilstrup-Sangiovanni and Sharman (2019), Gready and Robins (2017).

minimum legal requirements of the regulatory regimes they comply with',[302] International NGOs are: non-profit organisations operating in multiple countries established privately rather than by intergovernmental agreement to engage in different activities like human rights advocacy and service delivery.[303] Within the context of transitional justice, the interaction between local and international NGOs is akin to a transfer of expertise and practices from the global to local sites.[304] The UNSC also recognises the role of international actors within transitional justice, as manifested in the reports regarding particular contexts like Côte d'Ivoire.[305] With such a wide acknowledgement of NGO roles, it is important to understand how they impact on the legitimacy of other transitional justice actors like courts.

Erla Thrandardottir and Vincent Charles Keating observe a gap between 'the de facto and de jure legitimacy' of international non-governental organisations that 'requires more consideration from scholars studying their role in the international system'.[306] As a way of bridging this legitimacy gap, they recommend clarity in the legal status of international organisations as de facto international actors.[307] Ultimately, an understanding of NGO legitimacy may help explain their involvement in transitional justice, and ability to bring about normative change in the institutions.[308] However, this book seeks to explore how NGOs interact with transitional justice and how they impact on the legitimacy of its institutions.

The language of liberal peace-building and the huge involvement of Western governments in the work of international NGOs pose new challenges for their legitimacy within ongoing conflicts.[309] Victimology literature suggests that the legitimacy of transitional justice mechanisms is also bolstered by actors that capture the voices of victims, in what is termed self-legitimation.[310] This also relates to their construction of humanitarian and victims' narratives, which is what Schwobel-Patel calls

---

[302] For deeper engagement with the theoretical explanations on NGOs and accountability, see Thrandardottir (2015, p. 51).

[303] See Walton et al. (2016, p. 2771).

[304] Van Schaack (2020, p. 10).

[305] UN Security Council, Security Council Resolution 2062 (2012) [on Extension of the Mandate of the UN Operation in Côte d'Ivoire (UNOCI) until 31 July 2013], 26 July 2012, S/RES/2062 (2012). It emphasised:

> the urgent need for concrete measures to promote justice and reconciliation at all levels and on all sides, including through the active involvement of civil society groups, with the aim of addressing the underlying causes of the Cote d'Ivoire crises, encourages support for transitional justice mechanisms, including the Dialogue, Truth and Reconciliation Commission, to adopt a broad-based a broad-based and comprehensive programme and to increase its activities at the local level throughout the country.

[306] Thrandardottir and Keating (2018, pp. 207–220).

[307] Thrandardottir and Keating (2017).

[308] See Thrandardottir (2015, p. 109).

[309] Walton (2018, p. 645).

[310] See for example McEvoy and McConnachie (2013, p. 492).

'the fundraising image of victimhood'.[311] It is therefore recommended that scholars assist International non Governmantal Organisations (INGOs) in this regard, with an evaluation of their interactions with other stakeholders.[312] Contextually, cases like Bosnia-Herzegovina highlight the importance of an interdisciplinary analysis of the role of NGOs in transitional justice processes.[313]

Narratives on transitional justice provide a good basis for using the analytical framework of legitimacy, when assessing the impact of NGOs on transitional justice. As observed by Arnould, narratives 'can be produced, reproduced, and contested (or, in the negative, controlled) which can serve to challenge legitimising discourses used by actors or institutions linked to past abuses'.[314] For example, the capacity of NGOs to question and change discourses on transitional justice contributes to the formation of international norms.[315]

It is important to note that the extensive involvement of NGOs in transitional justice is contested, with critical perspectives from the Global South that view international NGOS as hegemonic actors.[316] This is exacerbated by the unequal power relations between domestic and international NGOs. As observed by Beijerman, 'the fact that NGOs have fixed positions based on their mission might obstruct, rather than facilitate any open debate'.[317] The relationships that NGOs (agents) have with their donors (principals) also necessitate some form of accountability, under the principal–agent market model.[318] In addition to donors, the demands placed on them by other actors like States, the media and international organisations put their legitimacy into question.[319] Within the context of conflict, Walton argues that local NGOs are particularly vulnerable to legitimacy questions, as they have to maintain relationships with both external and domestic actors.[320]

There is solid literature about NGOs and their engagement in international criminal justice, specifically hybrid tribunals and the ICC. International and local NGOs influenced local activities and discussions on the Extraordinary Chambers in the Courts of Cambodia (ECCC or Khmer Rouge tribunal) in a manner that not only legitimised the specialised justice mechanism but also opened pathways for debates on the implementation of the concept of transitional justice in general.[321]

More specifically, international law scholars have shown how INGOs promote the ICC, for example, through its formalised procedures like the *amicus curiae*

---

[311] Schwöbel-Patel (2016, p. 250).

[312] For further analysis see Walton et al. (2016, p. 2782).

[313] Kurze (2017, p. 27).

[314] Arnould (2015, p. 358).

[315] Beijerman (2018, p. 153).

[316] Beijerman (2018, pp. 147–173).

[317] Beijerman (2018, p. 154).

[318] Keating and Thrandardottir (2016, p. 136).

[319] Walton (2008, p. 134).

[320] Walton (2008, p. 137).

[321] See Stephan Parmentier's analysis on the ECCC and transitional justice in Cambodia in Fletcher and Weinstein (2018, p. 47).

and victims' procedures[322] This book lends support to Mégret's argument that this increased non-State and civil society participation contributes to the understanding about their legitimacy.[323] Similarly, Carsten Stahn argues that NGOs have 'become important advocates and voices of judicial action'.[324] However, their lines of inquiry are not specifically about the impact of transnational networks in ICL or transitional justice.

What comes closer to this book's line of inquiry is Leila Ullrich's empirical work which shows the emerging position of NGO intermediaries in ICL, revealing the ICC's dependence upon intermediaries to mitigate the challenges that come with lack of proximity with the affected communities.[325] More importantly, there is a legitimation of the ICC's work by NGOs within pluralist spaces of justice.[326] Such inquiry on ICC intermediaries links well with prior discussions, specifically on the uncertain working relationship between NGO intermediaries and the ICC.[327] One strand of research analyses the work of NGOs in international criminal justice from the lens of criminology and sociology, showing that they are advocates of humanity.[328] Most importantly, revealing how global NGO networks use victims in a way that legitimises international criminal justice. However, the findings are situated within a 'sociology of punishment' perspective.[329] On the other hand, this book approaches the work of the ICC from the scholarly discipline of transitional justice. Secondly, whilst Lohne uses and advocates for sociology of punishment as a frame for international criminal justice, this book shows how NGOs enhance or reduce the legitimacy of transitional justice institutions like the ICC.

Within the field of transitional justice, African scholars and local transitional justice practitioners offer useful insights on state-NGO relationships, indicating how the latter promote, reframe and challenge transitional justice processes.[330] For instance, the drafting and adoption of the African Union Transitional Justice Policy of 2019 was significantly led by Transnational Networks, notably the Centre for the Study of Violence and Reconciliation (CSVR) and the Institute for Justice and Reconciliation in South Africa.[331] Departing from studies that make a more generalised assessment of NGO work in Africa,[332] this book narrows down to the case studies

---

[322] Mégret (2012, p. 4).

[323] Mégret (2012, p. 7).

[324] Stahn (2018, p. 282).

[325] Ullrich (2016, 543).

[326] Ullrich (2016, 658).

[327] See for instance Haslam and Edmunds (2013, pp. 49–85).

[328] A good analysis on NGOs role within the field of International Criminal Justice is Lohne (2019).

[329] Lohne (2019) and Lohne (2021, pp. 3–23).

[330] For detailed exploration on the role of NGOs in shaping transitional justice approaches and policies in Africa, see Bosire and Lynch (2014, pp. 256–276), Dhizaala (2016, pp. 43–63) and Brankovic and van der Merwe (2016, pp. 225–243).

[331] See Mtero (2024, pp. 122–123).

[332] Brankovic and van der Merwe (2016, pp. 225–243), Brankovic and van der Merwe (2018), Moyo (2022, pp. 32–56).

of Uganda and Myanmar. Besides the analysis of transitional justice using the lens of legitimacy, the use of comparative methodology in the book always an in-depth exploration of the commonalities, but also differences in the international actors' involvement in transitional justice across different contexts. The empirical sections of this book will investigate how transnational networks and NGOs (de)legitimise the ICC and other transitional justice mechanisms in the Ugandan and Myanmar cases.

8 Conclusion

The purpose of this chapter has been to explore the link between NGOs and legitimacy, within the scholarly discipline of transitional justice. Preliminary discussions on legal theory have shown how liberalism is embedded within orthodox transitional justice elements of retribution. Similarly, the chapter has shown that global justice making transcends the narrow purview of legalism. More broadly, the chapter has explored critical discourse and practice within transitional justice, highlighting a gap between Global North and Global South understandings of aspects like retribution. It has also discussed the normative boundaries of ICL, specifically the ICC. An important normative question has been posed; who speaks for the victims? As such, NGOs are centralised in the discussions, as critical actors within transitional justice. In order to comprehensively explore the role of transnational networks and NGOs in transitional justice, the chapter has discussed the theory of legitimacy as a conceptual framework for transitional justice. Ultimately, the chapter has set the ground for examining transitional justice by situating NGOs as key actors. It has also created the foundation for assessing the impact of institutions like the ICC, using the theory of legitimacy.

References

Ainley K (2014) Transitional justice in Cambodia: the coincidence of power and principle. In: Jeffery R, Kim H (eds) Transitional justice in the Asia-Pacific. CUP, Cambridge, pp 125–156

Akhavan P (2013) The rise, and fall, and rise, of international criminal justice. J Crim Justice 11:527–536

Alter K, Helfer L, Madsen M (2018) How context shapes the Authority of International Courts. In: Alter K, Helfer L, Madsen M (eds) International Court Authority. OUP, Oxford

Ammann O (2019) How do and should domestic courts interpret international law? Insights from the jurisprudence of HLA Hart and Duncan Kennedy. Transnatl Legal Theory 10:3–4

Antkowiak T (2008) Remedial approaches to human rights violations: the Inter-American Court of human rights and beyond. Columbia J Transnatl Law 46:351–419

Archibugi D, Pease A (2018) Crime and global justice: the dynamics of international punishment, 1st edn. Polity Press, Cambridge

Arnould V (2015) Transitional justice and democracy in Uganda: between impetus and instrumentalisation. J East Afr Stud 9:354–374

Askin K (2003) Prosecuting wartime rape and other gender-related crimes under international law: extraordinary advances, enduring obstacles. Berkeley J Int Law 21:288–349
Barnett M, Duvall R (2005) Power in international politics. Int Org 49:39–75
Bayefsky R (2013) Dignity, honour, and human rights: Kant's perspective. Polit Theory 41:809–837
Beetham D (2013) The legitimation of power, 2nd edn. Macmillan Education, London
Beijerman M (2018) Conceptual confusions in debating the role of NGOs for the democratic legitimacy of international law. Transnatl Legal Theory 9:147–173
Bekou O (2015) Doing justice for the liberian victims of mass atrocity: NGOs in aid of universal jurisdiction. J Int Crim Justice 13:219–227
Boesenecker A, Vinjamuri L (2011) Lost in translation? Civil society, faith-based organizations and the negotiation of international norms. Int J Transitional Justice 5:345–365
Bosire L, Lynch G (2014) Kenya's search for truth and justice: the role of civil society. Int J Transitional Justice 8:256–276
Brankovic J (2010) Advocating justice: civil society and transitional justice in Africa. Workshop Report, African Transitional Justice Research Network and Centre for the Study of Violence and Reconciliation, Cape Town
Brankovic J, van der Merwe H (eds) (2018) Advocating transitional justice in Africa: the role of civil society. Springer, Cham
Buchanan A (2004) Justice, legitimacy, and self-determination: moral foundations for international law. OUP, Oxford
Buchanan A (2010) The legitimacy of international law. In: Besson S, Tasioulas J (eds) The philosophy of international law. OUP, Oxford
Buchanan A, Keohane R (2006) The legitimacy of global governance institutions. Ethics Int Aff 20:405–437
Buckley-Zistel S, Mieth F, Papa M (2016) Assessing the acceptance of international criminal justice in situation countries—a methodology. International Nuremberg Principles Academy, Nuremberg
Burrus B (1962) American legal realism. Howard Law J 8:36–52
Carlson K (2017) International criminal law and its paradoxes: implications for institutions and practice. J Law Courts 5:33–53
Carozza P (2008) Human dignity and judicial interpretation of human rights: a reply. Eur J Int Law 19:931–944
Cassese A (2008) Remarks on the present legal regulation of crimes of states. In: Gaeta P, Zappalà S (eds) The human dimension of international law: selected papers of Antonio Cassese, 1st edn. OUP, Oxford, pp 404–415
Chapman A, Ball P (2001) The truth of truth commissions: comparative lessons from Haiti, South Africa, and Guatemala. Hum Rights Q 23:1–42
Clark I (2005) Legitimacy in international society. OUP, Oxford
Clark J (2018a) Rape, sexual violence and transitional justice challenges lessons from Bosnia Herzegovina, 1st edn. Routledge, Abingdon
Clark J (2018b) Transitional justice, education, and sexual violence stigma: the results of a schools-based study in Bosnia-Herzegovina. J Law Soc 45:509–537
Constitutional Court of South Africa. The Citizen 1978 (Pty) Ltd and Others v. McBride. Case CCT 23/10, 2011, ZACC 11, 8 April 2011
Convention for the Protection of All Persons from Enforced Disappearance (20 December 2006) E/CN.4/2005/WG.22/WP.1/Rev.4, Entered into Force 23 December 2010
Convention on the Elimination of All Forms of Racial Discrimination Adopted and Opened for Signature and Ratification by General Assembly Resolution 2106 (XX) of 21 December 1965 Entry into Force 4 January 1969, in Accordance with Article 19
Convention on the Prevention and Punishment of the Crime of Genocide Approved and Proposed for Signature and Ratification or Accession by General Assembly Resolution 260 A (III) of 9 December 1948 Entry into Force: 12 January 1951

Daly K (2015) What is restorative justice? Fresh answers to a vexed question. Vict Offenders 11:9–29
Daly K, Stubbs J (2006) Feminist engagement with restorative justice. Theor Criminol 10:9–28
de Greiff P (2016) Unacknowledged past breeds manipulation and fear. International Center for Transitional Justice. International Center for Transitional Justice, New York
Delara M (2016) Social determinants of immigrant women's mental health. Adv Public Health 2016:1–11
Dempster L (2020) Quiet' transitional justice: 'publicness', trust and legitimacy in the search for the 'disappeared. Soc Legal Stud 29:246–272
De Silva N (2017) Intermediary complexity in regulatory governance: the international criminal court's use of NGOs in regulating international crimes. Ann Am Acad Pol Soc Sci 670:170–188
De Silva N (2018) International courts' socialization strategies for actual and perceived performance. In: Squatrito T, Young O, Follesdal A, Ulfstein G (eds) The performance of international courts and tribunals. CUP, Cambridge, pp 288–323
Devlin R (1997) The charter and anglophone legal theory. Rev Const Stud 4:19–79
Devlin R (2001) Jurisprudence for judges: why legal theory matters for social context education. Queen's Law J 27:161–206
Dhizaala J (2018) Transitional justice in liberia: the interface between civil society organisations and the liberian truth and reconciliation commission. In: Brankovic J, van der Merwe H (eds) Advocating transitional justice in Africa: the role of civil society. Springer, Cham, pp 43–63
Dothan S (2013) How international courts enhance their legitimacy. Theoret Inquiries Law 14:455–478
Dothan S (2015) Luring NGOs to international courts: a comment on CLR v. Romania. Zeitschrift Für Ausländisches Öffentliches Recht und Völkerrecht/Heidelberg J Int Law 3:635–669
Dudai R (2018) Transitional justice as social control: political transitions, human rights norms and the reclassification of the past. Br J Sociol 69:691–711
Duthie R, Seils P (eds) (2017) Justice mosaics: how context shapes transitional justice in fractured societies. International Center for Transitional Justice, New York
Drumbl M (2012) Reimagining child soldiers in international law and policy. OUP, Oxford
Drumbl M (2016) Victims who victimize. Lond Rev Int Law 4:217–246
Dyzenhaus D (2003) Transitional justice. Int J Const Law 1:163–176
Eilstrup-Sangiovanni M, Sharman J (2019) Enforcers beyond borders: transnational NGOs and the enforcement of international law. Perspect Polit First View 19:131–147
Factory at Chorzow (Germ. v. Pol.) (P.C.I.J 13 September 1928)
Fagan A (2009) Human rights: confronting myths and misunderstandings. Edward Elgar Publishing, Cheltenham
Findlay M (2013) International and comparative criminal justice: a critical introduction, 1st edn. Routledge, Abingdon
Finnis J (2011a) Human rights and common good: collected essays, vol III. OUP, Oxford
Finnis J (2011b) Natural law and natural rights, 2nd edn. OUP, Oxford
Fletcher G, Ohlin J (2005) Reclaiming fundamental principles of criminal law in the Darfur case. J Int Crim Justice 3:539–561
Fletcher L, Weinstein H (2018) 'North-South' dialogue: bridging the gap in transitional justice—workshop transcript. Berkeley J Int Law 36:218–333
Follesdal A (2019) Legitimacy criticisms of international courts not only fuzzy rhetoric? In: Sadurski W, Sevel M, Walton K (eds) Legitimacy: the state and beyond. OUP, Oxford, pp 223–237
Follesdal A (2020) Survey article: the legitimacy of international courts. J Polit Philos 24:476–499
Galbraith J (2009) The pace of international criminal justice. Mich J Int Law 31:79–155
Gavrielides T (2012) Contextualizing restorative justice for hate crime. J Interpers Violence 27:3624–3643
Gready P, Robins S (2014) From transitional to transformative justice: a new agenda for practice. Int J Transitional Justice 8:339–361

Gready P, Robins S (2017) Rethinking civil society and transitional justice: lessons from social movements and 'new' civil society. Int J Hum Rights 21:956–975

Grey R, Chappell L (2020) Re-writing sex and gender in international criminal law. In: deGuzman M, Oosterveld V (eds) The elgar companion to the international criminal court. Edward Elgar Publishing, Cheltenham, pp 363–386

Guest S (2012) Ronald Dworkin: Third Edition, vol 3. Stanford University Press, Stanford

Hall M (2017) Exploring the cultural dimensions of environmental victimization. Palgrave Commun 3:1–10

Hart HLA (1958) Positivism and the separation of law and morals. Harvard Law Rev 71:593–629

Hart HLA (2016) The new challenge to legal positivism (1979). Oxford J Legal Stud 36:459–475

Haslam E, Edmunds R (2013) Managing a new 'partnership': 'professionalization', intermediaries and the international criminal court. Crim Law Forum 24:49–85

Hillebrecht C (2020) International criminal accountability and the domestic politics of resistance: case studies from Kenya and Lebanon. Law Soc Rev 54:453–486

Holtermann J (2015) "One of the challenges that can plausibly be raised against them"? On the role of truth in debates about the legitimacy of international criminal tribunals. iCourts Working Paper Series, No. 36, 2015

Holtermann J (2017) One of the challenges that can plausibly be raised against them'? On the role of truth in debates about the legitimacy of international criminal tribunals. In: Hayashi N, Bailliet C (eds) The legitimacy of international criminal tribunals. CUP, Cambridge, pp 206–227

Holtermann J, Madsen M (2015) European new legal realism and international law: how to make international law intelligible. Leiden J Int Law 28:11–230

Holtermann J, Madsen M (2016) What is empirical in empirical studies of law? A European new legal realist conception. Retfærd: Nordisk Juridisk Tidsskrift 39

Horovitz S (2018) Rwanda's Kabgayi Trial between international justice and national reconciliation. In: Christensen M, Levi R (eds) International practices of criminal justice: social and legal perspectives, 1st edn. Routledge, Abingdon

Hoyle C, Ullrich L (2014) New court, new justice—the evolution of justice for victims at domestic courts and at the international criminal court. J Int Crim Justice 12:681–704

International Criminal Court (2004) Report on Participation of and Reparations to Victims. ICC-ASP/3/21

International Criminal Court (2010) Helping victims make their voice heard: the Office of Public Counsel for Victims. Office of Public Counsel for Victims (OPCV), International Criminal Court, The Hague

International Criminal Court (2018) Representing victims before the international criminal court: a manual for legal representatives, 5th edn. Office of Public Counsel for Victims, The Hague

International Law Commission (2001) Draft Articles on Responsibility of States for Internationally Wrongful Acts. Supplement No. 10 (A/56/10)

Kaitesi U (2013) Genocidal gender and sexual violence the legacy of the ICTR, Rwanda's ordinary courts and gacaca courts. Utrecht University, Utrecht

Karimova T (2014) What amounts to 'a serious violation of international human rights law'? An analysis of practice and expert opinion for the purpose of the 2013 Arms Trade Treaty. Geneva Academy of International Humanitarian Law and Human Rights, Academy Briefing No. 6, Geneva Academy

Karstedt S, Parmentier S (2012) Introduction to the Special Issue. Eur J Criminol 9: 465–467

Keating V, Thrandardottir E (2016) NGOs, trust, and the accountability agenda. Br J Polit Int Relat 19:134–151

Kelder J, Holá B, van Wijk J (2014) Rehabilitation and early release of perpetrators of international crimes: a case study of the ICTY and ICTR. Int Crim Law Rev 14:1177–1203

Kendall S, Nouwen S (2014) Representational practices at the international criminal court: the gap between juridified and abstract victimhood. Law Contemp Probl 76:235–262

Killean R, Moffett L (2017) Victim legal representation before the ICC and ECCC. J Int Crim Justice 15:713–740

Kingsbury B, Straumann B (2010) State of nature versus commercial sociability as the Basis of International Law: reflections on the roman foundations and current interpretations of the international political and legal thought of Grotius, Hobbes and Pufendorf. In: Besson S, Tasioulas J (eds) The Philosophy of Int Law. OUP, New York, pp 33–51
Kirabira T (2021) Surrender of Ali Kushayb and Paul Gicheru: new perspectives in Africa's relationship with the ICC. NY Univ J Int Law Polit 54:23–32
Knoops G (2014) An introduction to the law of international criminal tribunals: a comparative study, 2nd edn. Nijhoff, Leiden
Kurze A (2017) Time for change: aid, NGOs, and transitional justice in Bosnia-Herzegovina. Transit Justice Rev 1:35–62
Labenski S (2017) Female defendants in international criminal law and beyond. SOAS University of London, London
Laplante L, Theidon K (2007) Truth with consequences: justice and reparations in post-truth commission peru. Hum Rights Q 29:228–250
Lars W (2012) Anticipating the past: transitional justice and socio-economic wrongs. Soc Legal Stud 21:171–186
Leyh B (2021) The role of universities and law schools in documenting serious international crimes and advancing the rule of law. Utrecht Law Rev 17:87–101
Linton S (2016) Women accused of international crimes: a trans-disciplinary inquiry and methodology. Crim Law Forum 27:159–226
Lohne K (2019) Advocates of humanity: human rights NGOs in international criminal justice. OUP, Oxford
Lohne K (2021) Penal welfarism 'gone global'? Comparing international criminal justice to the culture of control. Punishment Soc 23:3–23
Luban D (2010) Fairness to rightness: jurisdiction, legality, and the. legitimacy of international criminal law. In: Besson S, Tasioulas J (eds) The philosophy of international law. OUP, Oxford
Lugano G (2023) Examining the domestic legal framework in selected African States that form part of the situational docket of the International Criminal Court. Afr J Int Crim Justice 7:46–78
Mack H, Leonardo M (2012) Editorial note: when transitional justice is not enough. Int J Transit Justice 6:175–181
Madsen M (2012) Explaining the power of international courts in their contexts: from legitimacy to legitimization. Robert Schuman Centre for Advanced Studies Policy Paper 2012/07. Courts, Social Change and Judicial Independence, Florence
Makau M (2016) Human rights standards: hegemony, law, and politics. SUNY Press, Albany
Mani R (2005) Rebuilding an inclusive political community after war. Secur Dialogue 36:511–526
McAuliffe P (2008) Transitional justice in transit: why transferring a special court for Sierra Leone trial to the Hague defeats the purposes of hybrid tribunals. Netherlands Int Law Rev 55:365–393
McAuliffe P (2019) The problem of elites. In: Evans M (ed) Transitional and transformative justice, 1st edn. Routledge, Abingdon
McCrudden C (2008) Human dignity and judicial interpretation of human rights. Eur J Int Law 9:655–724
McEvoy K, McConnachie K (2013) Victims and transitional justice: voice, agency and blame. Soc Legal Stud 22:489–513
Mégret F (2012) Private actor litigation and the evolving legitimacy of supranational adjudication. Robert Schuman Centre for Advanced Studies Policy Paper 2012/07. Courts, Social Change and Judicial Independence, Florence
Mégret F (2016) The anxieties of international criminal justice. Leiden J Int Law 29:197–221
Méndez J (1997) Accountability for past abuses. Hum Rights Q 19:255–282
Méndez J, Bariffi F (2012) Truth, right to, international protection. In: Wolfrum R (ed) Max Planck Encyclopedia of Public International Law. Heidelberg and OUP, Oxford
Mennecke M (2017) The African union and universal jurisdiction. In: Jalloh C, Bantekas I (eds) The International Criminal Court and Africa. OUP, Oxford, pp 10–37

Miralles A (2008) Practical reason, morality and law. In: Martínez A, Šilar M, Torralba J (eds) Natural law: historical, systematic and juridical approaches. Cambridge Scholars Publishing, Newcastle
Moyo K (2022) Civil society as a transitional justice litigation actor in Africa. Afr J Conflict Resolut 22:32–56
Mtero S (2024) African Union System and the African Union Transitional Justice Policy. In: Murithi T (ed) African Union and Transitional Justice: healing the past and restoring human dignity, Jacana Media, Sunnyside, pp 113–124
Murcia L (2013) Social policy or reparative justice? Challenges for reparations in contexts of massive displacement and related serious human rights violations. J Refugee Stud 27:191–206
Nell A (2018) Philosophical justifications in international criminal law jurisprudence: a systematic content analysis in pursuit of rule of law and institutional legitimacy. University of Birmingham, Birmingham
Ohlin J (2009) Towards a unique theory of international criminal sentencing. Cornell Law Faculty Publ Pap 23:373–404
Oomen B (2007) Transitional justice and its legitimacy: the case for a local perspective. Neth Q Hum Rights 25:141–148
Orentlicher D (1991) Settling accounts: the duty to prosecute human rights violations of a prior regime. Yale Law J 100:2539–2615
Parmentier S, Weitekamp E (2013) Punishing perpetrators or seeking truth for victims: serbian opinions on dealing with war crimes. In: Rothe D, Meernik J, Ingadóttir T (eds) The realities of international criminal justice. Brill | Nijhoff, Leiden, pp 43–62
Pillay N (2012) Establishing effective accountability mechanisms for human rights violations. Delivering Justice, no. 4, vol. XLIX Retrieved from UN website https://www.un.org/en/chronicle/article/establishing-effective-accountability-mechanisms-human-rights-violations
Prosecutor v. Jean-Paul Akayesu (Trial Judgement), ICTR-96-4-T, International Criminal Tribunal for Rwanda (ICTR) (2 September 1998) [Hereinafter Akayesu Case]
Prosecutor v Kordic and Cerkez (Appeal) IT-95-14/2-A (17 December 2004)
Prosecutor v Simic et al (Judgment) IT-95-9-T (17 October 2003)
Prosecutor v Thomas Lubanga Dyilo (Appeals Chamber) ICC-01/04-01/06-3129 (A A2 A3) (3 March 2015) [Hereinafter Lubanga Case]
Prosecutor v. Zlatko Aleksovski, Judgement, Case No. IT-95-14/1-A (24 March 2000)
Quinn M (2012) Feminist legal realism. Harvard J Law Gender 35:1–56
Raz J (1988) The morality of freedom. OUP, Oxford
Robinson P (2008) Competing conceptions of modern desert: vengeful, deontological, and empirical. Camb Law J 67:144–147
Robinson D (2013) A cosmopolitan liberal account of international criminal law. Leiden J Int Law 26:127–154
Robins S, Gready P, Aloui A, Andrieu K, Hamza H, Ferchichi W (2022) Transitional justice from the margins: collective reparations and Tunisia's truth and dignity commission. Polit Geogr 94:1–10
Roht-Arriaza N (1990) State responsibility to investigate and prosecute grave human rights violations in international. Calif Law Rev 78:451–513
Rome Statute of the International Criminal Court, U.N. Doc. No. A/ CONF.183/9" (1998)
Rowen J (2018) The Transformation of legal ideas: the globalization and politicization of transitional justice in the Middle East. In: Christensen M, Levi R (eds) International Practices of Criminal Justice, 1st edn. Routledge, Abingdon
Sabharwal G (2017) How can dialogue support reconciliation and transitional justice in post- conflict contexts? Norwegian Institute of Int Affairs, Issue No. 2/2017: 1–4
SáCouto S, Cleary K (2012) Investigative management, strategies, and techniques of the International Criminal Court's Office of the Prosecutor. War Crimes Research Office, Washington D.C.

Schwöbel-Patel C (2016) Spectacle in international criminal law: the fundraising image of victimhood. Lond Rev Int Law 4:247–274
Schwöbel-Patel C (2018) The "ideal" victim of international criminal law. Eur J Int Law 29:703–724
Sharp D (2018) Rethinking transitional justice for the twenty-first century beyond the end of history. CUP, Cambridge
Simpson A, Farrelly N, Holliday I (eds) (2017) Routledge handbook of contemporary Myanmar. Routledge, Abingdon
Slaughter A (1995) International Law in a World of Liberal States. Eur J Int Law 6:503–538
Smeulers A (2015) Female perpetrators—ordinary and extra-ordinary women. Int Crim Law Rev 15:207–253
Spalek B (2005) Crime victims: theory, policy and practice. Palgrave Macmillan, London
Stahn C (2012) Editorial: between 'faith' and 'facts': by what standards should we assess international criminal justice? Leiden J Int Law 25:251–282
Stahn C (2018) Legacy in International Criminal Justice. In: deGuzman M, Amann D (eds) Arcs of global justice: essays in Honour of William A. Schabas. OUP, Oxford, pp 271–287
Statute of the International Tribunal for the Prosecution of Persons Responsible for Serious Violations of International Humanitarian Law Committed in the Territory of the Former Yugoslavia since 1991, U.N. Doc. S/25704 at 36, Annex (1993) and S/25704/Add.1 (1993), Adopted by Security Council on 25 May 1993, U.N. Doc. S/RES/827 (1993)
Stensrud E (2009) New dilemmas in transitional justice: lessons from the mixed courts in Sierra Leone and Cambodia. J Peace Res 46:5–15
Stensrud E (2015) Transitional justice and the problem of legitimacy a study of the mixed courts in Cambodia and Sierra Leone. University of Oslo, Oslo
Taliaferro C (2001) God's Natural Laws. In: George R (ed) Natural law, liberalism, and morality: contemporary essays. OUP, Oxford
Tankebe J, Liebling A (2013) Legitimacy and criminal justice: an introduction. In: Tankebe J, Liebling A (eds) Legitimacy and criminal justice: an international exploration. OUP, Oxford
Teitel R (2002) Transitional justice in a new era. Fordham Int Law J 26:893–906
Teksen F (2019) Implementation of transitional justice initiatives in Bosnia and Herzegovina: the need for an inclusive approach'. J Muslim Minor Aff 39:199–215
The Prosecutor v. Jean-Pierre Bemba Gombo, Decision on Victim Participation, ICC-01/05-01/08-103-Para.10 (Pre-Trial Chamber III, 12 September 2008)
Thrandardottir E (2015) NGO legitimacy: four models. Representation 51:107–123
Thrandardottir E, Keating V (2017) Bridging the legitimacy gap—why INGOs should have clarity in their legal status as international actors. The Humanitarian and Conflict Response Institute
Thrandardottir E, Keating V (2018) Bridging the legitimacy gap: a proposal for the international legal recognition of INGOs. Int Polit 55:207–220
Uche M (2024) Bringing justice closer to victims and creating a community of practice? Some thoughts on ways to implement the ICC OTP's policy on complementarity and cooperation. EJIL:Talk! Blog of the European Journal of International Law. https://www.ejiltalk.org/bringing-justice-closer-to-victims-and-creating-a-community-of-practice-some-thoughts-on-ways-to-implement-the-icc-otps-policy-on-complementarity-and-cooperation/
Ullrich L (2016) Beyond the 'global–local divide': local intermediaries, victims and the justice contestations of the international criminal court. J Int Crim Justice 14:543–568
UN (2017) Report of the Special Rapporteur on the Promotion of Truth, Justice, Reparation and Guarantees of Non-Recurrence,' UN Docs. A/HRC/30/42 (2015), 6, and A/HRC/36/50
UN 'Basic Principles and Guidelines on the Right to a Remedy and Reparation for Victims of Gross Violations of International Human Rights Law and Serious Violations of International Humanitarian Law' (2006), A/RES/60/147. [Hereinafter UN Basic Principles 2005]
UN, Declaration of Basic Principles of Justice for Victims of Crime and Abuse of Power: Resolution/ Adopted by the General Assembly, 29 November 1985, A/RES/40/34
UN, Report of the Secretary-General, The rule of law and transitional justice in conflict and post-conflict societies (2004), S/2004/616

UN Security Council, Security Council resolution 2062 (2012) [on extension of the mandate of the UN Operation in Côte d'Ivoire (UNOCI) until 31 July 2013], 26 July 2012, S/RES/2062(2012)
UN, UN Commission on Human Rights, Report of the Independent Expert Diane Orentlicher, 'Updated Set of Principles for the Protection and Promotion of Human Rights through Action to Combat Impunity' (2005) E/CN.4/2005/102/Add.1 [hereinafter UN Updated Set of Principles]
UN, UN Commission on Human Rights, Study on the Right to the Truth, Report of the Office of the United Nations High Commissioner for Human Rights, (2006) E/CN.4/2006/91 (2006)
UN, Universal Declaration of Human Rights, 10 December 1948, 217 A (III)
van der Merwe H, Brankovic J (2016) The role of African civil society in shaping national transitional justice agendas and policies. Acta Juridica 1:225–243
Van Schaack B (2020) Transitional justice without transition: the International Community's Efforts in Syria. In Imagining Justice for Syria. OUP, New York
Voeten E (2013) Public opinion and the legitimacy of international courts. Theoret Inquiries Law 14:411–436
von Joeden-Forgey E (2017) Gender and the future of genocide studies and prevention. In: Randall A (ed) Genocide and gender in the twentieth century: a comparative survey, 1st edn. Bloomsbury Academic, London
Walton O (2008) Conflict, peacebuilding and NGO legitimacy: National NGOs in Sri Lanka. Confl Secur Dev 8:133–167
Walton O (2018) Beyond disaster framing: exploring multi-mandate INGOs' representations of conflict. Third World Q 39:642–660
Walton O, Davies T, Thrandardottir E, Keating V (2016) Understanding contemporary challenges to INGO legitimacy: integrating top-down and bottom-up perspectives. VOLUNTAS 27:2764–2786
Wemmers J, Amissi Manirabona A (2014) Regaining trust: the importance of justice for victims of crimes against humanity. Int Rev Victimol 20:101–109
War Crimes Research Office (2011) Ensuring effective and efficient representation of victims at the International Criminal Court. War Crimes Research Office, American University Washington College of Law
Wierda M, Nassar H, Maalouf L (2007) Early reflections on local perceptions, legitimacy and legacy of the special tribunal for Lebanon. J Int Crim Justice 5:1065–1081
Zaum D (2016) Legitimacy. In: Cogan J, Hurd I, Johnstone I (eds) The Oxford handbook of international organizations. OUP, Oxford
Zuber V (2019) Are human rights of religious origin? Int J Hum Rights 16:17–31
Zuckert M (2001) Is modern liberalism compatible with limited government? The case of rawls. In: George R (ed) Natural law, liberalism, and morality: contemporary essays. OUP, Oxford

The Case of Uganda: A Fusion of Domestic Transitional Justice and International Criminal Law

1 Introduction: Historical Overview of Conflict

Since gaining its independence in 1962, Uganda has experienced a turbulent political environment characterised by military rule, gross violations of human rights and civil unrest. Dozens of rebel movements surged between 1970 and 1990, with the aim of overthrowing 'dictatorial' regimes.[1] One of these groups, the Joseph Kony-led Lord's Resistance Army (LRA), came into being in 1987, when Northern Uganda erupted into in a civil conflict one year after President Yoweri Museveni took charge of the country.

Some researchers and local observers attributed the rise of this rebellion and conflict to the tenuous political environment in Uganda following President Museveni's rise to power, where native Acholi people from Northern Uganda were politically and economically alienated from the rest of Uganda.[2] The rebellion, therefore, could be seen as retaliation for the ethnic suppression of the people of Northern Uganda and suggests the deeply rooted regional divides.[3] It is important to note that there are still ethnic divisions in the Uganda, as the country still struggles with legacies of British colonial rule.

[1] Kanyeihamba (2010, p. 178).

Author note- The author note of this chapter must mention the overlap with this article JIHLS and that permission has been taken.

[2] For instance Lomo and Hovil (2004, p. 17). Zachary Lomo and Lucy Hovil worked at the Refugee Law Project of Makerere University in Uganda.

[3] Kirabira (2021, pp. 1143–1167). See also Lomo and Hovil (2004, p. 18).

There are some overlaps in this chapter with my doctoral thesis. Additionally, there are overlaps with my published work—Kirabira T (2021) Technology as a key tool for the prosecution of international crimes: Lessons from Uganda. Int Criminal Law Rev 22: 1143–1167, for which permission to re-use content was obtained.

© The Author(s), under exclusive license to Springer Nature Singapore Pte Ltd. 2025
T. R. Kirabira, *Transnational Networks and Justice in the Global South*, International Law and the Global South, https://doi.org/10.1007/978-981-95-3137-0_3

As noted elsewhere, 'the LRA were implicated in acts of sexual violence, murder and recruitment of children as soldiers. It is estimated that about 20,000 children were abducted and recruited into the military by the LRA between 1987 and 2002'.[4] Their atrocities caused the massive internal displacement of more than 440,000 persons in Northern Uganda.[5] They received ammunition and supplies from the neighbouring Sudanese government, due to existing political conflicts between Uganda and Sudan.[6]

In 1994, there was a temporary ceasefire and a peace agreement was close to being reached between the Ugandan government and the LRA.[7] However, the LRA returned to the bush and the violence escalated in subsequent years. In July 2006, the Ugandan government and the LRA commenced peace talks, convened in Juba,[8] the capital city of what is now South Sudan. However, they collapsed in December 2008.[9] Each side viewed the other with suspicion and the Ugandan government opted for a military operation to end the insurgency.[10]

Due to the pressing demands for peace, the Ugandan government had already enacted an Amnesty Act in 2000, which offered immunity and resettlement packages to LRA fighters who surrendered. Consequently, over 26,000 people in the whole country responded positively and returned home.[11] However, the situation changed in 2012 when the 2000 Amnesty law expired, and the new law did not envisage the application of amnesty towards the key LRA commanders.[12] It is important to note that the government's ambiguous approach towards amnesty was initially criticised by some observers—notably Ugandan lawyer and transitional justice expert Barney Afako—concerned that amnesty delayed the peace process.[13]

In 2002, the Ugandan government began an intensive military drive named 'Operation Iron Fist', exerting further pressure on the LRA.[14] Despite its initial success, the number of Internally Displaced People (IDPs) grew to over 800,000 by the end of 2003.[15] One year after the ICC commenced its work in 2002, the Ugandan government referred the conflict to the ICC for investigation. Subsequently, in 2005, arrest warrants relating to crimes against humanity and war crimes were issued for the LRA's top five commanders. Dominic Ongwen, one of LRA's top commanders,

---

[4] See report of Child Soldiers Global Report (2004).

[5] See report of the Office of the Special Representative of the Secretary-General for Children and Armed Conflict (2012).

[6] Lomo and Hovil (2004, p. 28).

[7] See Agreement between the Uganda Government and the Lord's Resistance Army (2004).

[8] Kirabira (2021, pp. 1143–1167).

[9] Hendrickson and Tumutegyereize (2012, p. 5).

[10] See newspaper article Newvision (2006).

[11] For a detailed analysis on amnesty in relation to the Lord's Resistance Army conflict see Afako (2012).

[12] McKnight (2015, p. 202).

[13] See Afako (2012).

[14] Macdonald (2017a, p. 631).

[15] Dunn (2004, p. 141).

surrendered in 2015, and his trial before the ICC commenced in 2016.[16] Backed by United States Special Forces and African Union (AU) troops, the Ugandan military pursued the LRA in DRC and the Central African Republic (CAR) between 2012 and 2017. The LRA gradually weakened due to the surrender and loss of top commanders. In 2017, the Ugandan government formally ended its military offensive against the LRA.[17] In the discourse on accountability for gross violations of human rights, it is thus imperative to examine the different transitional justice approaches in Northern Uganda. Although most stakeholders often speak the language of peace and reconciliation, the victims' perspectives need to be considered. The State's application of justice needs to be considered in line with the aspirations of the victims.

The Uganda context elicits key questions in respect to socio-contexts or political aims of criminal justice as a means of accountability. One question could be; whether States use international institutions and ICL for partisan reasons? For example, in neighbouring Rwanda, the State's use of gacaca courts was viewed by some researchers as a 'tool of social control'.[18] Similarly, as scholars have also pointed out, there are concerns about the nature and timing of the Ugandan government's self-referral to the ICC, which was instrumentalised as a weapon against the LRA?[19] Specifically, the ICC Prosecutor's selective focus on crimes committed by the LRA without investigating alleged crimes committed by government soldiers during the war left a gap in the transitional justice process.[20] Therefore, the questions concerning the ICC's selective intervention in Northern Uganda link well with the aspect of legitimacy that is analysed in this book, specifically how Transnational Networks and NGOs (de)legitimise transitional justice.

2 Framework for Transitional Justice

2.1 Amnesty as a Tool of Transitional Justice: Peace vs Justice

There are different competing philosophies on the role of amnesties as tools of transitional justice. The word amnesty is derived from the Greek word *amnestia*, meaning to 'cast into oblivion'.[21] This suggests a historical practice of cleaning the past whilst forging a new transition and socio-political order. However, there is no uniform definition of the notion of amnesty within socio-legal discourse. Whilst emphasising the

[16] See Statement of the Prosecutor of the ICC following the surrender and transfer of Ongwen (2015).

[17] See local newspaper report Musisi (2017).

[18] Heller (2008, p. 998).

[19] See for example Oloka-Onyango (2020), Heller (2008), Ten Kate and Nouwen (2018).

[20] For detailed explanation see Kasande (2024), first online.

[21] Freeman (2010, p. 13).

political context, Andreas O'Shea adopts the Oxford English Dictionary definition of amnesty as 'immunity in law from either criminal or civil consequences, or from both, for wrongs committed in the past in a political context'.[22] Freeman departs from the traditional conception of amnesty as *amestia* and defines amnesty as:

> an extraordinary legal measure whose primary function is to remove the prospect and consequences of criminal liability for designated individuals or classes of persons in respect of designated types of offenses irrespective of whether the persons concerned have been tried for such offences in a court of law.[23]

Beyond its definition, the application of amnesty in transitional justice draws mixed debates, due to a host of statutory limitations. Different treaties provide theoretical justifications for opposition to the notion and practice of amnesty. These outline State obligations to provide effective remedies under article 8 of the Universal Declaration of Human Rights (UDHR), article 2(3) of the International Covenant on Civil and Political Rights (ICCPR), article 6 of the Convention on the Elimination of All Forms of Racial Discrimination (CERD), article 14 of the Convention against Torture and Other Cruel, Inhuman or Degrading Treatment or Punishment (CAT), and article 39 of the Convention on the Rights of the Child (CRC).[24]

More importantly, in contexts like the Northern Ugandan civil war, article 29 of the Rome Statute bars the applicability of statute of limitations to crimes within the jurisdiction of the ICC.[25] Similarly, the Convention on Non-Applicability of Statutory Limitations to War Crimes against Humanity provides a firm limitation under article 4 that requires States to:

> Undertake to adopt, in accordance with their respective constitutional processes, any legislative or other measures necessary to ensure that statutory or other limitations shall not apply to the prosecution and punishment of the crimes referred to in articles I and II of this Convention and that, where they exist, such limitations shall be abolished.[26]

As a result of this normative framework, in the late 1980s and 1990s, the vast of transitional justice scholarship was opposed to the use of amnesties, whilst affirming criminal prosecution as the ideal way to achieve accountability for human rights violations.[27] However, the field has migrated significantly from this position towards reconciliation and restorative justice-based approaches. Nonetheless, it is important to acknowledge the theoretical gap between transitional justice and the notion of amnesty. A key question could be; whether the two notions are compatible?

---

[22] O'Shea (2002, pp. 1–10).

[23] Freeman (2010, p. 13).

[24] A more elaborate analysis is provided under the Preamble to the UN Basic Principles 2005.

[25] See Rome Statute.

[26] Convention on the Non-Applicability of Statutory Limitations to War Crimes and Crimes Against Humanity Adopted and Opened for Signature, Ratification and Accession by General Assembly Resolution 2391 (XXIII) of 26 November 1968 Entry into Force: 11 November 1970, in Accordance with Article VIII.

[27] For a comprehensive review of Freeman's book and the compatibility of amnesty and transitional justice, see Minogue (2010, p. 306).

Freeman presents an interesting argument to this debate. For example, he infuses 'non-amnesty-specific duties of states under international law', as a rationale to prevent and prosecute human rights violations. In response to the statutory limitations, Freeman argues that 'amnesties and statutes of limitations [are] different types of legal measures'.[28] In an attempt to reconcile the criticisms against amnesties, he recommends their application as a 'last recourse'.[29] This line of argument fits squarely within the Ugandan case.

The case of Uganda presents an interesting but yet underexplored nexus between transitional justice and amnesty. Amnesty is defined under Ugandan law as 'a pardon, forgiveness, exemption or discharge from criminal prosecution or any other form of punishment by the State'.[30] An Amnesty Commission was charged with the demobilisation, reintegration and resettlement of those who reported themselves to the Commission.[31] The key proponents of this amnesty argued that the judicial approach was not suited to LRA fighters, because many of the perpetrators were also victims.[32] Whilst scholarly discourse hinged on empirical studies, narratives were also founded on comparative analysis, based on practical lessons from the case of South Africa. For example, O'Shea argues that Uganda's amnesty aimed at securing peace and not democratic transition like the case in South Africa.[33] From the empirical research, findings suggest widespread societal support for the Amnesty Act in the LRA-affected areas of Northern Uganda.[34]

Whilst empirical studies suggest a tremendous social contribution of amnesty, some critics regard the Ugandan amnesty as a 'blanket amnesty' that did not allow for thorough investigations into gross human rights violations.[35] To others, it was largely a tool for discouraging rebellion and persuading rebels to surrender.[36] Despite these debates, amnesty remains intimately linked to the transitional justice process in Uganda. It complements other measures to promote justice and accountability as crucial aspects of transitional justice.

2.2 *Agreement on Accountability and Reconciliation: Peace or Justice?*

Reconciling peace and justice often presents tremendous conceptual challenges. The case of Northern Uganda is particularly interesting, due to the application of both

[28] See review in Minogue (2010, p. 308).

[29] Minogue (2010, p. 311).

[30] The Amnesty Act, Chapter 294, 31 December 2000, Sec 1.

[31] The Amnesty Act, Chapter 294, 31 December 2000, Sec 8.

[32] See Agger (2012, p. 4).

[33] O'Shea (2002, p. 38).

[34] Agger (2012, p. 4).

[35] O'Shea (2002, p. 44).

[36] O'Shea (2002, p. 22).

peace and justice mechanisms. Inevitably, tough compromises, including amnesty, are explored. However, victims need to be maintained as central subjects within the processes. In this regard, an important question could relate to the role of victims during peace processes.

Peace talks between the government and the LRA commenced in 2006, mediated by Sudanese Vice-President Riek Machar in Juba, South Sudan.[37] They raised some hope, through the signing of cessation of hostilities agreements.[38] The negotiations were based on five key elements: (i) cessation of hostilities; (ii) a comprehensive solution (including participation in national institutions and life; economic and social development of northern and eastern Uganda; resettlement of IDPs); (iii) accountability and reconciliation; (iv) demobilisation, disarmament and reintegration; and (v) a formal ceasefire agreement.[39] On 2 May 2007 and 29 June 2007, the parties signed agreements on comprehensive solutions to the conflict—the Agreements on Accountability and Reconciliation (AAR)—with recognition for reconciliation and accountability. These agreements raised the momentum for the peace talks, whilst maintaining the desire for justice.

Consequently, on 19 February 2008, the government and the LRA signed an important annex to the AAR.[40] Theoretically, it reinforced the element of accountability, by providing for trials for the most serious crimes, a truth commission, reparations and the application of traditional justice mechanisms.[41] These can be considered as positive elements for investigation, prosecution of crimes, accountability and the provision of reparations. In addition, victims' participation and reparations were outlined in both documents, which are key elements within transitional justice.[42]

The AAR incorporates the fair trial standards guaranteed under Uganda's constitution,[43] specifically 'the right of the individual to a fair hearing and due process' and 'a fair, speedy and public hearing before an independent and impartial court or tribunal established by law'.[44] In practice, essential fair trial standards are often violated in Uganda, due to acts of impunity[45] and legal ambiguities.[46] These challenges suggest a need for contextual and case specific approaches towards transitional

[37] See local newspaper report Tafeng (2006).

[38] See Report of the High Commissioner for Human Rights on the Activities of Her Office in Uganda (2007).

[39] Report of the High Commissioner for Human Rights on the Activities of Her Office in Uganda (2007).

[40] See Annex to the AAR (Annex to June 29 Agreement).

[41] See AAR (Addendum 4), 03/11/2007.

[42] See AAR (Addendum 4), 03/11/2007.

[43] See Constitution of the Republic of Uganda, 22 September 1995, Arts. 24–28.

[44] See AAR Clause 3.3.

[45] See Report of Human Rights Watch (27 July 2011).

[46] Nanima (2019, p. 661).

justice processes and accountability for gross violations of human rights. From a transitional justice perspective, the agreements outlined the recognised measures of: restitution, compensation, rehabilitation, satisfaction and guarantees of non-repetition.[47] The element of reparations is in line with international standards that accord victims of crimes against humanity, war crimes, torture, extrajudicial executions, enforced disappearances and other human rights violations, the right to full and effective reparations.[48]

Qualitative research done by the UN High Commissioner for Human Rights (OHCHR) in Northern Uganda between January and June 2007 is quite instructive in regard to the inclusion of transitional justice processes of accountability within the peace processes.[49] As much as this book does not set out to explore perceptions among the conflict-affected communities on the different transitional justice options, it is important to analyse how transnational networks and NGO work impact on the general local perceptions of transitional justice mechanisms like the ICC. As such, victims remain an important point of analysis. Within the Northern Uganda context, the rationale is to ensure that the rights of the victims are not entirely forgotten, as also highlighted in the previous empirical studies.[50] Whilst acknowledging the positive impact of the explicit provisions on reparations, research suggests that the proposed reparations process within the agreements lacked a 'victims focused approach' within the development and implementation stages.[51] The perceived shortcomings relate to the lack of explicit measures to rebuild their lives and also involving them in both planning and implementing the reparations programmes.

Another perplexing issue concerned the application of two strands of justice; traditional and community justice on one hand, complemented by criminal prosecution. The Annex to the 2007 Agreement established a special division of the High Court of Uganda, to try individuals who were alleged to have committed serious crimes during the conflict.[52] Procedurally, the legislation establishing the Court allowed for '[t]he recognition of traditional and community justice processes in proceedings'.[53] However, the provision is vague and presents a procedural dilemma regarding the specific role of community justice practices within contemporary courts, as also acknowledged by Amnesty International.[54] Moreover, empirical studies challenge the depictions of victims in Northern Uganda as reconciliatory.[55]

[47] See AAR Clause 9(1).

[48] See UN Basic Principles, Principle 3.

[49] See Report of the High Commissioner for Human Rights on the Activities of Her Office in Uganda (2007).

[50] See Report of the High Commissioner for Human Rights on the Activities of Her Office in Uganda (2007, p. 67).

[51] For a comprehensive analysis on the Agreement and Annex on Accountability and Reconciliation see Amnesty International (2008, pp. 21–22).

[52] See Annex to the AAR (n 404) clause 7.

[53] See Annex to the AAR (n 404) clause 9.

[54] Amnesty International (2008, p. 13).

[55] See report of the UN Office of the High Commissioner for Human Rights—OHCHR (2007, p. ii).

Despite these challenges, scholars ought to acknowledge the need for compromises like reconciliation within legally pluralistic contexts like Uganda. To some proponents of accountability, reconciling former LRA rebels with local society should only be used as an 'absolute last resort and with international endorsement on the basis that this is genuinely the only way of ending the suffering of the people of the region once and for all'.[56] Based on extensive empirical research, Dylan Hendrickson and Kennedy Tumutegyereize suggest that future efforts for peace talks should not seek to tackle complex issues simultaneously. Instead, they argue for peacebuilding as the most immediate goal.[57] Ultimately, the implementation of Global Justice requires multifaceted approaches, especially in pluralistic societies within the Global South.

The debate on peace vis-a-vis justice in Northern Uganda has attracted a great deal of scholarly interest in the past years. For example, scholars map out the role of criminal justice during the Juba peace negotiations, arguing that ICC processes partly shaped the political dynamics between the negotiating parties in Juba.[58] Regarding the issue of accountability, there is an argument that both the Ugandan government and the LRA perceived the ICC as 'a perplexing intervention that needed to be contained', thereby allowing cooperation during the peace talks.[59] In essence, the two parties were worried about this new international criminal justice process which was strongly supported by influential international State and Non-State actors. All in all, such observations lay a good foundation for analysing how NGOs impact on transitional justice mechanisms in this case study of Uganda.

The vast of literature on the conflict in Northern Uganda focuses on the culpability of the LRA as perpetrators of crime, without considering the crimes committed by the Ugandan government agents. This is acknowledged by Louise Mallinder, in her discussion on the military campaigns against the LRA.[60] In addition to reports of ethnic marginalisation of the Acholi,[61] qualitative research carried out by the OHCHR indicates that the people in Northern Uganda broadly believe 'that both the LRA and the Government—and specifically their leaders—should be held accountable for the harms they have caused during the conflict'.[62] With such complexities, it becomes vital to assess how NGOs impact on the work of accountability-oriented institutions like the ICC, within such contested spaces of transitional justice.

---

56 See International Crisis Group (2007, pp. 1–15).

57 Hendrickson and Tumutegyereize (2012, p. 7).

58 For more discussion see Macdonald (2017a, pp. 628–648), Gissel (2017, pp. 367–387).

59 Macdonald (2017a, p. 630).

60 Mallinder (2009, p. 13).

61 For more insights see Otunnu (2009).

62 See report of the UN Office of the High Commissioner for Human Rights- OHCHR (2007, p. ii).

2.3 *Regional and International Legal Framework: Enabling a Legal Environment for Accountability*

An important step towards achieving transitional justice by a State is the ratification of important international treaties that provide for accountability, whilst working towards the implementation of relevant provisions.

Theoretically, most human rights treaties hold the States as entities accountable for human rights violations, with corresponding duties to victims. There are strong legal arguments for treaties as sources of affirmative State obligations.[63] Moreover, where States fail to fulfil their responsibilities, international bodies and tribunals are considered viable alternatives in order to provide accountability.[64] It can therefore be argued that by ratifying key human rights treaties, Uganda makes positive steps towards achieving transitional justice and encouraging accountability for gross human rights violations.

However, there are diverse and conflicting views on the role of international treaties and legal frameworks in achieving transitional justice in local contexts. For example, in addition to explicit treaty-based obligations, Naomi Roht-Arriaza argues for a customary law basis for the state obligations to investigate and prosecute crimes.[65] Another scholarly line of argument places emphasis on democratic transitions. The debates address post-transition duties of the new governments that replaced regimes responsible for crimes and gross violations of human rights.[66] However, there are more contextual analyses on the role of international law in shaping domestic policy and transitional justice. In this regard, Anna Macdonald's critical scholarship identifies a problem of 'internationalization' and 'normalization' of transitional justice, within the Ugandan context.[67] She argues that it is 'detached from the politics and cultures of the societies in question'. In regard to the theory of democratic transition, she is skeptical about the international promotion of transitional justice in conflict-affected regions like Northern Uganda, a different context from a country under democratic transition.[68] In view of these debates, it is important to understand the international legal framework under which Uganda operates, within the transitional justice processes and accountability.

The information contained in Table 1 is significant in that it indicates that Uganda has committed itself to a number of accountability mechanisms under IHRL, IHL and ICL obligations, which are relevant in providing accountability to the victims of gross human rights.

In terms of domestic applicability, international treaties are not explicitly recognised as a source of law in Uganda, as they need to be domesticated through Acts

[63] See Méndez (1997, p. 259).

[64] Navanethem Pillay presents a summary of effective accountability mechanisms Pillay (2012).

[65] Roht-Arriaza (1990, p. 489).

[66] Orentlicher (1991, p. 2541).

[67] Macdonald (2019, p. 229).

[68] Macdonald (2019, p. 230).

Table 1 Relevant treaties and conventions signed, ratified or acceded to by Uganda

Treaty	Status
The Universal Declaration of Human Rights	Voted in favour of the UDHR in 1948
African Charter on Human and Peoples' Rights	Ratified in 1994
Protocol to the African Charter on Human and Peoples' Rights on the Rights of Women in Africa	Ratified in 2010
Convention for the Elimination against all form of discrimination against women	Ratified in 1985
Convention on the Rights of the Child	Ratified in 1990
Optional Protocol to the Convention on the Rights of the Child on the involvement of children in armed conflict	Acceded to in 2002
African Charter on the Rights and Welfare of the Child	Ratified in 1994
Convention on the Elimination of All Forms of Racial Discrimination;	Acceded to in 1980
International Covenant on Civil and Political Rights	Acceded to in 1995
International Covenant on Economic, Social and Cultural Rights	Acceded to in 1987
Convention Against Torture and Other Cruel, Inhuman and Degrading Treatment	Acceded to in 1986
African Union Convention on the Protection and Assistance of Internally Displaced Persons in Africa	Uganda was the first country to ratify this regional convention in 2010
Geneva Conventions	Acceded to in 1964
Additional Protocol (I) to the Geneva Conventions	Acceded to in 1991
Additional Protocol (II) to the Geneva Conventions	Acceded to in 1991
Additional Protocol (III) to the Geneva Conventions	Acceded to in 2008
Statute of the International Criminal Court, 1998	Ratified in 2002
Convention for the Protection of all Persons from Enforced Disappearance	Signed in 2007
Convention on the Prevention and Punishment of the Crimes of Genocide	Acceded to in 1995

of Parliament.[69] Nonetheless, whilst it does not provide an explicit application of international law, Uganda's Constitution obliges the State to observe its international treaty obligations ratified prior to the enactment of the constitution in 1995.[70] In summary, these regional and international treaties provide a firm foundation for accountability in Uganda.

Victims within the context of displacement have special protection under the African Union Convention for the Protection and Assistance of Internally Displaced Persons in Africa (Kampala Convention). This is an important instrument for accountability, in the context of the victims' vulnerability as a result of war and displacement in Northern Uganda. Quantitative and qualitative studies highlight human rights violations as among the key political dimensions of internal displacement in Uganda.[71] Up to 2006, more than 1.1 million people were displaced into hundreds of IDP camps within Acholi.[72] In the specific context of Northern Uganda, the atrocities of the LRA and the lack of accountability remained a part of the social narratives.[73] Besides the LRA atrocities, human rights researchers observe several violations committed by the Ugandan government, like the recruitment of IDPs into civil militias.[74] Ultimately, there is a need to thoroughly review the underlying protection for IDPs, whilst exploring the accountability mechanisms. The concept of IDPs is well-defined within the Kampala Convention. IDPs means:

> persons or groups of persons who have been forced or obliged to flee or to leave their homes or places of habitual residence, in particular as a result of or in order to avoid the effects of armed conflict, situations of generalized violence, violations of human rights or natural or human made disasters, and who have not crossed an internationally recognized State border.[75]

As provided under international legal instruments, States take primary responsibility for protecting and assisting IDPs.[76] However, there is a global normative gap regarding the protection of IDPs, a fact acknowledged by Adama Dieng.[77] In a novel way of achieving accountability, the Kampala Convention holds non-State actors like rebel movements liable for human rights violations leading to displacement and requires states to exercise criminal liability.[78] According to Dieng, it serves as a basis for a more comprehensive international instrument for the protection of IDPs.[79]

---

69 See the Judicature Act (Cap 13), Revised Laws of Uganda 2000, S. 14(2).

70 Constitution of the Republic of Uganda, 22 September 1995, Art. 287.

71 Kamara, Cyril and Renzaho (2017, pp. 444–473).

72 See Report of the UN High Commissioner for Refugees in respect to internal displacement in Northern Uganda. UNHCR (2010, p. 7).

73 UNHCR (2010, p. 466).

74 Janmyr (2014, p. 218).

75 See African Union Convention for the Protection and Assistance of Internally Displaced Persons in Africa (Kampala Convention), 23 October 2009. Art.1(k).

76 See Kampala Convention, Art 5, paras 6–7.

77 Dieng (2017, p. 99).

78 Dieng (2017, p. 99). Kampala Convention, Art 5, paras 7(4).

79 Dieng (2017, p. 292).

The other notable victim-centred approach relates to the remedial approach under the Convention. It creates an expansive remedial approach to victims within IDPs. States are required to provide effective remedies including 'just and fair compensation and other forms of reparations, where appropriate … in accordance with international standards'.[80] In addition, it provides special protection for vulnerable groups like persons with disabilities, women and the elderly.[81]

Despite the normativity and increased accountability for internal displacement, there is a scholarly concern about the lack of effective implementation of the Kampala Convention.[82] It is noted that there are limited criminal prosecutions relating to crimes under the Kampala Convention.[83] This limits the ability of victims of gross human rights violations, within the context of displacement, to achieve justice and accountability. There is a normative gap due to the absence of treaty law on the international human rights obligations of non-State actors, which is acknowledged by scholars.[84] In addition, the bulk of the literature focuses on human rights obligations of States.[85] However, human rights protection is important during armed conflict. This is acknowledged in modern international law literature, which extends human rights obligations to times of war.[86] In addition, obligations are derived from IHL, under the Geneva Conventions of 12 August 1949, stating; 'Persons taking no active part in the hostilities… shall in all circumstances be treated humanely'.[87]

Besides transnational networks and NGOs' roles in legitimating transitional justice, a brief understanding of the position of other actors within conflict areas is vital, within the IHL framework. In this respect, non-State actors like rebel movements have legal obligations under Additional Protocol II of 1977 to the Geneva Conventions and relevant minimum standards of protection.[88] These present a positive dimension in the accountability processes, because unlike under IHL, IHRL does not place explicit human rights obligations onto non-State actors.[89] However, there is a lack of academic consensus on the intersection and context of these different obligations. Yaël Ronen recognises the normative gap relating to human rights obligations of non-State actors like armed groups.[90] Yet, Andrew Clapham argues that non-State actors do already have international human rights obligations, depending

---

80 Kampala Convention, Art 12.

81 Kampala Convention, Art 9.

82 Asplet and Bradley (2012, pp. 1–5).

83 International Committee of the Red Cross (2017, p. 386).

84 Ronen (2013, p. 35).

85 See Méndez (1997, p. 266), Hillebrecht (2020, pp. 453–486).

86 See UN Report on International Legal Protection of Human Rights in Armed Conflict (2011, p. 5).

87 See Geneva Conventions of 12 August 1949 Art.3.

88 International Committee of the Red Cross (ICRC), Protocol Additional to the Geneva Conventions of 12 August 1949, and Relating to the Protection of Victims of Non-International Armed Conflicts (Protocol II), 8 June 1977, 1125 UNTS 609.

89 Ronen (2013, pp. 21–50).

90 Ronen (2013, p. 33).

on their capacity, context and commitments.[91] In a slightly similar manner, Ronen emphasises the aspect of territorial control as significant for the imposition of human rights obligations onto non-State actors.[92]

Away from the discussions on rebel movements, it is equally vital to understand the responsibilities of States. The Protocol to the African Charter on Human and Peoples' Rights on the Rights of Women in Africa (Maputo Protocol) sets out a number of State obligations. In addition to punishing perpetrators of violence against women, states are obliged to establish mechanisms for reparations and remedies like rehabilitation for victims of violence against women.[93] With regard to the situation of women and children in armed conflict, the African Commission expounded on the notion of accountability, to include 'the right to just and equitable reparation to victims in all forms (restitution, compensation, rehabilitation, satisfaction and guarantees of non-repetition)'.[94] Furthermore, rape in times of conflict is categorised as a crime against humanity and as a war crime, in line with international criminal law jurisprudence.[95] These provisions give women and child victims in Northern Uganda the right to a remedy and reparation as a form of accountability.

In the context of child victims, the CRC provides for the protection of child victims of violence, through reference to rules of IHL and remedies under IHRL.[96] At the regional level, the African Charter on the Rights and Welfare of the Child (African Children's Charter) complements the Optional Protocol to the Convention on the Rights of the Child on the involvement of children in armed conflict.[97] It obliges States to take necessary measures to protect children from hostilities, recruitment as soldiers, sexual abuse and violence.[98]

Still on State responsibility, transnational networks and NGOs can take important measures against to help push the former to fulfil their obligations. In 2005, a complaint was filed before the African Committee of Experts on the Rights and Welfare of the Child by representatives of several children in Northern Uganda.[99] Even though the Committee did not find explicit violations of Uganda's obligations

---

[91] Clapham (2019, pp. 11–36).

[92] Ronen (2013, p. 26).

[93] African Union, Protocol to the African Charter on Human and People's Rights on the Rights of Women in Africa, 11 July 2003 Arts. 4(e) (f), 25.

[94] African Commission on Human and Peoples' Rights, 283 Resolution on the Situation of Women and Children in Armed Conflict—ACHPR/Res.283 (LV) 2014.

[95] African Commission on Human and Peoples' Rights, 111 Resolution on the Right to a Remedy and Reparation for Women and Girls Victims of Sexual Violence—ACHPR/Res.111(XXXXII) 07, 28 November 2007.

[96] UN General Assembly, Convention on the Rights of the Child, 20 November 1989, United Nations, Treaty Series, vol. 1577, p. 3 Arts. 38–39.

[97] Optional Protocol to the Convention on the Rights of the Child on the Involvement of Children in Armed Conflict, 25 May 2000.

[98] Organisation of African Unity (OAU), African Charter on the Rights and Welfare of the Child, 11 July 1990, CAB/LEG/24.9/49 (1990) Arts 16, 22(2) and 27.

[99] African Committee of Experts on the Rights and Welfare of the Child (ACERWC), *Michelo Hunsungule and others (on behalf of children in Northern Uganda) v The Government of Uganda,*

under the African Children's Charter, it recommended the introduction of explicit legal provisions in Uganda's penal code, for protection and sanctions against the recruitment of children in armed conflict.[100]

Transnational networks and NGOs can equally advocate for transitional justice-related mechanisms and reforms under the UDHR[101] and the ICCPR,[102] affirming the right to a remedy and reparation, as important aspects of accountability. In addition, States are obligated to criminalise, investigate and, where there is sufficient evidence, prosecute acts of torture irrespective of its status under domestic law. Under the CAT, States are obligated to criminalise all acts of torture, including attempts to commit torture, and ensure those responsible are punishable by appropriate penalties considering their grave nature.[103] Torture is defined as:

> any act by which severe pain or suffering, whether physical or mental, is intentionally inflicted on a person for such purposes as obtaining from him or a third person information or a confession, punishing him for an act he or a third person has committed or is suspected of having committed, or intimidating or coercing him or a third person, or for any reason based on discrimination of any kind, when such pain or suffering is inflicted by or at the instigation of or with the consent or acquiescence of a public official or other person acting in an official capacity. It does not include pain or suffering arising only from, inherent in or incidental to lawful sanctions.[104]

As already pointed out, Uganda ratified the CAT in 1987, but did not criminalise torture until 2012 when it enacted the Prevention and Prohibition of Torture Act, to give effect to its obligations as a state party to the CAT.[105] Nonetheless, Uganda's Constitution offers extensive protection against torture, recognising the rights to freedom from torture as non-derogable rights.[106] In addition, the criminal laws offer a victim-centred approach to prosecutions. The Prevention and Prohibition of Torture Act has an expansive approach to victims, beyond the provisions under CAT. It outlines certain aggravating factors of torture, like when the offender uses or used sex as a means of torture and when the victim acquires HIV/AIDS.[107] Another key dimension within the accountability framework is the perception of torture as a crime against humanity. It can thus be argued that when committed in the context

---

Communication No 1/2005 Decision, Ethiopia, Twenty first Ordinary Session, 15–19 April 2013 para 11.

[100] *Michelo Hunsungule and others (on behalf of children in Northern Uganda) v The Government of Uganda,* para 81.

[101] Universal Declaration of Human Rights, 10 December 1948, 217 A (III) Art.8.

[102] International Covenant on Civil and Political Rights, 16 December 1966, United Nations, Treaty Series, vol. 999, p. 171 Art.2.

[103] Convention Against Torture and Other Cruel, Inhuman or Degrading Treatment or Punishment, 10 December 1984, United Nations, Treaty Series, vol. 1465, p. 85 Art 4.

[104] Convention Against Torture and Other Cruel, Inhuman or Degrading Treatment or Punishment, 10 December 1984, United Nations, Treaty Series, Vol. 1465, p. 85.

[105] Prevention and Prohibition of Torture Act, 2012 (No. 3 of 2012).

[106] Constitution of the Republic of Uganda 1995.

[107] Prevention and Prohibition of Torture Act, 2012 (No. 3 of 2012).

of a widespread or systematic attack against a civilian population, torture and other forms of violence may constitute crimes against humanity.[108]

In addition to the explicit provisions for torture as a crime against humanity under the Rome Statute,[109] genocide studies make a strong argument for the systematic and widespread nature of sexual crimes to be recognised as crimes against humanity.[110] Interdisciplinary empirical studies in Northern Uganda indicate a range of acts of torture and sexual violence among victims of armed conflict.[111] Within this context, rape and other forms of sexualised violence need to be effectively investigated and prosecuted.

Moreover, impunity by State actors might negatively affect the accountability processes, as researchers note a rampant violation of the freedom against torture based on actions by state actors in Northern Uganda.[112] As such, there is a need for accountability for acts of both State and non-State actors. The adoption of comprehensive anti-torture laws is an important step to ensure the necessary legal regime for domestic prosecutions of war crimes, consistent with international legal obligations and standards.

Although not explicitly recognised in Uganda's domestic laws, the right to the truth is an important element of the States' duty of accountability for gross human rights violations and transitional justice. The right to truth adds another layer to the State obligations to investigate gross violations of human rights. The Preamble of the International Convention for the Protection of All Persons from Enforced Disappearance (ICPPED), highlights 'the right of any victim to know the truth about the circumstances of an enforced disappearance and the fate of the disappeared person'.[113] Moreover, theoretical developments have led to the adoption of relevant resolutions and declarations by the UN General Assembly and the Human Rights Council. The latter affirmed that:

> '[i]t is important for states to provide appropriate and effective mechanisms for society as a whole and, in particular, for relatives of the victims, to know the truth regarding gross violations of human rights and serious violations of international Humanitarian law'.[114]

As such, Uganda is bound to adhere to international fair trial standards under international treaties, when implementing transitional justice and accountability measures. The fundamental principle underlying the right to a fair trial, is the right to equality before the law. The African Charter[115] and the ICCPR provide for this right, stating

---

108 See International Commission of Jurists (2019).

109 Rome Statute of the International Criminal Court (1998) Art.7 (1)(f).

110 Pohlman (2017, p. 586).

111 Gray, Stern and Dolan (2020, p. 206).

112 Okema (2007, p. 75).

113 See Convention for the Protection of All Persons from Enforced Disappearance (20 December 2006).

114 UN Human Rights Council, Right to the truth: resolution / adopted by the Human Rights Council, 10 October 2012, A/HRC/RES/21/7 p. 3.

115 See African Charter on Human and Peoples' Rights ('Banjul Charter'), 27 June 1981, CAB/LEG/67/3 rev. 5, 21 I.L.M. 58 (1982), Art. 3.

that 'all persons shall be equal before the courts and tribunals'.[116] Even in the course of investigations and judicial proceedings, the State is bound to respect the non-derogable prohibition on torture and other inhuman or degrading treatment or punishment.[117] The Rome Statute of the ICC provides concise benchmarks of fair trials like credibility, independence and adherence to international fair trial standards.[118]

Besides the procedural standards, the Rome Statute sets out important duties and obligations for Uganda as a member State. For example, the prohibition of the commission of crimes against humanity and accountability was also codified in the Rome Statute.[119] Uganda is therefore bound by both customary international law and the Rome Statute, in dealing with crimes against humanity and accountability measures. In this regard, Uganda's criminal laws prohibit crimes against humanity, with an explicit reference to the ICC definition, which is a great step towards fulfilling its international obligations.[120]

Moreover, ICL jurisprudence has adopted an expansive approach regarding victims and the definition of sexual violence. In the *Akayesu* case the ICTR defined sexual violence as 'any act of a sexual nature which is committed on a person under circumstances which are coercive'.[121] The ICTR further expanded the meaning of sexual violence to include acts that do not involve penetration or even physical contact with the victims.[122] Since acts of sexual violence constitute crimes against humanity, Uganda is therefore obliged to prosecute and provide redress to all categories of victims of sexual violence during the LRA conflict in Northern Uganda.

Moreover, IHRL is not limited to the rights enumerated in treaties, but also derives from customary international law. Some treaty obligations enjoy a special status as peremptory norms of customary international law *ius cogens*, and are therefore legally binding on all States, regardless of their ratification status.[123] Therefore, prohibitions of torture, slavery, genocide, racial discrimination and crimes against humanity are widely recognised as peremptory norms.[124]

More importantly, State obligations under human rights instruments do not cease in the case of armed conflict. In line with this theory, Uganda was held liable for human rights violations like torture and other forms of inhumane and degrading

---

[116] International Covenant on Civil and Political Rights, 16 December 1966, United Nations, Treaty Series, vol. 999, p. 171 Art. 14(1).

[117] See e.g. Article 55(1)(b) of the Statute of the International Criminal Court; Art. 2(2) of the Convention against Torture and Other Cruel, Inhuman or Degrading Treatment or Punishment and Art. 4(2) of the International Covenant on Civil and Political Rights.

[118] See Rome Statute, Art.64.

[119] Rome Statute, Art.7(1).

[120] International Criminal Court Act, 2010 Sect. 8.

[121] *Prosecutor v. Jean-Paul Akayesu* (Trial Judgement), ICTR-96–4-T, ICTR (2 September 1998), para 598.

[122] *Prosecutor v. Jean-Paul Akayesu* (Trial Judgement), ICTR-96–4-T, ICTR (2 September 1998), para 688.

[123] See generally Espinosa (2022, pp. 79–114).

[124] See International Law Commission, 'Draft Articles on Responsibility of States for Internationally Wrongful Acts' (2001) Supplement No. 10 (A/56/10) Art. 26.

treatment, arising from its armed activities in the DRC.[125] The Court concluded that the acts committed by Ugandan soldiers violated customary international law.[126] In addition, the court noted the relationship between IHL and IHRL, whilst stressing the applicability of IHRL instruments in armed conflict.[127]

Besides the State obligations, the comprehensive legal framework and human rights treaties facilitate litigation for individual criminal accountability for past human rights violations. In addition to ratification of key treaties, scholars highlight the need for the adoption of normative, policy and concrete measures at the national level in order to achieve justice and accountability.[128] Against this normative background, a critical analysis of the Northern Uganda conflict is made, with emphasis on the status of victims within the different transitional justice and accountability mechanisms.

3 The Gap Between Victims and Transitional Justice: Perceptions of Responsibility and Accountability

3.1 Understanding the Cultural and Social Narratives

Northern Uganda is inhabited by two major tribes, the Acholi and Langi. Like in many African countries, ethnicity is a key factor within the political discourses in Uganda.[129] Historical studies indicate close similarities between the Lango and Acholi tribes.[130] However, within the context of reconciliation, studies highlight inter-ethnic identities and hostilities between the Acholi and Lango.[131] These nuances suggest a need to take close consideration of the cultural narratives within the transitional justice process in Northern Uganda.

Historically, the traditional systems in Lango and Acholi were largely structured along clan systems.[132] The Acholi maintained a traditional governance structure led by spiritually anointed chiefs known as the *rwodi moo*.[133] The chiefdoms were based on a conglomeration of different clans and their leaders. The chiefs' powers are not absolute as they are subject to guidance from a democratically elected Council of clan elders, known as the *Ludito Kaka*, who also historically exercised judiciary

---

[125] For comprehensive details see Armed Activities on the Territory of the Congo (*Democratic Republic of the Congo v Uganda*), Judgment, ICJ Reports 2005 216.

[126] *Democratic Republic of the Congo v Uganda* para. 219.

[127] *Democratic Republic of the Congo v Uganda* paras 181–220.

[128] International Committee of the Red Cross (2017, p. 390).

[129] Amone (2015, p. 129).

[130] Uzoigwe (1973, p. 403).

[131] Shabdita and Okwir (2015, p. 23).

[132] Atim and Proctor (2013, p. 8).

[133] Latigo (2008, p. 102).

and legislative functions.[134] To emphasise the communal governance structure and relationship among the Acholi, we can draw close attention to the belief and practice of consensus among the elders, as opposed to individual decision-making.[135]

One notable cultural practice is the *Gwooko Dog Paco*, which is a central element of the Acholi ethno-cultural identity. It is a belief in communal responsibility for defending homesteads, with an emphasis on self-preservation.[136] However, most of the traditional and cultural practices were grossly disrupted with the introduction of British colonial rule, especially during the years 1894–1910.[137] Apart from traditional cultural beliefs and structure, most of the Acholi people are Christians. One could argue that Christianity and British colonial rule diminished the Acholi traditions. To some extent, this could be true, given the changing societal norms. Evidence-based research highlights these changing societal norms, with respect to aspects of gender and culture.[138] Despite these developments, cultural narratives are still relevant within conflict and peace processes.

Ethnographic discourse presents interesting dimensions within transitional justice literature. Whilst most Acholi are Christians,[139] ethnographic studies indicate that their religious beliefs still co-exist with their customary rituals.[140] Whilst he acknowledges these dynamic complexities between Acholi culture and modern religion, James Latigo observes the continued practice of traditional cultural beliefs among Acholi people.[141] This reinvigorates the debate on the role played by traditional justice mechanisms in dealing with the legacy of mass conflict and gross human rights violations, like the case of Northern Uganda.

One factor that is often overlooked during transitional justice processes is the dimension of culture and its ethno-social context. Apart from legal discourse, this important dimension is acknowledged by other transitional justice scholars, most notably in anthropology.[142] Anthropological engagement with transitional justice literature is critical that 'transitional justice mechanisms almost always have unexpected outcomes that emerge out of the 'frictions' between these global mechanisms and local realities'.[143]

In her exploration of the failure of international justice in East Timor and Indonesia, Elizabeth Drexler makes an interesting analysis regarding the fusion of the local context in transitional justice mechanisms.[144] She argues that criminal

---

[134] Latigo (2008, p. 103).

[135] Amone and Muura (2014, p. 42).

[136] Oloya (2012, p. 43).

[137] Harris (2017, p. 6).

[138] Shabdita and Okwir (2015, p. 19).

[139] Meier (2013, p. 35).

[140] Harris (2017, p. 17).

[141] Latigo (2008, p. 109.

[142] See for example Meier (2013, p. 35).

[143] See Hinton (2010, p. 9).

[144] Drexler (2010, p. 50).

trials create 'unintended consequences', due to legally constructed global narratives which differ from local contexts, thus undermining the legitimacy of transitional justice mechanisms.[145] However, this argument is refuted by Roger Duthie. Whilst he acknowledges the possibility of these unintended consequences, Duthie argues that transitional justice is inherently political and there are competing narratives within society that overlap across state, society, group, family and personal levels.[146] In addition, a number of scholars conceptualise transitional justice with a keen focus on transitional periods of political change.[147] Yet, as Tietel argues, beyond the political transitions, local factors affect the legitimacy of transitional justice mechanisms.[148] Nonetheless, researchers are advised to analyse how political processes are informed by specific cultural concepts.[149] The fusion of culture within transitional justice fits within Tietel's Phase 2 under the transitional justice history, with complex interactions between universal and local dimensions.[150] She relates the different cultural approaches and restoration mechanisms, to the goal of achieving rule of law and democracy.[151] However, this assertion might not perfectly fit within transitional justice processes during ongoing conflicts.

Away from the discourse to practice, transitional justice scholarship is more persuasive when focused on country-specific contexts like Sierra Leone, Cambodia and the Rwandan genocide. However, key questions could arise; to what extent do criminal trials help to bring about peace and reconciliation in society? To Tietel, this necessitates inquiries into the role of criminal trials under Phase 3 of the transitional justice history.[152] As has been highlighted in the introduction, the book explores how transnational networks influence justice in the Global South, particularly their impact on transitional justice in the different contexts. Within this context, the inquiry relates to the impact of NGOs on the legitimacy of the ICC, among other transitional justice avenues in Uganda. Put succinctly, case studies like Uganda remind us about the important role of ethno-social contexts within transitional justice.

The shift in transitional justice paradigms, from purely normative approaches to local-based approaches, has slowly gained ground. Political scientist Adam Branch regards this turn to traditional culture as an 'ethno justice agenda', where he equates the fulfilment of justice with the establishment of what he considers a traditional social order.[153] Besides Guatemala, Timor Leste and Rwanda, the Ugandan case was one of the first transitional justice approaches with a tremendous focus on local-based approaches, taking local realities into account during transitional justice.[154]

---

[145] Drexler (2010, p. 52).

[146] Duthie (2010, p. 253).

[147] More prominently among the scholars is Teitel (2003, pp. 69–94).

[148] Teitel (2003, p. 93).

[149] Meier (2013, p. 40).

[150] Teitel (2003, p. 81).

[151] Teitel (2003, p. 84).

[152] Teitel (2005, p. 857).

[153] Branch (2014, p. 614).

[154] See Hinton (2010, p. 5).

There was explicit reference to traditional forms of justice during the peace negotiations between the LRA and the government:

> Traditional justice mechanisms, such as *Culo Kwor, Mato Oput, Kayo Cuk, Ailuc and Tonu ci Koka* and others as practiced in the communities affected by the conflict, shall be promoted, with necessary modifications, as a central part of the framework for accountability and reconciliation.[155]

Crucially, a background overview of traditional reconciliation approaches within the region also helps in analysing the approaches taken by transnational networks and NGOs, in regard to the ICC intervention and transitional justice. Away from the peace negotiations, Acholi traditional leaders promoted traditional cultural ceremonies as a means of pursuing justice. Furthermore, anthropologists observe dominant cultural and religious discourses in the arguments against ICC intervention in the Northern Uganda conflict.[156] These nuances reaffirm the complex question of whether or not traditional justice is suited to dealing with contemporary challenges like war crimes.

The most widely discussed ritual is the *Mato Oput* or ‘bitter root’ ceremony, which affirms the *rwodi-moo*, or traditional elders’ roles in conflict resolution.[157] The first major scholarly argument for this approach is presented by Dennis Pain, upon his observation that the ‘principle of conflict resolution in Acholi is to create reconciliation which brings the two sides together’, with elements of compensation for harm done through the *Mato Oput*.[158] Put within the ambit of transitional justice, the local practices were viewed as complementary to the formal amnesty practice. There is a firm account of the traditional authority structure of the Acholi elders and traditional justice as a cultural approach to transitional justice.

Like many Global South contexts, religion has a key influence on aspects of justice and reconciliation. It is not surprising that besides the cultural relativist narratives in Uganda, arguments for traditional forms of justice were equally based on religious foundations of forgiveness.[159] In addition to the contextualisation of restorative justice premised on principles of Christian forgiveness, these narratives argued that forgiveness was a core transitional justice principle in the Ugandan context.[160] This was further reflected in the work of the Acholi Religious Leaders Peace Initiative (ARLPI), which drew upon traditional conflict resolution mechanisms as a means for reconciliation between the local communities and the LRA.[161] From a transitional justice perspective, they recognised Acholi rituals as a form of ‘social healing’.[162]

---

155 See Annex to the AAR Sec. 3(1).

156 Armstrong (2014, p. 601).

157 Branch (2014, p. 618).

158 See Pain (1997, p. 3). Commissioned by NGO International Alert following the engagements with Acholi in a London meeting, Pain’s Report contains rich anthropological observations and insights on Peacebuilding in Northern Uganda.

159 Armstrong (2014, pp. 599–601).

160 See Macdonald (2017b, pp. 286–311).

161 See Apuuli (2011, pp. 116–129).

162 Meier (2013, p. 42).

The treatment of former child soldiers of the LRA presented a cultural dilemma. In order to encourage former child combatants to return home, Acholi scholar Opiyo Oloya advocated for the revival of another Acholi cultural practice of *dwoogo paco*, translated as 'returning home'.[163] Juxtaposing this reconciliatory literature with the notion of accountability suggests a closer attention to victims of gross human rights violations within these ethnically diverse and pluralistic contexts. More importantly, as the book sets out, it is vital to understand how transnational networks and NGOs impact on the victims' perceptions of transitional justice and its various mechanisms.

One may argue that transitional justice is ineffective, without a regard for the cultural and contextual sensitivities. This argument could also debunk the discourse on international criminal justice vis-a-vis traditional justice systems. Reconciliatory discourse strongly argues for traditional justice processes, as they consider the 'unique experiences of victims and perpetrators'.[164] As Latigo observes, there are several strengths of the traditional justice mechanisms in Northern Uganda. Besides the inclusiveness and dialogue within the peacebuilding process, the process allows for wider communal participation and unity, generates community-focused outcomes, high levels of compliance.[165] He further places an emphasis on the unique role of traditional leaders and elders, as significant actors in the peacebuilding process in Northern Uganda.[166]

Despite the positive attributes of the Acholi traditional justice system, scholars are concerned about some contextual and structural dilemmas, which limit its effectiveness. For example, there is no practical way for combatants to provide compensation to victims and yet 'from their point of view, reconciliation cannot proceed without some form of compensation being provided'.[167] Furthermore, 'each Acholi clan is involved both as victim and perpetrator in numerous different cases'.[168] Therefore, the clan elders expect the State to provide the necessary compensation to the victims.[169]

Another complex issue regarding traditional justice mechanisms relates to the perceptions of transitional justice terms and theories. Anthropological studies observed this dilemma within the process of peace negotiations, where people in Northern Uganda had different ideas about what 'peace', 'violence' and 'justice' really meant, in comparison with the understanding of the mediators.[170] The fusion of Western and traditional narratives presents fundamental challenges to transitional justice within cultural contexts. The Acholi scholar Latigo observes a host of weaknesses associated with the traditional justice system. Among them is the lack of

---

[163] See generally Oloya (2012, p. 43).

[164] Shabdita and Okwir (2015, p. 38).

[165] Latigo (2008, p. 112).

[166] Latigo (2008, p. 97).

[167] Meier (2013, p. 40).

[168] Meier (2013, p. 40).

[169] Meier (2013, p. 40).

[170] Meier (2013, p. 36).

flexibility, the absence of a clear, written structure, delays and challenges of compliance, inconsistency and lack of uniformity among the different Acholi clan communities.[171] Within the broader context of the LRA conflict, he observes a fundamental weakness of the application of *mato oput* as a remedy, in that 'it wrongly projects the LRA insurgency as a local Acholi affair'.[172]

Other scholarly debates hover over questions of whether or not the Acholi were actually as forgiving as proclaimed by local leaders.[173] To Opiyo Oloya, Acholi society experienced severe cultural trauma,[174] and the self-healing capacity of Acholi culture was devastated by the war.[175] Based on these weaknesses, he concluded that the traditional practice approach lacked the capacity to support returning combatants due to culturally constructed identities.[176] This inevitably suggests a cultural dilemma that transcends the disciplines peacebuilding and reconciliation, closely associated with transitional justice.

Socio-legal studies present some contrasting views on practical relevance of traditional justice, forgiveness and reconciliation in Northern Uganda. Whilst anthropologist Barbara Meier emphasises the specific cultural contexts, Anna Macdonald argues they played a diminished role in the post-conflict interactions between the LRA and the community.[177] Instead, she argues that LRA rebels engaged in peace programmes due to 'political economies of survival' and not traditional justice, forgiveness or reconciliation initiatives.[178] Without being cynical, Barbara Meier recommends for research that analyses how political processes are informed by specific cultural concepts.[179] From an ICL standpoint, Ugandan scholar Emma Lubaale makes a case for legal pluralism, where traditional justice approaches and criminal justice can complement each other.[180]

One aspect of transitional justice that cannot be under looked relates to redress for Conflict-Related Sexual Violence, particularly the applicability of traditional mechanisms. Considering the patriarchal nature of the post-war societies, the gender inequalities leave women on the fringes of communal dialogues and decision-making processes. As equally observed by Ugandan scholars, victims of Conflict-Related Sexual Violence are often passive participants in the traditional mechanisms, making them unsuitable for addressing such crimes.[181]

It is thus not only possible to weigh the benefits of local traditional justice mechanisms vis-a-vis the formal judicial processes when implementing transitional justice,

---

[171] Latigo (2008, p. 113).

[172] Latigo (2008, p. 112.

[173] Armstrong (2014, p. 604).

[174] Oloya (2012, p. 161).

[175] Oloya (2012, p. 164).

[176] Oloya (2012, p. 164).

[177] See Macdonald (2017b, p. 299).

[178] Macdonald (2017b, p. 299).

[179] Meier (2013, p. 31).

[180] Lubaale (2020, pp. 180–202).

[181] See Ndagire (2024, p. 158) and Nakayi (2008, p. 19).

but also how the systems might complement each other. What can be gathered from the discussions is that traditional justice and other localised dispute resolution mechanisms are still relevant within Uganda's transitional justice, primarily for the achievement of restorative justice and communal relations. Therefore, it is important to explore how stakeholders like transnational networks and NGOs engage with the mechanisms in Uganda.

3.2 *Law and Policy: Closing the Gap Between Victims and Transitional Justice*

Having identified the gaps in Uganda's transitional justice process, it is vital to explore the relevant legal and policy avenues. As I have argued elsewhere, there is a need for a comprehensive transitional justice framework in order to inform future disaster and conflict response, but more importantly enhance the protection for vulnerable victims like IDPs.[182] Similarly, NGOs working on transitional justice in Uganda argue for comprehensive approaches in addressing systemic human rights abuses.[183] A good example for Uganda can be drawn from the UN's approach to transitional justice, which consists of:

> both judicial and non-judicial processes and mechanisms, including prosecution initiatives, facilitating initiatives in respect of the right to truth, delivering reparations, institutional reform and national consultations. Whatever combination is chosen must be in conformity with international legal standards and obligations.[184]

This approach suggests a structural relationship between IHRL and transitional justice, that could also be applicable to the context of Uganda. Whilst centralising the role of the UN, Leena Grover examines an important question on the implications of this structural relationship on the normative content of transitional justice.[185] Based on the UN's approach to transitional justice, she argues that States are bound by both international legal obligations and standards, referring to norms and policies established by the UN through soft law instruments.[186] As such, there is an adequate normative foundation for transitional justice in Uganda, also embedded in the soft laws.

Uganda is part of the member States of the AU. Regionally, the African conceptualisation of transitional justice is reflected in the AU's transitional justice framework, that broadens the notion of justice beyond retributive justice, to encompass

---

[182] Kirabira and Choukroune (2023).

[183] For more commentary on the National Transitional Justice Policy (2019) see Oola and Nono (2019).

[184] UN Secretary-General (UNSG), Guidance Note of the Secretary-General: United Nations Approach to Transitional Justice, March (2010, p. 3).

[185] Grover (2019, p. 360).

[186] Grover (2019, p. 375).

socio-economic elements of restoration, redistribution and transformation.[187] This elaborate focus on victims' participation is well grounded in transitional justice literature, which centralises victims' roles in designing and implementation of transitional justice.[188]

Studies of social psychology and victimhood greatly contribute to our understanding of the attitudes of different victims towards transitional justice policies.[189] For example, whereas refugees and IDPs are most likely to support restorative policies such as amnesty, victims of gross human rights violations like torture are more likely to support forms of retributive justice.[190] This might be true in the context of Northern Uganda, due to the long-lasting impact of the legacies of war crimes.

Reparation is one of the fundamental elements within transitional justice policies, due to the socio-economic effects of mass conflict. For example, forced displacement creates multiple socio-economic losses for both victims and states, thus creating a need for effective policies that centralise victims. A good example is the demand by victims of the LRA for a comprehensive reparations process from the state.[191] Against this background, it would be important to ascertain whether institutions like the ICC are considered as legitimate in the eyes of such victims. As this line of inquiry demands extensive empirical research, the focus of this book is on the work of transnational networks and NGOs that interact with the victims.

One would wonder how development and reparations policies link together in Northern Uganda. In terms of scholarship, we can draw differences between social development policy and reparations policy. To Naomi Roht-Arriaza and Katharine Orlovsky, in order for reparation policies to serve their symbolic functions, they should come primarily from perpetrators and states.[192] To refugee scholars, repairing the harm done to victims of displacement means recognising their vulnerability and accompanying reparations measures with specific messages, like acknowledgements of their suffering.[193] A central point of agreement is the position of victims as central actors during the design and implementation of transitional justice processes. Uganda is thus a good case study to assess whether and how reparations, in addition to the prosecution of perpetrators and other truth-seeking mechanisms, legitimise transitional justice. This legitimation effect is also construed in terms of 'creating a consciousness of survivors as rights-holders'.[194] Therefore, it is important to highlight the different approaches within Uganda's transitional justice police framework.

---

187 See African Union, Transitional Justice Policy, February 2019, paras 67–70.

188 For more details, see Fisher (2020, pp. 318–345), McEvoy and McConnachie (2013, pp. 489–513), and Orentlicher (1991, p. 19).

189 Hall et al. (2018, p. 347).

190 Hall et al. (2018, p. 347).

191 See International Center for Transitional Justice (2014). The NGO report highlights the need for reparations for war victims in Northern Uganda.

192 See for instance Roht-Arriaza and Katharine Orlovsky (2009, pp. 171–213).

193 See generally Murcia (2013, pp. 191–206).

194 Roht-Arriaza and Katharine Orlovsky (2009, p. 172).

In June 2019, Uganda adopted a National Transitional Justice Policy (NTJP),[195] three months after the adoption of the African Transitional Justice Policy. The policy was founded upon the peace negotiations in Juba and the AAR, that acknowledged the:

> need for an overarching justice framework that will provide for the exercise of formal criminal jurisdiction, and for the adoption and recognition of complementary alternative justice mechanisms.[196]

This Policy formed a national basis for the state's commitment to establishing concrete measures for accountability.

The formulation of the NTJP was mainly the work of the Justice, Law and Order Sector office (JLOS), within the Ministry of Justice and the Uganda Law Reform Commission. Their work was delayed by the shifting priorities of the national agenda and donors.[197] This dimension is equally acknowledged by Anna Macdonald in her analysis of the transitional justice implementation gap in Uganda.[198] Based on long-term qualitative fieldwork in Uganda, she indicates that the implementation gap is co-constituted by technical donor approaches and political bureaucracy by the Ugandan government.[199]

The NTJP encompasses globally accepted aims of transitional justice like ending impunity for serious crimes, restoration, retribution, reconciliation and institutional reforms.[200] In addition, the NTJP provides a framework for the operation of both formal and informal justice processes of the post-LRA conflict situation.[201] Another notable element is the contextualisation of victims, defined to include those who individually or collectively suffer physical or mental harm.[202] Besides the provision of a comprehensive framework for accountability, the adoption of a NTJP demonstrated the Ugandan government's commitment to pursuing transitional justice measures.[203] Moreover, some researchers related the shifting of transitional justice agendas to the government's 'tactics of narrative control and calculated stasis'.[204] It should be noted that despite this comprehensive NTJP, it's successful implementation is an issue that requires more study, largely due to the absence of a Transitional Justice Act. At the time of this writing, there were still pending legislative consultations about the Transitional Justice Bill 2022, which is the legal backing for this NTJP.

My previous research on the transitional justice implementation in relation to IDPs and Children Born of War (CBW) in Uganda highlights the gaps within the

---

195 Uganda National Transitional Justice Policy (2019).

196 See Annex to the ARR para. 5.2.

197 Quinn (2015, p. 24).

198 Macdonald (2019, p. 243).

199 Macdonald (2019, p. 243).

200 Uganda National Transitional Justice Policy (2019, para. iv).

201 Ajok (2019, p. 3).

202 Uganda National Transitional Justice Policy (2019, para. ix).

203 For more commentary on the National Transitional Justice Policy (2019) see Oola and Nono (2019).

204 Macdonald (2019, p. 245).

processes more broadly, for instance the limited access to Housing, Land and Property Rights (HLP).[205] Yet these rights fit within the broader pictures of customary practices and transitional justice, since they enable IDPs and CBW to integrate into the post-war communities. With the existing dilemmas, it is not a surprise that under the traditionally understood foundations of transitional justice based on democratic transitions, Uganda is perceived as a 'pre-transitional' State.[206] Based on extensive empirical studies in Uganda, Joanna Quinn observes key indications of the failure of transitional justice processes in Uganda.[207] Among other factors, she highlights the ethno-cultural differences as a barrier towards effective transitional justice policies.[208] Within the context of transition, Quinn argues that 'the effectiveness and impact of transitional justice practices and mechanisms is significantly less when they are invoked and/or implemented in pre-transitional states'.[209] As much as her arguments derive from a political science perspective, a social-legal approach towards transitional justice presents a clearer and more elaborate discussion on the impact of Uganda's NTJP.

4 Conclusion

What is the state of transitional justice in Uganda? The chapter has provided a historical analysis of the Northern Uganda situation, to set the stage for analysing the transitional justice mechanisms, for example, amnesties, traditional justice and formal criminal accountability. It has highlighted the tensions surrounding the application of traditional and formal justice mechanisms like the ICC intervention and prosecution. It also discussed the difficulties faced in relying on formal judicial systems and traced the cultural and social narratives around justice and reconciliation, whilst situating victims as the central subjects. Put succinctly, it is apt to suggest that Uganda is still a State under transition, from the emerging developments in transitional justice, including the adoption of a transitional justice policy. What will be interesting then is to examine the role of transnational networks and NGOs in the contested transitional justice processes.

References

[205] For more details on the existing post-war recovery framework in the light of HLP rights see Kirabira and Choukroune (2023).

[206] Quinn (2015, p. 14).

[207] Quinn (2015, p. 14).

[208] Quinn (2015, p. 16).

[209] Quinn (2015, p. 10).

Afako B (2012) Undermining the LRA: role of Uganda's Amnesty Act. Conciliation Resources. https://www.c-r.org/news-and-views/comment/undermining-lra-role-ugandas-amnesty-act
African Commission on Human and Peoples' Rights, 111 Resolution on the Right to a Remedy and Reparation for Women and Girls Victims of Sexual Violence—ACHPR/Res.111(XXXXII)07, 28 November 2007
African Commission on Human and Peoples' Rights, 283 Resolution on the Situation of Women and Children in Armed Conflict—ACHPR/Res.283(LV)2014, May 2014
African Committee of Experts on the Rights and Welfare of the Child (Acerwc), Michelo Hunsungule and Others (on Behalf of Children in Northern Uganda) v. The Government of Uganda, Communication No. 1/2005 Decision, Ethiopia, Twenty First Ordinary Session, 15–19 April 2013
African Union, African Union Convention for the Protection and Assistance of Internally Displaced Persons in Africa ('Kampala Convention'), 23 October 2009
African Union, Protocol to the African Charter on Human and People's Rights on the Rights of Women in Africa, 11 July 2003
African Union, Transitional Justice Policy, February 2019
Agreement on Accountability and Reconciliation between the Government of the Republic of Uganda and the LRA/M(Addendum 4), 03/11/2007
Agger K (2012) The end of amnesty in Uganda: implications for LRA defections. The Enough Project, Washington, pp 1–8
Ajok M (2019) Special report: the national transitional justice policy. The Justice, Law and Order Sector Secretariat, Kampala
Amnesty International (2008) Uganda: Agreement and Annex on Accountability and Reconciliation Falls Short of a Comprehensive Plan to end Impunity (AFR 59/001/2008). Amnesty International
Amone C (2015) Constructivism, instrumentalism and the rise of Acholi ethnic identity in northern Uganda. Afr Identities 13:129–143
Amone C, Muura O (2014) British colonialism and the creation of Acholi ethnic identity in Uganda, 1894 to 1962. J ImpAl Commonw Hist 42:239–257
Annex to the Agreement on Accountability and Reconciliation between the Government of the Republic of Uganda and the Lord's Resistance Army/Movement (Annex to June 29 Agreement), Juba, Sudan, June 29, 2007, February 19, 2008
Apuuli K (2011) Peace over justice: the Acholi Religious Leaders Peace Initiative (ARLPI) vs. The International Criminal Court (ICC) in Northern Uganda. Stud Ethn Natl 11:116–129
Armed Activities on the Territory of the Congo (Democratic Republic of the Congo v. Uganda) Judgment, ICJ Reports 2005
Armstrong K (2014) Justice without peace? international justice and conflict resolution in Northern Uganda. Dev Chang 45:589–607
Asplet M, Bradley M (2012) Strengthened protection for internally displaced persons in Africa: the Kampala convention comes into force. Am Soc Int Law (ASIL) Insights 16:1–5
Atim T, Proctor K (2013) Modern challenges to traditional justice: the struggle to deliver remedy and reparation in War-Affected Lango. Feinstein International Center, Tufts University, Medford, USA, pp 1–19
Branch A (2014) The violence of peace: ethnojustice in Northern Uganda. Dev Chang 45:608–630
Child Soldiers International (2004) Child Soldiers Global Report 2004—Uganda
Clapham A (2019) Human rights obligations for non-state actors: where are we now? In: Lafontaine F, Larocque F (eds) Doing peace the rights way: essays in international law and relations in honour of Louise arbour. Intersentia, Cambridge, pp 11–36
Constitution of the Republic of Uganda, 22 September 1995
Convention Against Torture and Other Cruel, Inhuman or Degrading Treatment or Punishment, 10 December 1984, United Nations, Treaty Series, vol 1465, p 85
Convention for the Protection of All Persons from Enforced Disappearance (20 December 2006) E/CN.4/2005/WG.22/WP.1/Rev.4, Entered into Force 23 December 2010

Convention on the Non-Applicability of Statutory Limitations to War Crimes and Crimes Against Humanity Adopted and Opened for Signature, Ratification and Accession by General Assembly Resolution 2391 (XXIII) of 26 November 1968 Entry into Force: 11 November 1970, in Accordance with Article VIII

Dieng A (2017) Protecting Internally displaced persons: the value of the Kampala convention as a regional example. Int Rev of the Red Cross 99:263–282

Drexler E (2010) The failure of international justice in East Timor and Indonesia. In: Hinton A (ed) Transitional justice: global mechanisms and local realities after genocide and mass violence. Rutgers University Press, New Brunswick

Dunn K (2004) Uganda: The Lord's resistance army. Rev Afr Polit Econ 31:139–142

Duthie R (2010) Afterword: the consequences of transitional justice in particular contexts. In: Hinton A (ed) Transitional justice: global mechanisms and local realities after genocide and mass violence. Rutgers University Press, New Brunswick

Espinosa JF (2022) The principle of non-recognition of states arising from serious breaches of peremptory norms of international law. Chin J I Law 21:79–114

Fisher K (2020) Messages from the expressive nature of ICC reparations: complex-victims in complex contexts and the trust fund for victims. Int Crim Law Rev 20:318–345

Freeman M (2009) Necessary evils: amnesties and the search for justice. CUP, Cambridge, pp 1–352

Geneva Conventions of 12 August 1949

Gissel L (2017) Legitimising the Juba peace agreement on accountability and reconciliation: the international criminal court as a third-party actor? J East Afr Stud 11:367–387

Gray H, Stern M, Dolan C (2020) Torture and sexual violence in war and conflict: the unmaking and remaking of subjects of violence. Rev Int Stud 46:197–216

Grover L (2019) Transitional justice, international law and the United Nations. Nord J Int Law 88:359–397

Hall J et al (2018) Exposure to violence and attitudes towards transitional justice. Polit Psychol 39:345–363

Harris C (2017) Some gender implications of the 'civilising mission' of the Anglican church for the Acholi peoples of Northern Uganda. Religions 8:1–20

Heller K (2008) Deconstructing international criminal law. Mich Law Rev 106:975–1000

Hendrickson D, Tumutegyereize K (2012) Dealing with complexity in peace negotiations: reflections on the Lord's resistance army and the Juba talks. Conciliation Resources 1–31

Hillebrecht C (2020) International criminal accountability and the domestic politics of resistance: case studies from Kenya and Lebanon. Law Soc Rev 54:453–486

Hinton A (2010) Introduction: toward an anthropology of transitional justice. In: Hinton A (ed) Transitional justice: global mechanisms and local realities after genocide and mass violence. Rutgers University Press, New Brunswick

Human Rights Watch (27 July 2011) Uganda: end Trials of Civilians in Military Courts Release Defendants or Send for Retrial to Protect Basic Rights

International Commission of Jurists (2019) Accountability through the specialized criminal chambers the adjudication of crimes under Tunisian and international law. International Commission of Jurists, Geneva

International Committee of the Red Cross (2017) Translating the Kampala convention into practice: a stocktaking exercise. Int Rev Red Cross 99:365–420

International Committee of the Red Cross, Protocol Additional to the Geneva Conventions of 12 August 1949, and Relating to the Protection of Victims of Non-International Armed Conflicts (Protocol II), 8 June 1977, 1125 UNTS 609

International Covenant on Civil and Political Rights, 16 December 1966, United Nations, Treaty Series, vol 999, p 171

International Criminal Court (2015) Statement of the Prosecutor of the International Criminal Court, Fatou Bensouda, following the surrender and transfer of top LRA Commander Dominic Ongwen, 21 Jan 2015

International Criminal Court Act, 2010

International Crisis Group (2007) Northern Uganda Peace Process: The Need to Maintain Momentum. Africa Briefing No. 46, Kampala/Nairobi/Brussels, pp 1–15
International Law Commission, 'Draft Articles on Responsibility of States for Internationally Wrongful Acts' (2001) Supplement No. 10 (A/56/10)
Janmyr M (2014) Recruiting internally displaced persons into civil militias: the case of Northern Uganda. Nord J Hum Rights 32:199–219
Kamara J, Cyril S, Renzaho A (2017) The social and political dimensions of internal displacement in Uganda: Challenges and opportunities—a systematic review. Afr Stud 76:444–473
Kanyeihamba G (2010) Constitutional and political history of Uganda: from 1894 to Present, 2nd edn. LawAfrica Publishing (K)Limited, Nairobi
Kasande S (2016) Kwoyelo and Ongwen trials show progress in fight against impunity. International Center for Transitional Justice, Kampala https://www.ictj.org/news/kwoyelo-ongwen-icc-uganda
Kasande S (2024) Beyond selective justice: confronting atrocities and delivering redress to victims in Northern Uganda. J Int Crim Justice 22:713–719
Kirabira T (2021) Technology as a key tool for the prosecution of international crimes: Lessons from Uganda. Int Crim Law Rev 22:1143–1167
Kirabira T, Choukroune L (2023) Uganda's post-war transitional justice process: have housing, land and property rights been restored? J Int HumItarian Leg Stud 14:156–181
Latigo J (2008) Northern Uganda: Tradition-based practices in the Acholi region. In: Huyse L, Salter M (eds) Traditional justice and reconciliation after violent conflict: learning from African experiences. International Institute for Democracy and Electoral Assistance, Stockholm, pp 85–119
Lomo Z, Hovil L (2004) Behind the violence: causes, consequences and the search for solutions in Northern Uganda. Refugee Law Project, Kampala, Working Paper No.11, pp 1–53
Lubaale E (2020) Legal pluralism as a lens through which to appreciate the role and place of traditional justice in international criminal justice. J Leg Plur Unoff Law 52:180–202
Macdonald A (2017a) In the interests of justice?" The International Criminal Court, peace talks and the failed quest for war crimes accountability in northern Uganda. J East Afr Stud 11:628–648
Macdonald A (2017b) Transitional justice and political economies of survival in post-conflict Northern Uganda. Dev Chang 48:286–311
Macdonald A (2019) 'Somehow this whole process became so artificial': exploring the transitional justice implementation gap in Uganda. Int J TransitAl Justice 13:225–248
Mallinder L (2009) Uganda at a crossroads: narrowing the amnesty? Working Paper from Beyond Legalism: Amnesties, Transition and Conflict Transformation, Institute of Criminology and Criminal Justice, Queen's University Belfast, pp 1–72
McEvoy K, McConnachie K (2013) Victims and transitional justice: voice, agency and blame. Soc Leg Stud 22:489–513
McKnight J (2015) Accountability in Northern Uganda: understanding the conflict, the parties and the false dichotomies in international criminal law and transitional justice. J Afr Law 59:193–219
Meier B (2013) 'Death does not rot': transitional justice and local 'truths' in the aftermath of the war in Northern Uganda. Afr Spectr 48:25–50
Méndez J (1997) Accountability for past abuses. Hum Rights Q 19:255–282
Minogue O (2010) "Peace vs. justice: the utility of amnesties. Crim Justice Ethics 29:306–314
Murcia L (2013) Social policy or reparative justice? challenges for reparations in contexts of massive displacement and related serious human rights violations. J Refug Stud 27:191–206
Musisi F (2017) The end of Joseph Kony? Daily Monitor, 8 May 2017
Nakayi R (2008) Reaching out for justice and reconciliation in Northern Uganda: the proposed war crimes court and 94 Traditional Justice. Centre for Civil and Human Rights, Working Paper no. 5: pp 1–31
Nanima R (2019) The (non) enforcement of the right to fair trial with regard to the admissibility of evidence obtained through human rights violations: Comment on Uganda's human rights (enforcement) act (2019). Afr J Int Comp Law 27:654–661

New Vision, Army doubts Kony peace offer (2006) Kampala, 25 May 2006
Ndagire J (2024) Rethinking the application of formal and informal justice responses to conflict related sexual violence in Uganda. Genocide Stud Prev: Int J 18:147–165
Office of the Special Representative of the Secretary-General for Children and Armed Conflict (2 June 2012) The Lord's Resistance Army and Children. Brussels
https://childrenandarmedconflict.un.org/2012/06/the-lords-resistance-army-and-children/
Okema S (2007) Assessing the implementation of the convention against torture in decentralised administration in Uganda: a case study of Gulu district. Makerere University, Kampala
Oloka-Onyango J (2020) Unpacking the African backlash to the International Criminal Court (ICC): the case of Uganda and Kenya. Strat Law J 4:41–68
Oloya O (2012) Child to soldier: stories from Joseph Kony's Lord's resistance army. University of Toronto Press, Toronto
Oola S, Nono F (2019) Uganda's transitional justice policy 2019: better late than never! new vision, 5 July 2009. https://www.newvision.co.ug/news/1502988/uganda-transitional-justice-policy-2019-late
Optional Protocol to the Convention on the Rights of the Child on the Involvement of Children in Armed Conflict, 25 May 2000
Organization of African Unity, African Charter on Human and Peoples' Rights ('Banjul Charter'), 27 June 1981, CAB/LEG/67/3 Rev. 5, 21 I.L.M. 58 (1982)
Organization of African Unity, African Charter on the Rights and Welfare of the Child, 11 July 1990, CAB/LEG/24.9/49 (1990)
Orentlicher D (1991) Settling accounts: the duty to prosecute human rights violations of a prior regime. Yale Law J 100:2539–2615
O'Shea A (2002) Amnesty for crime in international law and practice. Kluwer Law International, The Hague/London, pp 1–376
Otunnu O (2009) The secret genocide. Foreign Policy, 19 Oct 2009 https://foreignpolicy.com/2009/10/19/the-secret-genocide/
Pain D (1997) "The bending of spears": producing consensus for peace and development in Northern Uganda. International Alert/Kacoke Madit, London
Pillay N (2012) Establishing Effective Accountability Mechanisms for Human Rights Violations. Delivering Justice, No. 4, vol XLIX Retrieved from UN website https://www.un.org/en/chronicle/article/establishing-effective-accountability-mechanisms-human-rights-violations
Pohlman A (2017) Sexual violence as torture: crimes against humanity during the 1965–66 Killings in Indonesia. J Genocide Res 19:574–593
Prevention and Prohibition of Torture Act, 2012 (No. 3 of 2012)
Prosecutor v. Jean-Paul Akayesu (Trial Judgement), ICTR-964-T, International Criminal Tribunal for Rwanda (ICTR) (2 September 1998) [Hereinafter Akayesu Case]
Quinn J (2015) Failure to launch: The consequences of prematurely conceived transitional justice. In: A paper presented at the European Consortium for Political Research, Montreal, 27 August 2015
Report of the High Commissioner for Human Rights on the activities of her office in Uganda, U.N. Doc. A/HRC/4/49/Add.2), 12 February 2007
Roht-Arriaza N (1990) State responsibility to investigate and prosecute grave human rights violations in international. Calif Law Rev 78:451–513
Roht-Arriaza N, Orlovsky K (2009) A complementary relationship: Reparations and development. In: De Greiff P, Duthie R (eds) Transitional justice and development: making connections. Social Science Research Council and the International Center for Transitional Justice, Brooklyn, NY, pp 171–213
Rome Statute of the International Criminal Court, U.N. Doc. No. A/ CONF.183/9" (1998)
Ronen Y (2013) Human rights obligations of territorial non-state actors. Cornell Int Law J 46:21–50
Shabdita S, Okwir I (2015) Mapping regional reconciliation in Northern Uganda: a case study of the Acholi and Lango Sub-Regions. Justice and Reconciliation Project, Gulu, pp 1–49
Tafeng K (2006) LRA optimistic on peace talks. New Vision, 16 June 2006

Teitel R (2003) Transitional justice genealogy. Harv Hum Rights J 16:69–94
Teitel R (2005) The law and politics of contemporary transitional justice. Cornell Int Law J 38:837–862
Ten Kate W, Nouwen S (2018) The globalisation of justice: amplifying and silencing voices at the ICC. Handmaker J, Arts K(eds) Mobilising international law for 'global justice.' CUP, Cambridge, pp 46–62
The Amnesty Act, Chapter 294,Date of Consolidation: 31 December 2000
Uganda National Transitional Justice Policy (2019)
Uganda: War Victims Emphasize Urgent Need for Reparations. (24 June 2014) International Center for Transitional Justice, Kampala
UN, Basic Principles and Guidelines on the Right to a Remedy and Reparation for Victims of Gross Violations of International Human Rights Law and Serious Violations of International Humanitarian Law (2006), A/RES/60/147. [Hereinafter UN Basic Principles 2005]
UN (2011) International legal protection of human rights in armed conflict. United Nations Publications, New York and Geneva, pp 1–119
UN General Assembly, Convention on the Rights of the Child, 20 (November 1989) United Nations. Treaty Series 1577:3
UN Human Rights Council, Right to the Truth : Resolution / Adopted by the Human Rights Council, 10 October 2012, A/HRC/RES/21/7
UN Office of the High Commissioner for Human Rights (2007) Making peace our own: victims' perceptions of accountability. Reconciliation and Transitional Justice in Northern Uganda. OHCHR, Geneva, pp 1–74
Secretary-General UN (2010) Guidance note of the secretary-general: United Nations approach to transitional justice. UN Digital Library, New York, pp 1–11
United Nations High Commissioner for Refugees (2010) A time between: moving on from internal displacement in northern Uganda. UNHCR, Geneva, pp 1–29
Universal Declaration of Human Rights, 10 December 1948, 217 A (III)
Uzoigwe G (1973) The beginnings of Lango society: a review of evidence. J Hist Soc Niger 6:397–411

Actor-Oriented Analysis of Accountability Mechanisms in Uganda

1 Introduction

Having explored the framework for transitional justice in Uganda in the previous chapter, this chapter uses empirical legal research and data, to show the role of NGOs in transitional justice. It is informed by data from secondary sources like NGO reports and court documents, supported with interviews. A mapping of the principal stakeholders and actors is important in order to effectively determine the relevancy and legitimacy of the initiatives. Moreover, critical peacebuilding debates view transitional justice as 'the result of what individual groups and actors are able to negotiate, either with local governments or with external funders'.[1] Moreover, there is a contestable relationship between the legitimacy and relevance of international criminal justice.[2] This has a direct connection to the approach of this book—an actor-oriented analysis of transitional justice to establish how the different actors influence the existing initiatives.

As also pointed out in the introduction, the book takes a socio-legal approach towards transitional justice. This line of inquiry also helps in the actor-oriented analysis of the different transitional justice initiatives in Uganda. Therefore, the discussions in this chapter go beyond the legal lens, to include perspectives from social sciences. Murithi's insights are important to make a socio-legal analysis of the ICC's intervention in Africa. He uses a political prism to examine the instrumentalisation

[1] Baker and Obradovic-Wochnik (2016, p. 291).

[2] See generally Munkholm et al. (2019) and Findlay (2013).

Some sections in the chapter have overlaps with my doctoral thesis. This is some overlap with my book chapter Kirabira, T.R. (2023). NGOs and the Legitimacy of International Criminal Justice: The Case of Uganda. In: Jeßberger, F., Steinl, L., Mehta, K. (eds) International Criminal Law—A Counter-Hegemonic Project?. International Criminal Justice Series, vol 31. T.M.C. Asser Press, The Hague.

© The Author(s), under exclusive license to Springer Nature Singapore Pte Ltd. 2025
T. R. Kirabira, *Transnational Networks and Justice in the Global South*, International Law and the Global South, https://doi.org/10.1007/978-981-95-3137-0_4

of international criminal justice and in particular, the ICC, by different actors.[3] He argues that the ICC is a form of judicial imperialism, politicised by both global actors and national politicians, in order to pursue their own self-interests.[4] Whilst Murithi uses the theme of 'de-legitimation', this chapter and book utilise the key theme of the 'legitimisation' of the transitional justice initiatives. Legitimacy is emphasised since it is a key measure of transitional justice mechanisms, within the eyes of all stakeholders.[5] As such, the discussions on legitimacy are oriented towards victims and conflict-affected communities.

The chapter begins with a historical analysis of the Ugandan case at the ICC, highlighting the salient role of different actors and how they relate with the victims. Secondly, it maps out the roles of different actors in the establishment and functioning of Uganda's International War Crimes Division. The analysis closely associates with the conception of 'international justice proponents' used by Jaya Ramji-Nogales, referring to international organisations that influence transitional justice initiatives, for example Amnesty International (AI) and Human Rights Watch (HRW).[6] Most of the international justice proponents speak for victims, in what Madling refers to as the 'theft of victims' pain'.[7] Whilst I do not agree with this assertion, we are reminded that transitional justice is not always legitimate, based on the way in which NGOs interact with the primary stakeholders, i.e. the victims. In line with Nogale's argument of balancing the perspectives of internal stakeholders with those of international justice proponents,[8] the discussion includes a fair discussion on the views of the local actors.

2 The ICC as a Transitional Justice Institution: Mixed Perceptions

The previous chapter highlighted critical concerns in the way victims engage within transitional justice, based on the ethno-cultural dimensions, but also different perceptions of responsibility and accountability. It also highlighted the dominant cultural and religious discourses in the arguments against the ICC's intervention in the Northern Uganda conflict.[9] Similarly, we are reminded of Ramji-Nogale's theory of 'bespoke transitional justice', which challenges the dominant scholarship that dismisses the role of the ICC as a mechanism of transitional justice.[10]

---

[3] Murithi (2019, p. 3).

[4] Murithi (2019).

[5] Ramji-Nogales (2015, pp. 106–121).

[6] Ramji-Nogales (2015, p. 116).

[7] Madlingozi (2010, p. 211).

[8] Ramji-Nogales (2015, p. 116).

[9] Armstrong (2014, p. 601).

[10] Ramji-Nogales (2015, p. 121).

The analysis in this chapter does not seek to conceptualise the ICC as a transitional justice mechanism per se, but rather, to show how it is (de)legitimised by different actors within the ambit of transitional justice. These discussions are founded on the sheer amount of material devoted to non-ICC substance in the previous chapters. This emphasis is important since perceptions about the Court are endogenous to politics and relationships between domestic and international actors.[11] More specifically, this sub-section will explore the legitimacy of the ICC and the diverse actors that interact with it. This dual analysis is relevant, in order to understand how the different actors influence its work and the way it addresses situations.[12] This expansive approach is also recommended by Ugandan transitional justice practitioner and lawyer Stephen Oola, who argues that:

> understanding the broader implications of the Court's [ICC] work requires viewing it in relation to domestic transitional initiatives, political factors and the work of other actors in the Ugandan context.[13]

Before delving into the Ugandan context, a recap on the concept of legitimacy is necessary, in line with the theoretical underpinning of this book. Most scholarly discussions on the impact of the ICC are based on perceptions of legitimacy.[14] To Cassese, the notion of legitimacy encompasses different aspects. Firstly, in what he refers to as 'consent legitimacy', it means 'the moral and psychological acceptance of a body (or, more broadly, of a political system or an authority) by its constituency'.[15] The second aspect relates to 'universal values legitimacy', 'based on the values common to the whole community within which the institution lives and operates'.[16]

However, as Cassese rightly acknowledges, there are other factors that are relevant when assessing the legitimacy of the ICC. In what he refers to as 'performance legitimacy', he notes aspects like the accountability to the institution's constituency and 'answerability' to the founding authority.[17] Within the context of Northern Uganda, Mégret questions the legitimacy of the ICC's efforts to represent victims, due to frustrations raised by some victims, regarding how the court engaged with them.[18] Likewise, scholars in political science equally allude to legitimacy concerns and the politicisation of institutions of international criminal justice, notably the ICC.[19] From a legal perspective, proponents of the ICC perceived it as the beginning of a new era in ensuring peace through justice, within the African context.[20] It is thus imperative to establish how the ICC is perceived, and the kind of actors involved.

---

[11] For a more detailed analysis see Hillebrecht (2020, pp. 453–486).

[12] De Vos et al. (2015, p. 4).

[13] Oola (2015, p. 149).

[14] Wierda et al. (2007, p. 1075).

[15] Cassese (2012, pp. 490–493).

[16] Cassese (2012, p. 492).

[17] Cassese (2012, p. 493).

[18] Mégret (2015, p. 42).

[19] See for example Findlay (2013).

[20] Nsereko (2011, p. 353).

According to Ugandan jurist and ICL expert Daniel Nsereko, the ICC is an appropriate mechanism for justice, as most African States are not always capable of holding perpetrators accountable domestically.[21] More specifically, his analysis helps to understand the interplay between the ICC and the protection of human rights in Africa.[22] As discussed in the previous chapter, the Ugandan government invited the ICC to intervene, in order to exert pressure on the LRA rebels in Northern Uganda. The statement of Solicitor General of Uganda at the time of the referral, as summarised by the ICC Pre-Trial Chamber, is instructive in this regard.[23] Whilst recognising the fairness, impartiality and effectiveness of the national judicial system, he stated that the ICC was:

> the most appropriate and effective forum for the investigation and prosecution of those bearing the greatest responsibility for the crimes within the referred situation. This view was based on several considerations, including (i) the scale and gravity of the relevant crimes; (ii) the fact that the exercise of jurisdiction by the Court would be of immense benefit for the victims of these crimes and contribute favourably to national reconciliation and social rehabilitation; (iii) Uganda's inability to arrest the persons who might bear the greatest responsibility for the relevant crimes.

In a highly politicised situation like Uganda's, it is necessary to understand how the ICC intervention impacted on transitional justice in general. To Tietel, the ICC symbolises the entrenchment of the Phase 1 Model of transitional justice, based on the Nuremburg Trials.[24] A general discussion would be on how international trials impact on transitional justice. Within the Northern Uganda context, the discourse would explore if the ICC has solidified transitional justice. The empirical data in this book is thus helpful to understand how transnational networks and NGOs impacted on the work of the ICC in Uganda, and the perceptions on its legitimacy.

As already shown in the previous chapter and previous empirical work in Uganda, the ICC processes and the issuance of the arrest warrants against the top LRA commanders partly shaped the political dynamics between negotiating parties in Juba.[25] Generally speaking, the ICC was also viewed as 'a perplexing intervention that needed to be contained', something that would consequently drive cooperation from the LRA, during the peace talks.[26] This illustrates what Anna Macdonald refers to as the 'unintended effects' of the ICC, 'such as the alteration of conflict narratives'.[27] Consequently, it is important to examine the interests of the negotiating parties and actors, in line with the notion of accountability.

From the onset, the ICC intervention in Uganda was seen as a contest between peace and justice. Initially, there were strong voices of dissent by local NGOs against

---

[21] Nsereko (2011, p. 353).

[22] Nsereko (2011, p. 355).

[23] See Decision on the Admissibility of the Case under Article 19(1) of the Statute, ICC-02/04-01/05-377, Pre-Trial Chamber II, 10 Mar. 2009 at para 37.

[24] Teitel (2003, pp. 585–606).

[25] For more explanation see Macdonald (2017, pp. 628–648) and Gissel (2017, pp. 367–387).

[26] Macdonald (2017, p. 360).

[27] Macdonald (2017), p. 360).

the ICC intervention in Uganda. The Acholi Religious Leaders Peace Initiative (ARLPI), an influential organisation at the time, opposed the ICC investigations because they were only aimed at the LRA activities and not the crimes that were allegedly committed by government forces.[28] Such opposition created an intimidating environment for domestic NGOs, as ICC proponents and some international NGOs (INGOs) were critical of the local peace initiatives. An NGO founder interviewed, recalled the tense environment, noting: 'some of us were accused of undermining ICC work [sic]'.[29] As noted from the discussions during the Review Conference of the Rome Statute in 2010, the peace vs justice debate polarised the engagements among the different transitional justice stakeholders in Uganda.[30]

Ultimately, Hovil's experience of working with the local NGO, the Refugee Law Project (RLP) during the initial years of the ICC in Uganda provides useful insights regarding the ICC's impact on transitional justice. She argues that the ICC intervention did not live up to the goals of transitional justice, because of the dynamics, but also the neglect of local NGOs.[31] In line with these dynamics, one wonders how local and INGOS were able to work together, within the process of transitional justice, including the ICC.

Addressing these important transitional justice questions requires empirical examination, specifically, the voices of key NGO actors in Northern Uganda. As rightly pointed out by Marieke Wierda, a vast of scholarship in relation to the ICC is often done remotely, without empirical studies in the situation countries and affected communities.[32] Marieke's scholarship and views are particularly relevant due to her extensive work as a transitional justice advisor in Uganda. The next sub-sections assess the situation from a more empirical perspective, to show how NGOs contribute to the (de)legitimisation of the ICC and the International Crimes Division (ICD) in Uganda.

3 Legitimisation of the ICC: Power of Transnational Networks

An analysis of the legitimation power of transnational networks involves an exploration of different local, domestic and international NGOs. The primary subject of analysis, in the context of the Ugandan context, relates to history and politics surrounding the ICC intervention. In resonance with the aim of this book, it is important to understand how the Court was legitimised as a form of transitional justice.

---

[28] Apuuli (2011, pp. 116–129).

[29] Interview with NGO founder, 26 February 2021.

[30] Hovil (2010).

[31] Hovil (2010).

[32] For an expansive assessment on the Impact of the ICC in Situation Countries see generally Wierda (2023).

As mentioned in the previous sub-section, Lucy Hovil worked with the RLP during the period when the LRA situation was referred to the ICC in 2004, and the subsequent issuance of arrest warrants against top commanders in 2005.[33] One of the reasons she gives for the initial strong condemnation by local NGOs of the ICC intervention was the limited knowledge and involvement:

> No prior warning of the announcement [ICC referral] and minimal consultation from the Court, the Government of Uganda or international NGOs who had particularly urged the intervention.[34]

In a transitional justice environment like Northern Uganda, it is impossible for local NGOs to operate alone without the financial and technical support of INGOs. As highlighted in Hovil's report, local NGOs and Ugandan-based officers working for INGOs had to make choices between keeping their stances against the new transitional justice mechanism or risk losing their funding and international partnerships.[35] For example, the RLP, the local NGO that Hovil worked for, was unable to acquire funding for research on the impact of the ICC, as it was perceived by INGOs and donors as negative towards the Court.[36] She makes an intriguing view on the perplexing relationship between local NGOs and INGOs at the time:

> This negative reaction also created considerable concern among international human rights groups [INGOs] who, understandably, were extremely concerned about the negative interaction surrounding the Court's first country situation. However, from the ground this only made the situation more intimidating for local civil society as the international human rights community and the Court appeared to be joining forces against us.[37]

An important event that united local NGOs and INGOs was the ICC Review Conference held in Uganda in June 2010. The Human Rights Network Uganda (HURINET–U) and No Peace Without Justice (NPWJ), an INGO headquartered in Rome, were quite instrumental in advocating for the ICC Review Conference in Uganda, as evidenced from their involvement in the Eighth Session of the Assembly of States Parties (ASP) in 2008.

Existing research shows that during the first years of the Court's existence, ICC Chief Prosecutor Moreno-Ocampo faced enormous pressure from external actors, including transnational networks and judges in The Hague to kick start the Court's operations with a first case.[38] With such an observation, an important question would be; what would such an international criminal case look like, considering the complex situation prevailing in Northern Uganda at the time? Inevitably, we are drawn to the work of transnational networks, NGOs and perceptions of the locals.

HRW carried out field interviews and observations in 2007 and reported that:

33 Hovil (2010, p. 2).

34 Hovil (2010).

35 Hovil (2010).

36 Hovil (2010, p. 3).

37 Hovil (2010, p. 3).

38 For an expansive assessment on the Impact of the ICC in Situation Countries see generally Wierda (2023).

> Nearly all those we met in displaced camps expressed an intense desire to return to their homes. A number conveyed real concern that prosecution of LRA leaders could further delay their departure and therefore saw the ICC as an obstacle. A distinct vocal minority, however, declared a desire to see those most responsible brought to trial, although they questioned how the ICC could arrest those it had charged.[39]

Despite the negative perception about the role of the ICC, HRW provided a justification for the Court's intervention, noting that:

> By issuing its arrest warrants against four senior LRA leaders, the International Criminal Court (ICC) has taken an important step to seeing that justice is done for the crimes committed in northern Uganda.[40]

Nonetheless, the report also acknowledges the complementary role of the ICC, albeit with a reference to the lack of capacity at the domestic level. It was noted that:

> Sham national proceedings aimed at shielding the accused from responsibility, unfair trials, or even meaningful prosecutions accompanied by a slap-on-the-wrist sentence will not pass muster with the ICC judges who will ultimately decide whether a trial in Uganda is an acceptable alternative.[41]

Amnesty International took a more skeptical view about any possibility for domestic prosecution of the LRA. Christopher Keith Hall, the senior legal adviser in AI's International Justice Project, reckoned that:

> At the moment, we have no evidence to suggest that even a new court established in Uganda to deal with these cases would be able and willing to do so in fair proceedings that are not a sham.[42]

Avocats Sans Frontières (ASF), an INGO headquartered in Brussels, operates an office in Uganda. In 2010, the organisation launched a multi-country project entitled 'Promoting the Rome Statute System and enhancing the effectiveness of the ICC'.[43] It carried out a baseline study in Uganda, interviewing lawyers, transitional justice practitioners, JLOS and local NGOs, to gather their views on the Rome regime.[44] More importantly, the study indicates that local NGOs did not view the ICC as a primary transitional justice avenue. As noted by ASF:

> The main challenge revealed by these interviews is that despite the CSO groups in this area recognizing that the ICC played an important role in peace building in the region, many of them now advocate for restorative justice tenets of forgiveness, reconciliation and truth-telling as avenues to bring about sustainable peace. This is parallel to the tenets of the ICC which pursues a retributive model of justice that aims at punishing those that commit serious human rights violations.[45]

---

[39] See Human Rights Watch report by Dicker (2007).

[40] Human Rights Watch report by Dicker (2007).

[41] Human Rights Watch report by Dicker (2007).

[42] For a summarised report on the reactions and mixed perceptions of Transnational Networks and NGOs in respect to the proposed domestic prosecution see IRIN (2008).

[43] Avocats Sans Frontières (2011, p. 6).

[44] Avocats Sans Frontières (2011, p. 6).

[45] Avocats Sans Frontières (2011, p. 6).

The above observation indicates that the ICC needed to enhance its legitimacy within the conflict-affected communities, but also, work with local NGOs. With regards promoting the ICC in Northern Uganda, an NGO representative noted; 'Our purpose was that we did not speak for the court. We could bash, if necessary'.[46] However, she noted a cordial working relationship, saying, 'we worked closely with the ICC outreach office…We had good working relationships with them and carried out joint activities'.[47]

One prominent transnational network is exemplified in the work of the Uganda Victims' Foundation (UVF) and the Redress Trust since the inception of the case of the *Prosecutor v. Joseph Kony, Vincent Otti, Okot Odhiambo, Dominic Ongwen* at the ICC. The two NGOs, jointly filed *amicus curiae* in support of the admissibility of the case, based on their involvement in the transitional justice in Northern Uganda.[48] An important aspect of their work at the pre-trial stages related to their submissions on the extent to which the ICC investigations and prosecutions proposed, satisfied the victims' needs for justice, accountability and reconciliation under the Ugandan context.[49]

From a legal standpoint, it is important to note that the *amici curiae* submissions filed by the UVF and Redress Trust persuaded the Court to admit the case, following concerns that the ICC process would jeopardise the exiting peace agreement and the proposed domestic prosecution.[50] Similarly, as alluded to by the judges, the *amici curie* also revealed the limited capacity of the Ugandan justice system to assert jurisdiction over members of the LRA due to the Amnesty Act.[51]

Another domestic coalition that closely engaged with INGOs and the ICC was the Northern Ugandan Transitional Justice Working Group (NUTJWG), a collation of over sixty NGOs formed in 2008 to engage with transitional justice mechanisms.[52] Their legitimation work is identified from their activities, which linked directly with the existing transitional justice mechanisms, including the ICC. For example, workshops convened under the auspices of NUTJWG aimed at 'Building consensus among civil society in northern Uganda to promote collective and collaborative engagement on issues of transitional justice'.[53] Inevitably, this broad mandate triggers questions about the role of NGO coalitions within the prism of transitional justice.

---

[46] Interview with NGO representative, 2 March 2021.

[47] Interview with NGO representative, 2 March 2021.

[48] See *The Prosecutor v. Joseph Kony* et al. (Application by the Uganda Victims' Foundation and the Redress Trust for Leave to Submit Observations to the Pre-Trial Chamber II of the International Criminal Court, Pursuant to Rule 103 of the Rules of Procedure and Evidence, 2008).

[49] Application by the Uganda Victims' Foundation and the Redress Trust for Leave to Submit Observations to the Pre-Trial Chamber II of the International Criminal Court, Pursuant to Rule 103 of the Rules of Procedure and Evidence, 2008.

[50] See Decision on the Admissibility of the Case under Article 19(1) of the Statute, ICC-02/04-01/05-377, Pre-Trial Chamber II, 10 Mar. 2009.

[51] Decision on the Admissibility of the Case under Article 19(1) of the Statute, ICC-02/04-01/05-377, Pre-Trial Chamber II, 10 Mar. 2009.

[52] See Justice and Reconciliation Project Annual Report (2009, p. 7).

[53] Justice and Reconciliation Project Annual Report (2009, p. 9).

When the ICC intervention built momentum within Northern Uganda, the coalitions, with the support of INGOs, hosted consultative dialogues within the affected communities to reflect on process. Following Ongwen's surrender and initial appearance before the ICC, the Refugee Law Project highlighted perspectives from Northern Uganda, raising key dilemmas within the context of transitional justice.[54] On the basis of Ongwen's previous experience as a victim turned perpetrator of crimes, there was an Ongwen 'Justice Dilemma' and an emphasis on the importance of both the ICC and domestic justice mechanisms. A key observation in the transitional justice process in Uganda relates to the significant diminishing of NUTJWG's work, as the ICC case progressed.[55] One possible reason for the redundancy of the coalition can be attributed to the shifting of donor and international NGO priorities in the preceding years, as revealed earlier from Macdonald's empirical work in Northern Uganda.[56]

On a transnational level, the victims work was part of a wider network under the Victims' Rights Working Group (VRWG) hosted by REDRESS in London. NGO representatives from the UVF participated in meetings of the ASP to the ICC.[57] ASP meetings are important avenues for NGOs to interact with States that support the ICC, including the Ugandan case. The UVF's activities also involved facilitating local dialogues and 'Victim Empowerment Training' in Northern Uganda.[58] It is important to note that due to the sensitivity about the ICC intervention, the UVF operated under a broad coalition of NGOs named Uganda Victims' Rights Working Group (U-VRWG). In an interview, a founding member of the UVF recalled the polarised situation at the time, noting that: 'There were fears from retaliation when talking about the ICC in the North [the conflict-affected communities in Northern Uganda]'.[59]

Another important avenue that linked domestic and international NGOS was the Ugandan Coalition for the International Criminal Court (UCICC), which was formed in 2004 and hosted by the HURINET–U. It was a broad network, envisaged:

> to bring together ... key players in civil society, government and the international community to pursue map out criminal accountability for the victims in Northern Uganda, as well as endorse a strategy to be employed in the campaign for the ICC in Uganda.[60]

A range of activities were also undertaken during the Review Conference of the Rome Statute that took place in 2010 in Uganda, where organisations like the UCICC directly engaged with both ICC staff and delegations. Among other goals, they aimed 'to bring ICC closer to the people affected'.[61] In addition, local events and seminars

---

54 Odong (2015, pp. 1–17).

55 Interview with NGO representative, 2 March 2021.

56 Macdonald (2019, pp. 225–248).

57 Interview with a Legal Representative for Victims in the Dominic Ongwen case, 12 April 2021.

58 See TrustAfrica (2019).

59 Interview with founding member of the UVF, 12 March 2021.

60 See UCICC statement and speech to the Fifteenth session of the Assembly of State Parties to the Rome Statute 2016.

61 See the Coalition for the International Criminal Court website <https://www.coalitionfortheicc.org/country/uganda>.

debunked the perception of the ICC as biased against African countries.[62] To the NPWJ, the ICC Review Conference provided:

> an unprecedented opportunity to conduct a stock-taking that can set the policy tone and direction for the Court in the years to come as well as to enhance ICC States Parties' understanding of the justice needs and experiences of communities affected by the Court's work.[63]

Field visits and local outreach are important tools for legitimising transitional justice and its mechanisms. The NPWJ collaborated with local NGO coalitions UCICC and HURINET–U to organise field visits by ICC State Parties delegates to the war-affected Northern Uganda between January and June 2010.[64] An explicit legitimising impact is seen in the way in which the NGOs directly supported ICC outreach activities, which had an impact of reducing the initial hostility towards the Court within the victims and war-affected communities. According to a local NGO founder, 'the ICC begun to strengthen their local presence' within the affected communities.[65] He recalled that 'during the first ICC Conference in 2010, we [the NGO] took the ICC president to Lukodi'.[66] Lukodi is one of the places in Northern Uganda where Ongwen committed crimes against humanity in 2004. Crucially, the perceptions on the ICC's legitimacy were enhanced in the process.

Furthermore, the empirical study indicates that the UCICC was equally instrumental in the ratification and domestic implementation of the Rome Statute in Uganda. An NGO member of the UCICC affirmed that they trained Members of Parliament on the subject of the Rome Statute.[67] A notable observation from the empirical research concerned the contestations among local NGOs regarding who should host the UCICC.[68] Besides not having a permanent home, the coalition largely implemented activities of INGOs and donors. As revealed by one of its former coordinators, 'the coalition was just implementing activities, yet it was supposed to be synergising NGO efforts'.[69] This anomaly points to an implicit legitimation strategy for the ICC intervention amidst the contested spaces of transitional justice in Northern Uganda. The paradigm shift also opens up space for closer analysis of the interaction between NGO networks and transitional justice in general.

At the time of writing this book, the UCICC was technically not in operation. Two reasons are provided for this situation: First, as has been revealed in the proceeding paragraphs, the UCICC did not have a permanent home, and so its operations were largely done by one NGO, HURINET–U, which created conflicts among member

[62] For perspectives from Ugandan students see Coalition for the International Criminal Court (2017).

[63] See Statement of NPWJ (2010).

[64] See HURINET-U, NPWJ and the UCICC (2010, pp. 1–65).

[65] Interview with NGO co-founder, 4 May 2021.

[66] Interview with NGO co-founder, 4 May 2021.

[67] Interview with a former Coordinator of the UCICC, 12 March 2021. The country adopted the International Criminal Court Act (ICC Act 2010) in June 2010.

[68] Interview with a former Coordinator of the UCICC, 2 March 2021.

[69] Interview with a former Coordinator of the UCICC, 2 March 2021.

NGOs.[70] The other critical aspect relates to the funding. As explained by a former coordinator: 'The priorities of donors changed along the way ... There were some serious challenges'.[71] This is akin to Kendall's observation regarding the Special Court for Sierra Leone (SCSL), in what she terms 'donors' justice.[72] The observations highlighted a significant influence of international donors on the work of the criminal tribunal, which became a major face of transitional justice in the country.

Transnational NGO networks equally had a turning impact on the work of the Coalition for Reconciliation in Uganda (CORU), whose priorities were reconciliation and healing. CORU was established by NGOs, academics, religious leaders and other actors in 2006, as a forum to build reconciliation in Northern Uganda.[73] A key activity was the proposed National Reconciliation Bill by the member NGOs, whilst maintaining strong discourses against the ICC intervention.

Oola points out that: 'It was clear to many CSOs at this stage that formal trials would not address the full extent of impunity in Uganda'.[74] However, just like the observation with the NUTJG, CORU became redundant following the shifting of donors' attention towards domestic prosecution and formal accountability mechanisms. Consequently, the shifting of local NGO priorities in line with external donor preferences has implications on the mode of justice. One can thus argue that NGO networks are implicitly tied to the structures that promoted international criminal justice as a form of transitional justice in Uganda.

The International Center for Transitional Justice (ICTJ), an INGO headquartered in New York (NY), has maintained targeted engagements with local NGOs in Uganda since 2005. A key theme of their work involves helping victims seek redress and advocating for accountability for the perpetrators. The ICTJ also facilitated NGOs to form the NUTJWG, by organising community dialogues within the conflict-affected areas of Northern Uganda, and roundtable meetings with policy makers like JLOS in Kampala in 2009.[75] These events are all important avenues for legitimising the Rome regime and work of the ICC.

Dissemination of the Dominic Ongwen trial at the ICC plays a significant role in the legitimation of the Court. The Open Society Justice Initiative, a part of the Open Society Foundations that was established in 2003, publishes an International Justice Monitor. The publication aims:

> to expand awareness and understanding of the role of international justice in holding accountable those responsible for atrocities, particularly war crimes, crimes against humanity, and genocide.[76]

---

[70] Interview with a former Coordinator of the UCICC, 2 March 2021.

[71] Interview with a former Coordinator of the UCICC, 12 March 2021.

[72] Kendall, (2011, pp. 585–606). See also Kirabira (2021)The Role of NGOs in the Domestic Implementation of the African Union Transitional Justice Policy Framework: Perspectives From Uganda, 180–201.

[73] Oola (2010, pp.1–10).

[74] Oola (2010, pp.1–10).

[75] See Justice and Reconciliation Project (2009).

[76] See International Justice Monitor website https://www.ijmonitor.org/about-this-website/

Lino Owor Ogora, the Director and Co-Founder of the Foundation for Justice and Development Initiatives (FJDI), a local NGO based in Northern Uganda, has been reporting on the Ongwen trial at the ICC. Ogora's reports are published by the International Justice Monitor. Together with cultural and religious leaders from Northern Uganda, Ogora, on behalf of other local NGOs, attended the opening of Ongwen's trial in December 2016 at The Hague.[77] Ogora quotes one of the members of the local delegation to The Hague, indicating a positive perception about the ICC:

> I am privileged to have travelled and confirmed with my own eyes that the ICC in fact exists. I saw Ongwen in the court, and this means we have not been told lies about his trial. Even if not all people were able to come, they have at least been represented by us.[78]

From the positive experiences of the Ugandan delegation at the opening of the Ongwen trial, Ogora concludes that:

> the initiative by the ICC field office and Danish Embassy in Uganda achieved its intended impact of promoting community participation and increased the community representatives' understanding and appreciation of the ICC. Furthermore, community representatives will be expected to engage in public outreach and share their experiences back home.

The above text, from a local NGO founder opens up sightlines for exploring the work of other NGOs that interacted with the ICC and INGOs. The next sub-section will carry the analysis forward by exploring aspects of victim-oriented work and technical capacity building, as legitimisation factors in transitional justice.

4 Legitimisation Through Victim-Oriented Work and Technical Capacity Building

It is important to recall that besides the ICC case, Uganda also operates a specialised domestic criminal justice system akin to ICL. Within the ICC complementarity framework, Uganda domesticated the Rome Statute into its legal regime, by enacting the International Criminal Court Act of 2010 (ICC Act).[79] In 2009, the JLOS in collaboration with *pro bono* law firm Public International Law Policy Group (PILPG), held public consultation meetings in different regions of Uganda, in relation to the proposed ICC Bill.[80] The Bill was later passed into law by the Parliament in 2010.

Crucially, the domestication of the Rome Statute of the ICC through the enactment of the ICC Act in 2010 set a normative foundation and framework for accountability for international crimes in Uganda. In previous years, the 'positive complementarity' discourse by the ICC has triggered scholarly debates as to whether the role of the

[77] Ogora (2016c).

[78] Ogora (2016c).

[79] Theoretically, the ICC implements a positive complementarity approach, where it complements and supports domestic prosecutions, instead of serving as the primary option for justice.

[80] See Justice and Reconciliation Project (2009).

ICC in developing domestic capacity for trying international crimes.[81] Oftentimes, scholars quote the vision perceived by the first prosecutor, Luis Moreno Ocampo:

> [t]he effectiveness of the International Criminal Court should not be measured by the number of cases that reach the Court. On the contrary, the absence of trials by the ICC, as a consequence of the effective functioning of national systems, would be a major success.[82]

Uganda established a hybrid court in form of the International Crimes Division (ICD) in 2008.[83] It is also important to note that the creation of a specialised court to try war crimes was initially proposed during the failed peace talks between the Ugandan government and the LRA in 2008. Delegates from the Ugandan government and the LRA agreed that a special division of the high court be set up to try war crimes committed during the LRA war.[84] Therefore, the ICC complementarity regime only served as a formal legal framework in which the proposal would be implemented. According to Oola:

> From the beginning, the success of the talks and the highly wrought contents of the agreements attracted pro- ICC funders to pour money into Uganda, seeing a potential case study for positive complementarity between the ICC and domestic peace processes.[85]

A notable observation is the perception held by some leaders in Northern Uganda, about the ICD being an extension of the ICC. As noted by a local journalist, 'the ICD is the smaller version of the ICC which is done here in Uganda. They both try the same crimes but at different levels'.[86] Originally, it was referred to as the War Crimes Division of the Ugandan High Court, before rebranding to the ICD.

ASF's baseline study in 2011 also reveals a limited engagement by local NGOs with the ICD, in the initial stages:

> All the NGOs interviewed were unfamiliar with the critical role they can play in the investigative processes of the newly created International Crimes Division. Further, many of them have neither interacted with the DPP nor the Registrar of the ICD. This shows a very critical lacuna in the ICD outreach process because such organizations are an important tool in mobilizing support for the newly created division of the High court of Uganda.[87]

What is more intriguing in ASF's study is the engagement between local NGOs and key stakeholders at the ICD, i.e. victims and witnesses. ASF notes:

> Our general impression from the interviews with the CSOs [local NGOs] is that many of them are not aware that they are already playing a role as intermediaries through the provision

---

[81] De Vos et al. (2015, pp. 1–20).

[82] De Vos et al. (2015, pp. 1–20).

[83] See the High Court (International Crimes Division) Practice Direction, Legal Notice No. 10 of 2011, Section 6(1).

[84] See (Annex to the Agreement on Accountability and Reconciliation between the Government of the Republic of Uganda and the Lord's Resistance Army/Movement (Annex to June 29 Agreement), Juba, Sudan, June 29, 2007, February 19, 2008.

[85] Oola (2010, pp.1–10).

[86] Interview, 8 May 2021.

[87] Avocats Sans Frontières (2011, p. 15).

> of psycho-social support, protective measures, safe and secure contact that are interventions of a witness management process.[88]

The observation shows that NGOs are not only intermediaries of victims, but also directly impact on their livelihoods through rehabilitation and protection. Not forgetting that victims are important stakeholders at the ICD.

Foreign donors and international civil society are observed to have a key role in the creation and operations of the ICD. PILPG offered technical support regarding the ICC Bill, as acknowledged by the Court's Registry:

> The Public International Law and Policy Group (PILPG) are assisting the Government with the setting up of the Special Division within the context of a wider Transitional Justice Program, [REDACTED]. In this respect, they are advising the Government on the legislative framework needed, which may take the form of amending the ICC Bill, and on the issue of the retrospective application of crimes. They are also advising on the Ugandan Authorities' obligations under the Rome Statute, including the ongoing admissibility review. PILPG are of the view that the LRA commanders could be tried nationally, in the Special Division, without breaching Uganda's obligations under the Rome Statute.[89]

As mentioned in the previous sub-section of this chapter, the UVF played an important role in relation to the ICC case. According to their application at the ICC:

> UVF is a registered nongovernmental organization based in Uganda which serves as a coalition of human rights and civil society nongovernmental organisations working with victims and on victims' rights issues in Uganda. The objectives of the UVF are to advocate for victims' rights especially with respect to the conflict in northern Uganda.[90]

The above text describes the work of the local NGO, but also points to the existence of a collation of different organisations. The UVF was formed in 2006 initially under the UVRWG, by victims' representatives, acknowledging 'the absence of an independent victims' rights advocacy group in the country'.[91]

Right from the admissibility stage of the cases, the UVF and Redress Trust brought to the ICC's attention the experiences of victims, showing their inability to obtain justice in the Ugandan domestic criminal jurisdictions.[92] In a nutshell, the position was that the Ugandan judiciary could not afford to provide justice to victims of serious international crimes.

It is also observed in the empirical interviews that victim-related work was a key priority within NGO networks, as reflected in the victims' participation process at the ICC. As one local leader and NGO representative noted:

---

[88] Avocats Sans Frontières (2011, p. 16).

[89] See *The Prosecutor v. Dominic Ongwen,* (ICC 2015).

[90] See Application by the Uganda Victims' Foundation and the Redress Trust for Leave to Submit Observations to the Pre-Trial Chamber II of the International Criminal Court, Pursuant to Rule 103 of the Rules of Procedure and Evidence, 2008.

[91] Application by the Uganda Victims' Foundation and the Redress Trust for Leave to Submit Observations to the Pre-Trial Chamber II of the International Criminal Court, Pursuant to Rule 103 of the Rules of Procedure and Evidence, 2008.

[92] Application by the Uganda Victims' Foundation and the Redress Trust for Leave to Submit Observations to the Pre-Trial Chamber II of the International Criminal Court, Pursuant to Rule 103 of the Rules of Procedure and Evidence, 2008.

> Many of the international partners wanted the victim's voices to be heard and some of them even facilitated the victims to the Hague so that they can be part of the process. They also wanted the court to put in consideration of the victim's feelings. Some victims were also facilitated in the court seat so that they can watch the trial and be a part of it.[93]

Crucially, the issue of victims' rights remains central, within the transitional justice-related work in Uganda.

NGOs were also influential in their pursuit of transitional justice, including the ICD, through the attraction of funds and resources. The impact of funding dynamics is that local NGOs had to re-strategise and align their work towards ICD-oriented initiatives. As one local leader revealed:

> The availability of resources makes certain modes of justice be preferred like for example the traditional leaders don't even have facilities to conduct their local reconciliation processes and yet the court process have very many parties willing to support[them] making it[international criminal justice] more preferred than the traditional ones.[94]

The only case involving transitional justice at the ICD is that of Thomas Kwoyelo, a former LRA commander who was captured by the government forces in 2009. In 2010, whilst in detention, he renounced rebellion and subsequently sought amnesty from Uganda's Amnesty Commission, under the Amnesty Act. In the same year, the Director of Public Prosecutions (DPP) charged him with crimes under the Geneva Conventions Act. He was subsequently committed for trial at the ICD.[95]

Kwoyelo's trial at the ICD initially stalled in 2011 when the Constitutional Court ruled that he was entitled to amnesty.[96] It was not until the Supreme Court overturned the decision in 2015 that the trial resumed. More generally, there remains a blurred line between the transitional justice concepts of amnesty and accountability, as noted in Justice Bart Katureebe's lead judgement:

> Therefore, it seems to have been the view which I agree with, that accountability for grave crimes is not exclusive of reconciliation and peace. The person who commits such crimes may be eligible for grant of amnesty for the act of rebellion or waging war on Uganda, under the Act, but he is not, in my view, entitled to amnesty for the grave crimes he may have committed.[97]

In 2013, ASF advocated for the rescission of the renewed amnesty law, and also wrote official correspondence to the Ministry of Internal Affairs.[98] Their argument was that the majority of victims in post-war Northern Uganda had not been adequately redressed, and did not play an active role in the national transitional justice process.[99] Against this background, the Supreme Court decision upholding Kwoyelo's trial

---

[93] Interview with local leader and NGO representative, 6 May 2021.

[94] Interview with local leader, 4 July 2021.

[95] *Uganda v Thomas Kwoyelo*, HCT-00-ICD-SC-02 OF 2010.

[96] See *Thomas Kwoyelo alias Latoni v Uganda* (Constitutional Petition 36 of 2011) 22 September 2011.

[97] *Uganda v Kwoyelo* (Constitutional Appeal 1 of 2012) Supreme Court, 8 April 2015, para 25.

[98] Avocats Sans Frontières (2013).

[99] Avocats Sans Frontières (2013).

ignited the ICD, as it was the only case involving transitional justice before the court.

In August 2024, Kwoyelo was convicted of war crimes and crimes against humanity and subsequently sentenced to 40 years imprisonment in October 2024. The Court delivered its reparations decision in December 2024, awarding reparations to the 103 victims.[100] The 15 year duration of the case and trial suggests that even though the Court was operational, there needs to be in place adequate legal, policy and financial resources for the effective implementation of domestic accountability and transitional justice.[101]

Sarah Kasande, the head of ICTJ's office in Uganda, considered Kwoyelo's trial a potential gateway for domestic prosecution of international crimes in Africa:

> Kwoyelo's trial will attract significant scrutiny of its compliance with international standards, jurisprudence, and any innovative practices it develops. It has the potential to offer important lessons to other states contemplating the prosecution of serious crimes in their national courts and to demonstrate the ability of African states to carry out national proceedings in their own courts.[102]

The above text indicates that the legitimacy of domestic or hybrid courts prosecuting international crimes is equally as important as that of the ICC.

Community outreach is another form in which transitional justice mechanisms are legitimised. For courts, it is important that their processes are clearly known and understood by the communities and victims. It is important to note that the ICC's legitimacy in the eyes of the war-affected communities and victims was significantly influenced by the operations and strategies of the Court's outreach office in Uganda. Whilst it is notable that the Office, working with local NGOs, enhanced local awareness about the *Ongwen* case, it's mandate does not include assistance to victims or reparations. Ultimately, some victims' expectations about the Court from the Ongwen case could not be addressed by the Outreach office. This dilemma was equally observed by Dennis Jjuuko and Francis Opio, viewed as a 'misinterpretation of the ICC's justice by victims' and 'disconnect between victims' conceptualization of justice and the Court's own vision'.[103] Ultimately, the ICC's legitimacy within the local communities depends on other actors, besides its own staff and agents.

Transnational networks and NGOs were important stakeholders during the outreach processes. In both the Ongwen and Kwoyelo trials, NGO field outreach narrowed the physical distance between the victim communities and courts. For example, FJDI carried out focus group discussions in 2016, gathering views from the conflict-affected and victim communities, in the run up to the Ongwen and Thomas Kwoyelo trials:

---

[100] *Laker & 102 Others v Uganda & Kwoyelo v Attorney General* (Miscellaneous Application 35 of 2024) [2024] UGHCICD 15 (16 December 2024).

[101] See Lubaale E (2025) for a summary of the Kwoyelo case before the ICD and how it compares to the Ongwen case before the ICC. See also Ruhweza (2022, pp. 427–468).

[102] Kihika (2016).

[103] See generally Jjuuko and Opio (2024). Jjuuko and Opio previously worked as NGO representatives from the Refugee Law Project, where they had significant interactions with victims during the course of the Ongwen case.

> A third factor which affected how the communities related to the trials appeared to be an ever-present information deficit, i.e. the informational gap between the communities and the trials. This followed in large part from the physical and subject matter distance already highlighted above. The focus groups in fact demonstrated that much information is still sought by the communities locally in order for them to understand the dynamics of the two trials but also to simply remain informed about them and to enable them to 'feel included'.[104]

NGOs thus contributed to the legitimacy of the trials as key dimensions of the transitional justice. FJDI, in collaboration with ASF, facilitated community representatives to attend the pretrial hearing of the *Kwoyelo* case in Uganda's capital city, Kampala. They also organised community dialogues and radio talk shows in Gulu town, to create more awareness about the upcoming trial, as reported by Ogora:

> In light of the fact that many of them would not be able to be physically present in the courtroom, community representatives then asked if ASF and FJDI could sponsor the broadcast of proceedings on radio. This, they argued, would enable victims to follow proceedings even in their villages. This concern demonstrates the importance of mass media, and in particular radio, in conducting community outreach. Any stakeholders who set out to conduct outreach must recognize radio as a vital tool for communication.[105]

Patricia Bako, the ASF Project Officer for transitional justice, expounded on the technicalities involved in victim-oriented support:

> I personally attended this community outreach and what I sensed is the need for outreach before the trial of Kwoyelo starts. We are trying as ASF to see how we can support the views to participate but the challenge is that we don't know who the exact victims are. It is important to draw a clean line between the victims who are witnesses and those who are just victims and probably do not wish to participate in the court proceedings which I think has not been done.[106]

As one of the ways of dealing with the victims' legal dilemma before the ICD, Bako suggested the use of the ICC as a guideline.[107] In 2018, Romain Ravet, ASF Country Director for Uganda, offered this clarification on their work at the ICD:

> ASF supports the two counsels appointed by the Court to represent the victims. We have filed applications for 98 victims to participate in the proceedings but their approval is still pending. We also support the counsels in reaching out to the victims to update them about the proceedings and collect their expectations. Victims are eager to participate in the case, yet their participation raises questions of material facilitation and security.[108]

It is important to note that when the *Kwoyelo* case commenced, there was no legal criteria for obtaining victim status at the ICD. As a result, there was a gap that NGOs needed to fill, in order to realise their aims of victim participation. ASF, ICTJ and UVF developed the relevant criteria in victim status in 2018. One NGO leader involved in the process notes that: 'We decided to call this the Kwoyelo initiative'.[109]

---

104 Gawronski and Ogora (2017, p. 37).

105 Ogora (2016b).

106 Ogora (2016b).

107 Ogora (2016b).

108 See Avocats Sans Frontières (2018).

109 Interview with local leader, 6 March 2021.

As discussed in chapter three of the book, Uganda adopted a National Transitional Justice Policy (NTJP) in June 2019.[110] A Transitional Justice Working Group (TJWG) under the JLOS worked to implement proposals on transitional justice that were envisaged under the Juba agreement. TJWG also prepared the first draft of the NTJP. Whilst local and international NGOs including REDRESS and ICTJ were largely excluded from the initial drafting stage of the NTJP, they continued to advocate for victims' participation and consultation in the proposed transitional justice framework. An NGO reports that:

> No input from victims has been solicited into the content and format that the Bill should take. Instead, there is an over-reliance on CSOs to conduct outreach and share public information, a responsibility which should not be totally delegated to them by the State.[111]

NGOs also recommended that diplomatic missions in Uganda continue their financial support towards victim-led groups and NGOs, as a way of implementing the ongoing transitional justice processes.[112] Reports by REDRESS and its local partners Emerging Solutions Africa (ESA) and the UVF indicate that, 'victims remain on the fringes of the proceedings and there is little resolve by either the bench or the counsel to challenge their absence from the courtroom'.[113] These reports reinvigorate the argument that NGOs are vital players in the legitimisation of international justice through victim-oriented work.

Besides the explicit victim-oriented work, the aspect of capacity building and technical support is also central. Ravet reveals that:

> ASF is also giving technical assistance to the Court and has mobilized civil society to cover some of these needs, but we [ASF] cannot substitute for the State's duty to implement the 2016 pre-trial ruling. Uganda, the issue of victims is not dealt with in detail and probably we could have to refer to the ICC and borrow some aspects but mindful of position of the ICD.[114]

Ravet's position resonates with the remarks made by ASF's Uganda transitional justice expert, Patricia Bako, during the opening of Kwoyelo's trial in 2016.[115]

Witness protection is an important aspect that drew attention at the ICD in the *Kwoyelo* case. For example, in order to protect witnesses, audiences, mostly the war-affected communities, are restricted from attending live court sessions. These measures illustrate the limited technical capacity at the ICD. As a result, NGOs have to fill the void and provide mitigating alternatives. For example, local NGO RLP facilitated the Court to make live broadcasts of hearings outside the court, and also use face and voice distortion technology for witnesses.[116] As I have pointed out in previous literature, such technological measures also enhance the legitimacy of the

---

[110] See Uganda National Transitional Justice Policy 2019.

[111] REDRESS (2020, p. 29).

[112] REDRESS (2020, p. 12).

[113] REDRESS (2020, p. 8).

[114] See Avocats Sans Frontières (2018).

[115] Ogora (2016b).

[116] Avocats Sans Frontières (2019).

Court before the affected communities.[117] My argument is basically that the use of technology makes it easier to store evidence and present it in the Courts, but also protect witnesses during the trials.

Generally, it was observed that NGOs are a primary and important component of the work at the ICD, especially covering the administration gaps during the *Kwoyelo* case. However, there is also a duplication of victim-oriented work among the NGOs. This is also highlighted in ASF's report, where they argue other NGOs to 'increase their collaboration to avoid duplicating efforts in supporting victims and their Counsel as well as the ICD'.[118]

The above text illustrates that NGOs are important stakeholders for both advocacy and supporting of victims during the trials. The NGO work also shows that the aspect of Courts' legitimacy within the conflict-affected communities is a matter that also requires legal compromises. As seen from the victims' dilemma at the ICD, the ICC Rules are presented as useful guideline for not only the domestic court, but also implicitly tied to the expectations of victims.

NGOs were pivotal in the victims' participation process at the ICC, opening up spaces for direct engagement between victims' representatives and The Hague. A local leader and NGO recalled:

> Many of the international partners wanted the victim's voices to be heard and some of them even facilitated the victims to the Hague so that they can be part of the process. They also wanted the court to put in consideration of the victim's feelings. Some victims were also facilitated in the court seat so that they can watch the trial and be a part of it.[119]

Victim participation is also seen in the form of live screening of the trial in The Hague, before victim communities. At the commencement of the *Ongwen* case, the ICC Outreach Unit partnered with local NGOs, including FJDI and provided a live screening of the trial in Northern Uganda, as reported by Ogora:

> The live screening of court proceedings by the ICC in Northern Uganda has set a precedent for victim participation. It is the first time such an initiative has been undertaken, and many victims and stakeholders in Northern Uganda looked at the event as a way of increasing victim participation. Many victims we spoke to seemed to be happy that they were able to follow proceedings as they unfolded, thus giving them a chance to participate in large numbers.[120]

Before the commencement of the Ongwen trial, the UVF unsuccessfully requested leave to submit *amicus curiae* observations before the Pre-Trial Chamber, claiming a 'lack of proper and effective legal representation that they [victims] … [had] received from the OPCV'.[121] Furthermore, the UVF averred that:

---

[117] Kirabira (2022, pp. 1143–1167).

[118] See Avocats Sans Frontières (2018). For detailed understanding of victims' perspectives on the reparations framework see Avocats Sans Frontières (2017, pp. 1–36).

[119] Interview with local leader and NGO representative, 6 March 2021.

[120] Ogora (2016a).

[121] See Application by the Uganda Victims Foundation to Submit Amicus Curie Observations Pursuant to Rule 103 of the Rules of Procedure and Evidence, 2015, para 11.

> Ongwen allegedly committed several crimes in many parts of Northern Uganda which have not been included in the case and victims are eager to speak with the Office of the Prosecutor in order to furnish them with further information on attacks including those that occurred in regions such as Lango and Teso.[122]

In essence, the UVF sought to represent the victims before the Court, and also expand the scope of the trial, to include a wider network of victims across the conflict-affected communities.

As the *Ongwen* case progressed at the ICC, INGOs further engaged in support for victims. For REDRESS, important aspects relate to the issue of reparations. REDRESS works with local intermediaries to build capacity in the domestic accountability for international crimes.[123] Between November 2017 and March 2020, REDRESS and its local partners carried out research and field activities under the project: 'Strengthening Victim Participation in the Fight against Impunity for International Crimes'.[124] REDRESS's work on victim participation at the ICD somewhat overlaps with that of ASF and ICTJ. Nonetheless, NGOs were pivotal in the *Ongwen* case, as revealed by Benjamin Gumpert, the lead prosecutor in the trial:

> The experience was mixed. Some NGOs were supportive and prepared to provide information and assistance, since they believed this would be for the benefit of their clients. Others were defensive and uncooperative. They did not always give reasons. My feeling was that it depended very much upon the pre-formed attitudes of influential NGO staff to the ICC and its work in Uganda.[125]

NGOs provided legal and factual analysis for the Court in respect to the identification of eligible victims in Ongwen's case, reinvigorating the book author's earlier highlights on the situation of children born out of sexual and gender-based crimes.[126] The *Amicus Curiae* was submitted by a transnational network comprising of: Avocats sans Frontières (ASF) Emerging Solutions Africa (ESA) Essex Transitional Justice Network at the University of Essex Global Survivors Fund (GSF) Gulu Women's Economic Development and Globalization (GWED-G) Institute for Peace and Strategic Studies at Gulu University International Federation for Human Rights (FIDH) REDRESS Watye Ki Gen, and Women Advocacy Network.

It is impossible to discuss transitional justice in Northern Uganda without referring to traditional justice mechanisms. As already discussed in chapter three of the book, there are mixed perceptions of responsibility and accountability within the victim communities in Northern Uganda.[127] Against this background, the empirical study

---

[122] Application by the Uganda Victims Foundation to Submit Amicus Curie Observations Pursuant to Rule 103 of the Rules of Procedure and Evidence, 2015, para 15.

[123] See REDRESS (2020, pp. 1–61).

[124] REDRESS (2020, pp. 1–61).

[125] Interview, 6 May 2021.

[126] See *The Prosecutor v Dominic Ongwen*, Amicus Curiae brief pursuant to article 75 of the Statute and Rule 103 of the Rules of Procedure and Evidence, No.: ICC-02/04-01/15, 4 February 2022, para 34. For a summarised commentary see Kirabira and Choukrone (2020).

[127] See Meier (2013, pp. 25–50), Latigo (2008, pp. 85–119), Shabdita and Okwir (2015, pp. 1–49).

also explored the work of a local NGO, the Justice and Reconciliation Project (JRP), that works with victims within the framework of reconciliation.

JRP was founded in 2005, following a collaboration between the Gulu District NGO Forum and the Liu Institute for Global Issues, University of British Columbia, Canada. Since then, JRP and its international partners have been pivotal in engaging victims of the LRA, on the relevance of traditional justice mechanisms. They also mobilised local NGOs to participate in the NUTJWG.

According to Boniface Ojok, a co-founder of JRP, it was vital to mobilise local actors to debate about the prevailing justice systems, with the use of traditional justice as a starting point.[128] In fact, JRP published the very first report on Dominic Ongwen's double victimhood in 2008, which also raised questions regarding the effectiveness of individual criminal responsibility mechanisms within the context of collective victimisation.[129] By articulating traditional practices as viable modes of transitional justice, JRP's work can be said to delegitimise the ICC as a transitional justice mechanism.

However, on closer scrutiny of the work in its initial years, JRP played a role in Uganda's domestication of the Rome Statute in 2010 and the *Kwoyelo* case.[130] Whilst not supporting victims directly in the *Kwoyelo* and *Ongwen* cases, JRP often collaborated with local NGOs that worked on the aspect of formal accountability as a transitional justice mechanism in Northern Uganda. Ultimately, the avenue of reconciliation through traditional justice did not have any substantial impact on the progress of the criminal prosecutions.

Finally, the work of ICC's Trust Fund for Victims (TFV) in Northern Uganda also adds a layer on the Court's legitimacy. The TFV was created in 2004 by the ASPs, with a goal of assisting victims in two broad ways; implementing Court-Ordered reparations and providing psycho-social rehabilitation.[131] The TFV has an office in Uganda where they have been implementing their assistance mandate since 2008. The TFV has more than 25 domestic NGO implementing partners, whose work has benefited more than 56,000 people across Northern Uganda.[132] The Fund also created an opportunity for domestic NGOs to engage in issues of victims' support. An NGO representative affirms that, 'NGOs had to strategise their work and work around the ICC'.[133]

Scott Bartell, TFV's Programme Manager for Uganda, noted a connection between rehabilitation and justice, noting that 'victims indicate that receiving rehabilitation is a form of justice'.[134] Generally, there was a positive impact of the TFV within the affected communities, through NGO intermediaries that offered rehabilitation services. At the same time, an independent local researcher and analyst

128 Interview, 3 May 2021.

129 Justice and Reconciliation Project (2008, pp. 1–19).

130 Justice and Reconciliation Project (2015 pp. 1–27).

131 See TFV website: https://www.trustfundforvictims.org/.

132 Interview with TFV Programme Manager for Uganda, 23 March 2021.

133 Interview with NGO Representative, 26 February 2021.

134 Interview, 23 March 2021.

who worked with implementing NGOs notes that the TFV 'served as a good public relations role for the ICC. It helped in control and management of their expectations – emphatically gave them false hope'.[135] This narrative shows a link between the TFV and the legitimacy of the ICC. The findings show that NGO discourses helped to situate the potential reparative remedies from the ICC within the aspirations of the victims.

The conviction of Ongwen in February 2021 opens avenues for further examination of the legitimacy of the ICC in Uganda. It will be interesting to explore how local NGOs articulate victims' interests, following the ICC's reparations order. The TFV's reparations mandate will be an important avenue for local NGOs to engage in the implementation of awards for reparations. Whilst it is practically impossible for all victims to receive individual reparations, the implementation of collective awards would further enhance the legitimacy of the ICC intervention.

5 Conclusion

The chapter has drawn on empirical legal research to explore the work of transnational networks and NGOs in transitional justice in Northern Uganda. Linkages have been shown to exist among the principal stakeholders and actors at the local, domestic and international levels. Moreover, the discourses of these transnational networks and NGOs have been shown to enhance the legitimacy of the domesticated International Court which is the ICD and the ICC in Uganda. More specifically, key avenues for NGO work and engagement with international criminal justice are revealed in their victim-oriented work and in the technical and capacity-building initiatives around the courts. In line with the comparative angle of this book, the second part will examine the case study of Myanmar.

References

Annex to the Agreement on Accountability and Reconciliation between the Government of the Republic of Uganda and the Lord's Resistance Army/Movement (Annex to June 29 Agreement), Juba, Sudan, June 29, 2007, February 19, 2008

Application by the Uganda Victims' Foundation and the Redress Trust for leave to submit observations to the Pre-Trial Chamber II of the International Criminal Court, pursuant to Rule 103 of the Rules of Procedure and Evidence (ICC-02/04-01/05) (2008) ICC

Application by the Uganda Victims Foundation to Submit Amicus Curie Observations pursuant to Rule 103 of the Rules of Procedure and Evidence (ICC-02/04-01/05). (2015) ICC

Apuuli K (2011) Peace over justice: the Acholi Religious Leaders Peace Initiative (ARLPI) vs. The International Criminal Court (ICC) in Northern Uganda. Stud Ethn Natl 11:116–129

[135] For a summarised local commentary on the Trust Fund for Victims' 3 year assistance programme in the Gulu region of Northern Uganda see Matsiko (2020).

Armstrong K (2014) Justice without peace? international justice and conflict resolution in Northern Uganda. Dev Chang 45:589–607
Avocats Sans Frontières (2011) Baseline survey report: evaluation of knowledge and expertise in International Criminal Justice in Uganda. Avocats Sans Frontières, Brussels
Avocats Sans Frontières (2013) Towards a comprehensive and holistic transitional justice policy for Uganda: Exploring linkages between transitional justice mechanisms. Advocates Sans Frontiers, Brussels
Avocats Sans Frontières (2017) A Beggar has no choice: victims' perspectives on a reparations framework for Uganda. Advocates Sans Frontiers, Brussels, pp 1–36
Avocats Sans Frontières (2018) A trial for history: Thomas Kwoyelo in Uganda. Advocates Sans Frontiers, Brussels. https://asf.be/thomas-kwoyelo-in-uganda-a-trial-for-history/
Avocats Sans Frontières (2019) Reflections on victim participation before the International Crimes Division in Uganda, Policy Brief, Avocats Sans Frontières, Brussels
Baker C, Obradovic-Wochnik J (2016) Mapping the Nexus of transitional justice and peacebuilding. J Interv Statebuilding 10:281–301
Cassese A (2012) The legitimacy of international criminal tribunals and the current prospects of international criminal justice. Leiden J Int Law 25:491–501
Coalition for the International Criminal Court (2017) ICC challenges: perspectives from Uganda's student community. Coalition for the International Criminal Court, The Hague
Decision on the Admissibility of the Case under Article 19(1) of the Statute, ICC-02/04-01/05-377, Pre-Trial Chamber II, 10 March 2009
De Vos CM, Kendall S, Stahn C (2015) Introduction. In: De Vos CM, Kendall S, Stahn C (eds) Contested justice the politics and practice of international criminal court interventions. CUP, Cambridge, pp 1–20
Findlay M (2013) International and comparative criminal justice: a critical introduction, 1st edn. Routledge, Abingdon
Gawronski M, Ogora L (2017) A renewed momentum for trial justice?: perceptions of conflict-affected communities in Northern Uganda in the run up to the Dominic Ongwen and Thomas Kwoyelo Trials. Foundation for Justice and Development Initiatives, Gulu, pp 1–44
Gissel L (2017) Legitimising the Juba Peace Agreement on accountability and reconciliation: the International Criminal Court as a third-party actor? J East Afr Stud 11:367–387
Hillebrecht C (2020) International criminal accountability and the domestic politics of resistance: case studies from Kenya and Lebanon. Law Soc Rev 54:453–486
Human Rights Network-Uganda (HURINET-U), No Peace Without Justice (NPWJ) and the Ugandan Coalition for the ICC (UCICC) (2010) Visits by ICC State Parties Delegates to Uganda: Final Report-January to June 2010. HURINET – U, UCICC, NPWJ, Brussels, pp 1–65
ICC (2015) Public redacted version of "The Registry's Report on the mission to Uganda" (ICC-02/04-01/15-152-Conf-Exp) (ICC-02/04-01/15)
IRIN (2008) Uganda: Peace, justice and the LRA. Geneva. https://www.refworld.org/docid/47cbc61fc.html
Jjuuko D, Opio F (2024) The Ongwen Case at the International Criminal Court as a test of the court's outreach programming in Northern Uganda. J Int Crim Justice (online first).
Justice and Reconciliation Project (2008) Complicating Victims and Perpetrators in Uganda: On Dominic Ongwen, Justice and Reconciliation Project, Gulu, JRP Field Note 7, pp 1–19
Justice and Reconciliation Project (2009) Justice and Reconciliation Project: Annual Report 2009. Justice and Reconciliation Project, Gulu
Justice and Reconciliation Project (2015) Annual Report 2015. Justice and Reconciliation Project, Gulu
Dicker R (2007) Trading Justice for Peace in Uganda Won't Work. Human Rights Watch, New York. https://www.hrw.org/news/2007/05/02/trading-justice-peace-uganda-wont-work
Hovil L (2010) The ICC's engagement in Uganda from a local NGO perspective. NGOs and the International Criminal Court: The State of the Union? Panel discussion at the Review Conference of the International Criminal Court (ICC), Kampala.

Kihika S (2016) Kwoyelo and Ongwen trials show progress in fight against impunity. International Center for Transitional Justice, Kampala. https://www.ictj.org/news/kwoyelo-ongwen-icc-uganda

Kirabira T (2021) NGO influence in global governance: achieving transitional justice in Uganda and beyond. Cambridge Int Law J 10:280–299

Kirabira T (2022) Technology as a key tool for the prosecution of international crimes: lessons from Uganda. Int Crim Law Rev 22:1143–1167

Kirabira T, Choukrone L (2020) Uganda: how to bring justice for thousands of children born of war. The Conversation, London

Latigo J (2008) Northern Uganda: tradition-based practices in the Acholi region. In: Huyse L, Salter M (eds) Traditional justice and reconciliation after violent conflict: learning from African experiences. International Institute for Democracy and Electoral Assistance, Stockholm, pp 85–119

Lubaale E (2025) The Conviction and Sentencing of Ex-rebel, Thomas Kwoyelo, 15 Years On. Opinio Juris, Geneva https://opiniojuris.org/2025/02/12/the-conviction-and-sentencing-of-ex-rebel-thomas-kwoyelo-15-years-on/

Macdonald A (2017) "In the interests of justice?" The International Criminal Court, peace talks and the failed quest for war crimes accountability in northern Uganda. J Eastern African Stud 11:628–648

Macdonald A (2019) 'Somehow this whole process became so artificial': exploring the transitional justice implementation gap in Uganda. Int J Transit Justice 13:225–248

Madlingozi T (2010) On transitional justice entrepreneurs and the production of victims. J Hum Rights Pract 2:208–228

Matsiko G (2020) ICC Trust Fund: "A good day today is better than a bad day tomorrow" (Uganda) Justice Info, Lausanne

Mégret F (2015) In whose name? The ICC and the search for constituency. In: De Vos CM, Kendall S, Stahn C (eds) Contested justice the politics and practice of International Criminal Court interventions. CUP, Cambridge, pp 23–45

Meier (2013) 'Death does not rot': transitional justice and local 'truths' in the aftermath of the war in Northern Uganda. Afr Spectr 48:25–50

Munkholm L, Pelaudeix C, Kristiansen B (2019) Conclusion: transnationalisation and legal actors: legitimacy in question. In: Kristiansen B et al (eds) Transnationalisation and legal actors: legitimacy in question. Routledge, Abingdon, pp 230–245

Murithi T (2019) Judicial imperialism: the politicisation of International Criminal Justice in Africa. Fanele, Johannesburg, pp 1–240

No Peace Without Justice (2010) ICC Review Conference: NPWJ calls for a stronger International Criminal Justice system, Brussels

Nsereko D (2011) The International Criminal Court and Africa. In: Ssenyonjo M (ed) The African regional human rights system: 30 years after the African charter on human and peoples' rights. Martinus Nijhoff Publishers, Leiden, pp 337–354

Odong J (2015) Ongwen's justice dilemma: perspectives from Northern Uganda. Refugee Law Project, Kampala, pp. 1–17

Ogora L (2016a) Live screening of Ongwen hearing in Northern Uganda: lessons learned. International Justice Monitor, Washington, DC. https://www.ijmonitor.org/2016/01/live-screening-of-ongwen-hearing-in-northern-uganda-lessons-learned/

Ogora L (2016b) Views on the trial of Thomas Kwoyelo and the need for community outreach. International Justice Monitor, Washington, DC. https://www.ijmonitor.org/2016/04/views-on-the-trial-of-thomas-kwoyelo-and-the-need-for-community-outreach/

Ogora L (2016c) Ongwen ICC trial: 'opportunity of a lifetime' for community leaders from Northern Uganda. International Justice Monitor, Washington, DC. https://www.ijmonitor.org/2016/12/an-opportunity-of-a-lifetime-for-community-leaders-from-northern-uganda/

Oola S (2010) The Coalition for Reconciliation in Uganda (CORU): important lessons for proactive civil society engagement in catalyzing transitional justice discourse. Advocating justice:

civil society and transitional justice in Africa. African Transitional Justice Research Network Workshop, Johannesburg, pp 1–10

Oola S (2015) In the shadow of Kwoyelo's trial the ICC and complementarity in Uganda. In: De Vos CM, Kendall S, Stahn C (eds) Contested justice the politics and practice of International Criminal Court interventions. CUP, Cambridge, pp 147–170

Ramji-Nogales J (2015) Bespoke transitional justice at the International Criminal Court. In: De Vos CM, Kendall S, Stahn C (eds) Contested justice the politics and practice of International Criminal Court interventions. CUP, Cambridge, pp 106–121

REDRESS (2020) Not with us: strengthening victim participation in transitional justice processes in Uganda. REDRESS, London, pp 1–61. https://redress.org/wp-content/uploads/2020/07/Not-Without-Us-Report-for-Web.pdf

Shabdita S, Okwir I (2015) Mapping regional reconciliation in Northern Uganda: a case study of the Acholi and Lango sub-regions. Justice and Reconciliation Project, Gulu, pp 1–49

Teitel R (2003) Transitional justice genealogy. Harv Hum Rights J 16:69–94

Kendall S (2011) Donors' justice: recasting international criminal accountability. Leiden J Int Law 24:585–606

Ruhweza D (2022) Wild Goose Chase, or a Quest for Genuine Prosecution? Lessons from Uganda's Ongoing Trial of Thomas Kwoyelo. In: Lubaale E, Dyani-Mhango N (eds) National Accountability for International Crimes in Africa. Palgrave Macmillan, Cham, London. pp 427–468

The Prosecutor v Dominic Ongwen, Amicus Curiae brief pursuant to article 75 of the Statute and Rule 103 of the Rules of Procedure and Evidence, No.: ICC-02/04-01/15, 4 February 2022

Thomas Kwoyelo Alias Latoni v. Uganda (Constitutional Petition 36 of 2011) 22 September 2011

TrustAfrica (2019) Strengthening victim participation in accountability processes: learning from the experiences of the Victim Support Initiative (VSI), Dakar

Uganda National Transitional Justice Policy 2019

Uganda v Kwoyelo (Constitutional Appeal 1 of 2012) Supreme Court, 8 April 2015

Uganda v Thomas Kwoyelo, HCT-00-ICD-SC-02 OF 2010

Wierda M (2023) The local impact of the International Criminal Court: from law to justice. CUP, Cambridge

Wierda M, Nassar H, Maalouf L (2007) Early reflections on local perceptions, legitimacy and legacy of the special tribunal for Lebanon. J Int Crim Justice 5:1065–1081

Achieving Transitional Justice in Myanmar: Between Accountability and National Reconciliation

1 Introduction

Myanmar, also known as Burma, presents another complex case of transitional justice, due to decades of ethnic conflicts, civil wars and military rule.[1] There is growing scholarly attention over how to address Myanmar's legacy of military repression and armed conflict.[2] In order to explore the prospects of transitional justice in Myanmar, it is important to understand country's political and social history.

Since the independence of the Union of Burma from British colonial rule in 1948, the military have been a central feature of the country.[3] Ethno-linguistic divisions have negatively impacted on the process of democratic transition in Myanmar. The historical background of these divisions is rooted in the heterogeneous population under the British colonial rule.[4] A series of bilateral ceasefire agreements were signed in the years after independence between the military government and ethnic insurgent groups. These ethnic groups included:

> [T]he Kachin Independence Organization (KIO), New Democratic Army (Kachin), Palaung State Liberation Organization, Myanmar National Democratic Alliance (MNDA – Kokang), Kachin Defense Army, Myanmar National Solidarity Party (Wa), National Democracy Alliance Army – Military Local Administration Committee (Shan/Akhar), Shan State Army (SSA), Pa-O National Organization, Shan State Nationalities People's organization, Mong Tai Army (MTA), Kayan National Guard, Kayinni National Progressive Party (KNPP),

[1] Prior to 1989, Myanmar was referred to in English as Burma. This book uses the name Myanmar because it deals with events after the name change.

[2] Dukalskis (2015, pp. 83–97) and Manley (2017, pp. 610–616).

[3] See Aung-Thwin (2017, pp. 15–24).

[4] Ganesan (2017, pp. 111–129).

This chapter has some overlaps with my doctoral thesis.

© The Author(s), under exclusive license to Springer Nature Singapore Pte Ltd. 2025

T. R. Kirabira, *Transnational Networks and Justice in the Global South*, International Law and the Global South, https://doi.org/10.1007/978-981-95-3137-0_5

Kayan New Land Party, Kayinni National People's Liberation Front and New Mon State Party (NMSP). The agreement with the KIO broke down in June 2011.[5]

The ethnic conflicts are further exacerbated by the involvement of Myanmar's neighbouring States and regional powers, with ethnic groups like the Rohingya and Kachin.[6] Dissidents from Myanmar are also harboured in these countries, i.e. Thailand, India, Bangladesh and China.[7] It is believed that the primary objective of the Tatmadaw (Myanmar armed forces) is to avoid the disintegration of Myanmar into smaller States.[8]

A central aspect of Myanmar's democratic transition relates to the promulgation of a new constitution in 2008, against the background of what is perceived as a 'stage-managed constitutional referendum'.[9] In the previous years, there was mainly direct military rule through the use of decrees.[10] The 1948 Constitution was revoked in 1974 under the Burma Socialist Programme Party, and there was rule by decree, until another military coup in 1988.[11] In what she refers to as 'Pre-emptive constitution-making' and 'military-state constitutionalism', Crouch argues that the Tatmadaw used the constitution to maintain control over the state.[12]

In addition to control over the ministries dealing with security related issues, the 2008 constitution secured the Tatmadaw 25 per cent of the seats in Parliament.[13] In a nutshell, the Tatmadaw maintain a 'national ideology that would prevent the right to self-determination, federalism and secession, and consolidate the military's role in maintaining political and territorial unity'.[14] From a general perspective of constitutionalism, the 2008 constitution remains a key feature of the authoritarian regime in Myanmar.

The three 'Main National Causes' grounded in the national ideology are non-disintegration of the Union, non-disintegration of national solidarity and the perpetuation of sovereignty.[15] The 2008 constitution also ushered institutional contestations due to the new power centres, for example the National Defence and Security Council, the Election Commission and the Constitutional Tribunal.[16] Succinctly, the orthodox pillars of the state remained as the executive, the legislature, the judiciary and the military.[17]

---

[5] Ganesan (2017, p. 127).

[6] Steinberg (2012, pp. 220–237).

[7] Steinberg (2012, pp. 220–237).

[8] See generally Steinberg (2012, pp. 220–237).

[9] Dukalskis (2015, p. 84).

[10] Crouch (2020, pp. 487–515).

[11] See Harding and Oo (2017).

[12] Crouch (2020, pp. 498–508).

[13] Waters and Panyakom (2021, p. 320).

[14] See Crouch (2020, p. 499).

[15] Crouch (2020, p. 500).

[16] See Farrelly and Win (2016, pp. 38–47).

[17] Farrelly and Win (2016, pp. 38–47).

The beginning of 2011 is viewed as an important democratic transition period due to the dissolution of the Than Shwe-led State Peace and Development Council (SPDC) and the taking of office by a new president Thein Sein.[18] From 2011, the military-backed civilian administration of Thein Sein tried to improve relations with ethnic armed groups, political opposition and the international community.[19] In what can be regarded as a positive move, Thein Sein publicly acknowledged the important role of NGOs in the country's development.[20] Local NGOs also gained some ground in initiatives for reconciliation and conflict Resolution.[21] Overall, Stein's administration saw a significant relaxation of State control over society, including NGO work.

In 2015, there was a positive step in terms of democracy, following general elections that were won by Aung San Suu Kyi's National League for Democracy (NLD). The outcome of the 2015 elections was seen as an opportunity for post-authoritarian transition.[22] It is important to note that the NLD had previously won elections in 1990, but the military had then re-asserted control over the State.[23] Even though the NLD overwhelmingly dominated the 2015 elections, the outcome was still considered as a 're-affirmation of the military's version of democracy'.[24]

Suu Kyi undertook a number of peace-building initiatives to address the ethnic divisions, for example, establishing a coordinating body named the National Reconciliation and Peace Centre (NRPC).[25] As the State Counsellor with important political and administrative power, Suu Kyi was equally considered as being well placed to resolve the ethnic divisions.[26] Consequently, Suu Kyi had the political legitimacy within the ethnic groups in Myanmar.

On 1 February 2021, the Tatmadaw seized power once more in Myanmar, a move that throttled the democratic transition in the country. Daw Aung San Suu Kyi and other NLD leaders were arrested and detained before they could sit for their first session in Parliament. Pro-democracy protests by civil society activists, ethnic minority representatives, and members of Parliament under the National Unity Government (NUG) were brutally suppressed by the Tatmadaw.[27]

Human rights observers reported cases of widespread and systematic attacks, e.g. enforced disappearances, torture, sexual abuse and arbitrary detentions by the Tatmadaw.[28] In a nutshell, there is a legacy of gross human rights violations against civilians by military perpetrators. Like I have highlighted, the Tatmadaw's

---

[18] Badgley and Holliday (2017, p. 39).

[19] See Dukalskis (2015, pp. 83–97).

[20] Kramer (2011, pp. 1–54).

[21] Kramer (2011, pp. 1–54).

[22] Farrelly and Win (2016, pp. 38–47).

[23] Dukalskis (2015, pp. 83–97).

[24] Huang (2017, pp. 25–26).

[25] Ganesan (2017, pp. 111–129).

[26] Ganesan (2017, pp. 111–129).

[27] See Human Rights Watch (2022, p. 474).

[28] Human Rights Watch (2022, p. 475).

actions have had serious ramifications for the country's transitional justice pathways, particularly those involving ethnic minorities including the Rohingya.[29]

In response to the February *coup d'état,* there was a rise in new militias across the country, as a form of resistance. Among these are the Chinland Defence Force in Chin State, Kalay Civil Army in Sagaing Region and Karenni Nationalities Defence Force in Kayah State.[30] More generally, the failure to address the problem of military impunity in Myanmar is viewed as diminishing the potential for transitional justice.[31] The military repression following the coup also created a turn of events, as ethnic prejudices were eroded, with sections of Bamar civilians becoming sympathetic towards ethnic minorities.[32] Nonetheless, it is still vital to address the wider ethnic divisions across the country. For a successful democratic transition to happen in Myanmar, there needs to be structural reforms to get rid of the social barriers that have long affected the processes of democratisation and development.[33] The pathways for transitional justice remain dim.[34]

The contemporary problems around race and identity in Myanmar can be traced back to the colonial period, where the British maintained racial categories.[35] The processes of classification and enumeration by the British involved the use of the gazettes and censuses that emphasised ethnic identities.[36] Giving an example of the Karen ethnic movements, Cho argues that the colonial period enhanced literacy and language within the communities, which served as tools for minorities to advocate for self-determination.[37] Shortly after independence, there were revolts by religious- and ethnic-based armed groups, including the Karen National Union.[38]

As Cho rightly points out, ethnic identity is crucial to the people as it involves claims for aspects like citizenship, political power and resources.[39] She argues that ethnic divisions and conflicts also work in the interest of the military, viewed as the only actor that can keep the country stable.[40] Against this background, the Rohingya situation is analysed as part of the wider ethno-political context in Myanmar.

---

[29] See Lee-Winter et al. (2021); see also Simpson and Farrelly (2023a, b) for more detailed analysis of the coup and its impact on the country's prospects for democracy.

[30] International Crisis Group (2021, pp. 1–20).

[31] For deeper explanation see Cheesman et al. (2016, p. 50).

[32] Thawnghmung and Noah (2021, p. 306).

[33] Badgley and Holliday (2017, p. 42).

[34] For more explanation see Simpson and Farrelly (2023a, b, pp. 284–304).

[35] Cho (2017, p. 43).

[36] Cho (2017, p. 44).

[37] Cho (2017, p. 45).

[38] Waters and Panyakom (2021, p. 317).

[39] Cho (2017, p. 49).

[40] Cho (2017, p. 49).

2 The Rohingya Question: Background of the Problem

In order to explore the contemporary Rohingya crisis, it is important to understand the process of statehood and nation building in post-colonial Myanmar. It is important to note that the Rohingya were called 'Indo-Arakanese' during the period of British colonial rule, residing in 'Arakan' or present-day Rakhine State.[41] The post-colonial era also ushered in armed resistance from separatist movements within the region, resisting the incorporation of Arakan into the new State of Burma.[42] As a result, there were also ethnic conflicts between the Rakhine Buddhists and the minority Rohingya Muslims.

The term 'Rohingya' remains controversial in Myanmar, with an official State policy of not using that nomenclature. Instead, the Rohingya are referred to as 'Bengali foreigners' and are excluded from the 135 ethnic groups recognised by the government.[43] From an international law perspective, the incorporation of Arakan into Burma further disempowered the Rohingya in the post-colonial statehood.[44] In theory, the right to self-determination for ethnic minorities like the Rohingya is limited by post-colonial State-building.

The 1982 citizenship law had a negative impact on the status of the Rohingya, rendering them stateless.[45] Nurul Islam, chairman of the Arakan Rohingya National Organisation (ARNO), points out vis-à-vis the Burma Citizenship Act of 1982 that the Rohingya had been treated as citizens since Myanmar's independence in 1948.[46] This criticism is not without merit, considering the changes in the categorisation of citizens.

The Citizenship Act of 1982 established a three-tiered system of citizenship: full, associate and naturalised.[47] As much as Rohingya activist Nurul Islam is critical of this type of citizenship due to its discriminatory nature, he also argues that the Rohingya are natural citizens of Myanmar by virtue of their ties to Arakan.[48] In theory, the Citizenship Act of 1982 is the most notable legal dilemma regarding the Rohingya's legal status in the country. However, there are also indications that the Rohingya faced discrimination prior to the Citizenship Act of 1948, as different indigenous ethnic groups contested over citizenship.[49] Ronan Lee's ethnographic work offers illuminating perspectives on Rohingya history, politics and rights—affirming the need for their acquisition of citizenship rights.[50] The Rohingya suffer additional challenges associated with their statelessness and lack of legal status

[41] Shahabuddin (2019, pp. 334–347).

[42] Shahabuddin (2019, p. 375).

[43] Kipgen (2013, p. 300).

[44] Shahabuddin (2019, p. 358).

[45] Kipgen (2020, p. 47).

[46] Islam (2017, p. 268).

[47] Islam (2017, p. 276).

[48] Islam (2017, p. 276).

[49] Chowdhory and Mohanty (2020, p. 5).

[50] Lee (2021).

within the country and neighouring countries like Bangladesh—vulnerable to slavery, prostitution, human trafficking and smuggling.[51]

Besides the legal dilemma on citizenship, an exploration of the ethno-religious landscape and conflicts within the Rakhine State is crucial to understanding the hostility towards the Rohingya. The Rakhine State has been politically unstable following a deadly rebel attack against police posts in August 2017, forcing many Rohingya to cross to Bangladesh.[52] This kind of violence was only an escalation of similar incidents in the past in the same region.

Refugee Influx into Bangladesh

The discrimination and violence against the Rohingya in Myanmar are largely embedded in Islamophobic and anti-Muslim discourses by Buddhist nationalists inside the country.[53] Qualitative reports reveal patterns of consistent persecution against the Rohingya since 2012, forcing many to flee to Bangladesh.[54] Human rights observers reported the major violence that occurred in June and October 2012 as a campaign of 'ethnic cleansing' against Rohingya Muslims.[55] Between 2012 and 2013, the violence in Rakhine State was believed to have caused up to 1,000 deaths and forced many others into long-term displacement.[56] The humanitarian situation in the State further worsened when the UN and some humanitarian organisations withdrew from the region in March 2014, following attacks by Buddhist militias[57] (Fig. 1).

In 2015, the International State Crime Initiative (ISCI), an interdisciplinary forum of researchers, released a report of their ethnographic fieldwork in Myanmar.[58] A Rakhine woman interviewed by the ISCI presented a vivid picture of the ethno-religious tensions and anti-Muslim propaganda:

> The main intention of the Muslims is to invade our land, Muslim people want the Arakan land to become a Muslim land... I have no idea how to solve the conflict but I don't want to live with Muslim people. Malaysia and Afghanistan used to be Buddhist lands, same with Indonesia, but now they've become Muslim.[59]

Similar assertions were made by a senior Ma Ba Tha monk interviewed by the ISCI:

> I heard that some Muslim extremists are demanding autonomous Muslim villages, i.e. in Maungdaw and Buthidaung where there is a Muslim majority. This is dangerous for authorities and Buddhists. Because Buddhists then feel afraid and like they have to leave because

[51] Lee-Winter and Kirabira (2021, pp. 1–8).

[52] UNHCR (2022).

[53] See Lee (2024, pp. 233–254).

[54] For a more detailed factual and legal analysis on documented atrocities committed against the Rohingya in Myanmar's Rakhine State see Public International Law & Policy Group (2018, pp. 1–92).

[55] See Human Rights Watch World Report (2015).

[56] Burke (2016, pp. 258–283).

[57] See Report of the Special Rapporteur on the situation of human rights in Myanmar, UN Human Rights Council, 23 March 2015, A/HRC/28/72, para. 44.

[58] Green et al. (2015, pp. 1–107).

[59] Green et al. (2015, p. 32).

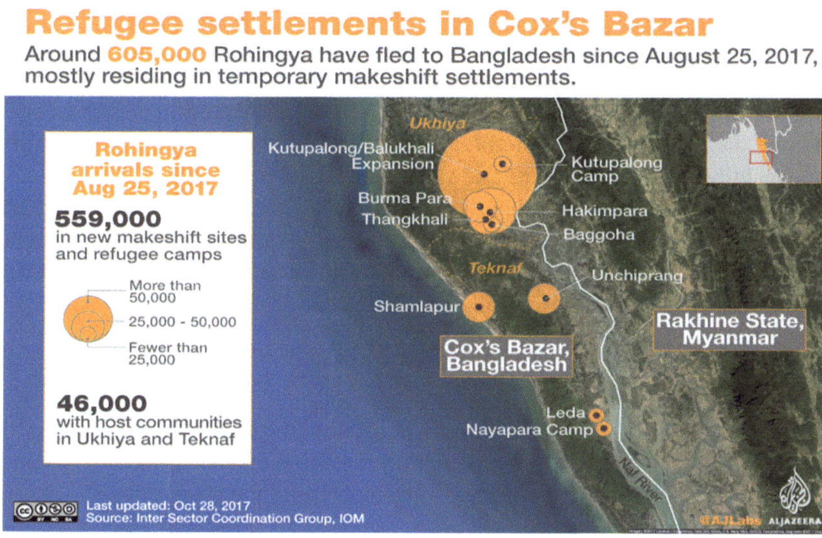

Fig. 1 Rohingya influx into Bangladesh. *Source* Al Jazeera

> of strong cultural differences. You cannot tame Muslim youth because they don't respect monks like Buddhists do.[60]

The ISCI also discovered a plan designed by the regime in 1988, to exterminate the Rohingya, under the auspices of the State Peace and Development Council's (SPDC).[61] Reports reveal that Myanmar military operated a 'clearing operation' following purported attacks by the ARSA in October 2016.[62] In addition to enforced disappearances and mass detention, there was documentation of acts of humiliation and degradation by the military against Rohingya women.[63]

As indicated in the preceding paragraphs, the denial of citizenship for the Rohingya also serves as a tool for systemic isolation, premised on Myanmar's 1982 Citizenship Law. In 1989, a national citizen verification programme stripped many Rohingya of national recognition.[64] Even with full recognition of citizenship, research indicates that ethnic minorities are still subjected to discrimination.[65] Against this background, it is argued that the formal grant of citizenship would not stop the State from eliminating the Rohingya.[66] As such, it is important to consider the implementation of long-term restorative transitional justice mechanisms.

---

[60] Green et al. (2015, p. 64).

[61] Green et al. (2015, p. 36).

[62] Public International Law & Policy Group (2018, p. 19).

[63] Public International Law & Policy Group (2018, p. 22).

[64] Green et al. (2015, p. 57).

[65] Green et al. (2015, p. 58).

[66] Green et al. (2015, p. 58).

An independent international fact-finding mission on Myanmar established by the Human Rights Council reported patterns of gross violations of human rights in Rakhine State, committed by the military.[67] It is important to note that the government of Myanmar did not cooperate with the Mission. In addition to crimes against humanity, the Mission highlighted that there was sufficient information to warrant the prosecution of genocide in relation to the situation in Rakhine State.[68]

Legal analysts assessed whether the crimes against the Rohingya amount to genocide.[69] From an IHRL perspective, the State duty to prevent genocide is based on customary international law and the Genocide Convention which obligate States to prevent genocide. Specifically, article I provides that:

> The Contracting Parties confirm that genocide, whether committed in time of peace or in time of war, is a crime under international law which they undertake to prevent and to punish.[70]

Within the context of Myanmar, reports reveal State responsibility for acts of genocide committed against Rohingya by both the military and non-State actors.[71] The empirical research and legal analyses provide a strong base for the pursuit of accountability mechanisms for the Rohingya.

Even though the NLD tried to ease the mistrust within ethnic minority groups towards the State, the conflict in Rakhine State persisted since the Rohingya were still excluded from national recognition and citizenship.[72] Aung San Suu Kyi was criticised by the international community for her silence about the flight of the Rohingya.[73] The independent international fact-finding mission on Myanmar faulted her for not using her de facto position as Head of Government to protect the civilian population in the Rakhine State.[74] However, Mon Myat describes two dissonances in relation to the legitimacy of Aung San Suu Kyi:

> That of the West which saw her as a human rights activist, and that of the Bamar majority of Myanmar which saw her as a protector of their rights and prerogatives as citizens against foreign interlopers such as the Bengali or the Rohingya.[75]

---

[67] See Report of the Detailed Findings of the Independent International Fact-Finding Mission on Myanmar, UN Human Rights Council, A/HRC/39/CRP.2, 17 September 2018.

[68] Report of the Detailed Findings of the Independent International Fact-Finding Mission on Myanmar, UN Human Rights Council, A/HRC/39/CRP.2, 17 September 2018, paras 87–88.

[69] See for example Lowenstein (2015, pp. 1–72).

[70] Convention on the Prevention and Punishment of the Crime of Genocide, Approved and proposed for signature and ratification or accession by General Assembly resolution 260 A (III) of 9 December 1948 Entry into force: 12 January 1951 [Genocide Convention].

[71] Lowenstein (2015, p. 32).

[72] Cho (2017, p. 49).

[73] Myat (2019, p. 4).

[74] Report of the Detailed Findings of the Independent International Fact-Finding Mission on Myanmar, UN Human Rights Council, A/HRC/39/CRP.2, 17 September 2018, para 93.

[75] Report of the Detailed Findings of the Independent International Fact-Finding Mission on Myanmar, UN Human Rights Council, A/HRC/39/CRP.2, 17 September 2018, para 4.

Without denying the critical role Aung San Suu Kyi played in facilitating democratic transition in Myanmar, Mon Myat argues that her political trajectory had a big influence on her approach towards the Rohingya.[76] In other words, Aung San Suu Kyi worked in an environment of deep Buddhist sentiments towards the Rohingya.

Amidst the socio-political dilemma surrounding the situation of the Rohingya within Myanmar, it is vital to explore the reactions from the international community. The violence against the Rohingya and their humanitarian situation since 2017 has attracted growing scholarly concern. For example, the international community is faulted for not adequately responding to the Rohingya crisis.[77] Besides a lack of political will on the part of the Association of Southeast Asian Nations (ASEAN), Myanmar remains on the fringes of the UNSC due to Russia's and China's veto powers.[78]

A notable initiative by the NLD government to address the problems in Rakhine State was the appointment of a nine-member State Advisory Commission on 24 August 2016. Headed by former UN secretary-general, Kofi Annan, the commission was tasked with analysing the situation in Rakhine State and 'Develop recommendations within five thematic areas: conflict prevention, humanitarian assistance, reconciliation, institution building and development'.[79] Considering the failure of previous commissions of inquiry in Myanmar, the Annan-led commission was considered as a more reliable mechanism to solve the protracted problems.[80] Among its recommendations, the commission urged the government to revise the 1982 Citizenship Law and abolish the distinctions between different types of citizens.[81]

In response to the Report, the government formed a ministerial-led committee to implement the commission's recommendations, assisted by an Advisory Board for the Committee for Implementation of the Recommendations on Rakhine (Advisory Board).[82] Hon. Lord Darzi of Denham, a member of the Advisory Board, stressed the need for dialogue 'within Myanmar and more importantly between international community and Myanmar towards securing a lasting peace in Rakhine'.[83]

In effect, the commission also enhanced the legitimacy of the NLD government before the international community. U Zaw Htay who served as the director-general for the Office of State Counselor Daw Aung San Suu Kyi and was spokesman for the President's Office made intriguing remarks about the commission: 'Whenever there is an accusation from the international community, we say we are taking action in

[76] Report of the Detailed Findings of the Independent International Fact-Finding Mission on Myanmar, UN Human Rights Council, A/HRC/39/CRP.2, 17 September 2018, para 7.

[77] See generally Morada (2020, pp. 64–85).

[78] Morada (2020, pp. 64–85).

[79] See Final Report of the Advisory Commission on Rakhine State (2017, p. 12).

[80] See Kipgen (2016).

[81] Final Report of the Advisory Commission on Rakhine State (2017, p. 31).

[82] For a news report on the governments' response to the Commission's Final Report and Recommendations see The Irrawaddy (2017); See also Kipgen (2020, p. 56).

[83] See Myanmar Digital News (2019) for a media report on the Committee for Implementing the Recommendations on Rakhine State.

line with the recommendations of the Kofi Annan commission. The commission is serving as a shield for us'.[84]

In sum, it is apt to say that the Annan-led commission provided a foundation for reconciliation in Rakhine State, based on the envisaged follow-up by the State. However, the peace and reconciliation processes are largely constrained by ethnic and religious divisions and rivalries within the local communities.[85] As has already been noted, the presence of armed-separatist groups and the lack of recognition for minority groups makes their relationship with the State further complicated.[86] Ultimately, an important question arises as to whether the Rohingya can pursue transitional justice.

3 Can the Rohingya Pursue Transitional Justice?

Having discussed the ethno-political history of Myanmar and the contemporary Rohingya crisis, it is important to explore the pathways for transitional justice. An important question, within this perspective, is whether transitional justice can be achieved for the Rohingya? As has been highlighted elsewhere, the Tatmadaw's actions since the military coup in 2021 diminished possibilities for potential transitional justice avenues, particularly in respect to ethnic minorities including the Rohingya.[87] Violent clashes between Arakan Rohingya Salvation Army (ARSA) and the military government forces since the 2021 coup have exacerbated the situation in Rakhine, driving more Rohingya across the border to Bangladesh.[88] With this reality, then the next issue is to find or explore the most suitable transitional justice avenues or mechanisms, if any.

Whilst discussing the critiques of transitional justice in chapter "Navigating Justice, Transitional Justice and Global North–South Dimensions" of the book, a dilemma was shown in relation to the stages of transition. Complex cases like Myanmar make it possible to validate scholarly concerns about the use of transitional justice mechanisms as a tool by actors like NGOs to promote their goals.[89] The previous discussions have highlighted gaps in the process of democratic transition in Myanmar. Even though transitional justice is not a direct feature of Myanmar's democratisation process,[90] the contemporary debates on its democratic transition

[84] See Myint (2017) for a media analysis of the Commission's work before the publication of its final Report.

[85] Aung-Thwin (2017, p. 23).

[86] Aung-Thwin (2017, p. 23).

[87] Lee-Winter et al. (2021).

[88] See Al Jazeera Report (2024). https://www.aljazeera.com/news/2024/5/25/some-45000-rohingya-flee-amid-allegations-of-beheading-burning-in-myanmar; for more explanation on the armed group, see Leider (2023, pp. 217–232).

[89] Rowen (2018, pp. 50–65).

[90] Renshaw (2019a, b, p. 386).

help to situate avenues for justice for the Rohingya. Similarly, the context of Myanmar broadens our understanding of whether transitional justice can be achieved where there is no transition.

Catherine Renshaw's analysis on human rights and democratisation in Myanmar offers illuminating insights when thinking of transitional justice in the country, particularly what she calls 'Myanmar's troubled transition towards a limited form of constitutional democracy' from 2008 to 2018.[91] As she rightly observes, owing to Myanmar's complex history, the transition did not involve the traditional transitional justice aspects like criminal prosecutions, truth-telling and reparations.[92] The aspect of national reconciliation is equally important in Myanmar's transitional justice. However, as noted by Yanghee Lee, former UN Special Rapporteur on the situation of Human Rights in Myanmar, there is a need for both peace and justice.[93]

Similarly, contentious laws like the 1982 Citizenship Law were not amended, or annulled. Nonetheless, the government established institutions like the National Human Rights Commission to strengthen the rule of law.[94] However, to some NGO observers, the formation of the Commission was merely to enhance Myanmar's legitimacy before ASEAN and the international community.[95] Generally, the country did not deal with the previous legacy of massive human rights violations by the military. The applicability of formal transitional justice approaches like amnesty, criminal trials and truth-seeking would be ideal, but the complex political situation does not offer an enabling ground for these measures. Recalling that previous Commissions of Inquiry instituted in the country in respect to the violence in the Rakhine region were largely perfunctory. Nonetheless, measures like truth commissions, amnesty and criminal prosecution can be envisaged for future approaches in order to deal with the long legacy of atrocities committed against the Rohingya.[96]

Beyond the traditional notions of transitional justice and the role of the State, it is equally important to understand the local perspectives and beliefs regarding justice. Empirical studies indicate that local people's experiences of justice in Myanmar are mostly influenced by the country's history of ethnic divisions and ongoing transitions.[97] In Myanmar, disputes and injustices are resolved through a distinctly plural range of justice processes—some formal court adjudications, others mediated settlements.[98] This legal pluralism could be useful, where the formal justice system is ill-equipped. However, it could also raise concerns about the readiness or legitimacy to deal with legacies of gross human rights violations. Moreover, reports indicate

[91] Renshaw (2019a, b, p. 397).

[92] Renshaw (2019a, b, p. 382).

[93] See Lee and Drake (2018).

[94] Renshaw (2019a, b, p. 386; 2020, p. 434).

[95] De Lang (2012, p. 11).

[96] For deeper analysis see generally Hossain (2024, pp. 1–23).

[97] For detailed study on local experiences of justice in Myanmar and levels of dispute resolution (study conducted in two parts of Myanmar—Mon State and Yangon Region) see Denney et al. (2016, p. 17).

[98] Denney et al. (2016, p. 15).

that there is little trust in the formal justice system, due to the military influence in all the structures of the State, including the judiciary.[99]

Varied local understandings of justice and limited literacy could also mean that many people simply do not actively seek to enforce their human rights. Observers note that 'many people equate justice with the reduction and disappearance of a problem, with people accepting whatever path that leads to closure most quickly'.[100] Such an understanding of justice would equally have an impact on transitional justice. It is noted that: 'Even more challenging for those working to strengthen justice outcomes in Myanmar is that people may not want the kind of justice outcomes that the international development community generally favours'.[101]

Qualitative research also raises concerns about high expectations regarding externally led transitional justice programmes in Myanmar.[102] The empirical reality in this is that external actors have little control over the application and implementation of transitional justice in Myanmar, as the country is yet to achieve democratic transition. As such, it is recommended to embrace the local reconciliatory justice processes, whilst working with locally grounded actors.[103] This view is not without merit, considering the increasing emphasis on local ownership in matters of transitional justice.[104]

Using Myanmar as a case study, interdisciplinary scholarship would provide a more contextualised perspective for transitional justice in Myanmar. For example, scholars from the field of international relations are more concerned about the rising level of impunity in the country, yet mainstream transitional justice mostly deals with measures like establishing truth commissions and removing blanket amnesties.[105] In what is referred to as 'everyday impunity', the scholars draw attention towards the impossibility of holding State officials accountable for their crimes.[106] In other words, it is important to identify and deal with modes of impunity in Myanmar that have emerged from earlier periods of military rule, if transitional justice is to be a reality in the country.

Previously, I have emphasised that transitional justice requires the implementation of a wide range of truth-seeking and reparative mechanisms for victims.[107] Renshaw provides three key reasons for the failure of transitional justice in Myanmar—military control, an ill-equipped judiciary, and the persistence of civil war in parts of the country.[108] Upon evaluating the existing accountability measures initiated by the

---

[99] Denney et al. (2016, p. 18).

[100] Denney et al. (2016, p. 44).

[101] Denney et al. (2016, p. 44).

[102] Denney et al. (2016, p. 47).

[103] Denney et al. (2016, p. 48).

[104] Sharp (2014, pp. 71–117).

[105] See for example Cheesman et al. (2016, pp. 48–61).

[106] Cheesman et al. (2016, pp. 48–61).

[107] See Kirabira (2020, p. 149) for a legal analysis of the accountability mechanisms.

[108] Renshaw (2019a, b, p. 382).

State, I concur with Renshaw and show that the situation of the Rohingya has not been remedied, due to lack of meaningful accountability measures.[109]

For meaningful transitional justice in Myanmar, Renshaw argues for a shift in the relationship and contours of understanding between the people and the state, in respect to past.[110] She calls for:

> broad public debate about the morality of the military's actions during the years of dictatorship, wide-scale deliberative reflection about society's existing political culture, and a period of deep national self-examination about the effects of long-term repression.[111]

As Renshaw argues, the acts of mass atrocity and violations against the Rohingya are also enhanced by the government's failure to recognise and acknowledge the historical wrongs and past legacy of crimes.[112] Truth commissions are an important aspect of conflict resolution and transitional justice. More generally, effective truth-seeking mechanisms would potentially help to counter the denial of atrocities committed against the Rohingya, within Myanmar.[113] As already discussed, the Annan-led commission provided a foundation for reconciliation in Rakhine State, but there are still key gaps in the implementation of its Reports.[114] From a transitional justice perspective, the five thematic areas of the commission: conflict prevention, humanitarian assistance, reconciliation, institution building and development, did not reflect a truth-seeking process.

It is important to note that the Annan-led Commission was not the only formal State-initiated inquiry into the Rohingya situation. An Inquiry Commission on Sectarian Violence in Rakhine State was set up in 2012, to investigate the recent violence in Rakhine State.[115] In 2016, there was an Investigation Commission into the violence in Rakhine state's Maungdaw township, led by Vice-President U Myint Swe. Its interim report indicated that there was insufficient evidence to support allegations of genocide or religious persecution of Rohingya Muslims.[116] Little wonder, the report was strongly denounced and rejected by Rohingya activists and NGOs.[117]

The government instituted another Independent Commission of Inquiry on 30 May 2018, to investigate acts of violence that occurred in Rakhine State in August 2017.[118] The Commission's mandate included the goal of 'seeking accountability and formulating recommendations on steps to be taken to ensure sustainable peace

---

[109] Kirabira (2020, p. 159).

[110] Renshaw (2020, p. 435).

[111] Renshaw (2020, p. 435).

[112] Renshaw (2020, p. 470).

[113] Hossain (2024, p. 6).

[114] See Myint (2017) for a media analysis of the Commission's work before the publication of its final Report.

[115] The New Light of Myanmar (2012, pp. 1–16).

[116] See Global New Light of Myanmar (2017).

[117] See Progressive Voice Myanmar (2017).

[118] See the Government's Executive Summary of the Independent Commission of Enquiry, Office of the President (2020).

and development in Rakhine State'.[119] However, according to some observers, the Commission was ineffective and its report did not address the massive human rights violations by the military against the Rohingya.[120] In sum, it can be argued that the State-sanctioned commissions of inquiry were not in line with international accountability standards, and don't provide redress for the Rohingya.[121]

Bearing in mind that the primary responsibility for investigating and prosecuting crimes under international law lies with the State, in this case the government of Myanmar.[122] However, this accountability measure only works if the State is able and willing to fulfil its duty. For the case of Myanmar, it is argued that there would be a need for 'an overhaul of the entire national justice and security sectors' in order to achieve accountability.[123] Due to the failure to achieve accountability in Myanmar, the international forum is seen as a suitable avenue for transitional justice.[124] However, as indicated in the introduction of the book, there needs to be an assessment of the impact of transnational networks and NGOs on the legitimacy of such accountability mechanisms. It is important to note that the book explores external transitional justice processes (Argentina/ICJ/ICC).

Prosecuting crimes against humanity at both domestic and international levels requires an enabling legal framework, in terms of relevant laws. There are limited chances of prosecuting military perpetrators of crimes against civilians in Myanmar, due to prevailing environment of impunity.[125] Aung San Suu Kyi and the NLD's reluctance to implement truth-seeking or retributive measures, was also attributed to their desire for democratisation and peace.[126] From a normative perspective, Myanmar is not a State party to the Rome Statute of the ICC. As a result, it would take the intervention of the UN Security Council, in order to trigger ICC jurisdiction over international crimes committed against the Rohingya within Myanmar. Nonetheless, international interventions have been triggered, and they will be explored in greater detail in the next chapter.

In a nutshell, there are no appropriate or meaningful mechanisms for responding to international crimes against the Rohingya within Myanmar, as the government prioritises peace over justice.[127] Despite this challenging legal context, there have been efforts to seek for justice for the Rohingya, at the international level.

---

[119] Office of the President (2020, p. 1).

[120] Human Rights Watch (2020).

[121] Kirabira (2020, pp. 152–153).

[122] For more explanation see Kirabira (2020, pp. 152–153), Sharp (2015), and Roht-Arriaza (1990, pp. 451–513).

[123] See Report of the Detailed Findings of the Independent International Fact-Finding Mission on Myanmar, UN Human Rights Council, A/HRC/39/CRP.2, 17 September 2018, para. 98.

[124] Report of the Detailed Findings of the Independent International Fact-Finding Mission on Myanmar, UN Human Rights Council, A/HRC/39/CRP.2, 17 September 2018.

[125] Palmer (2020, p. 202).

[126] Renshaw (2019a, b) Myanmar's transition without justice, p. 134.

[127] Palmer (2020, p. 202).

In September 2018, the Human Rights Council established an Independent Investigative Mechanism for Myanmar (IIMM). The broad mandate was to:

> collect, consolidate, preserve and analyze evidence of the most serious international crimes and violations of international law committed in Myanmar since 2011, and to prepare files in order to facilitate and expedite fair and independent criminal proceedings, in accordance with international law standards, in national, regional or international courts or tribunals that have or may in the future have jurisdiction over these crimes, in accordance with international law.[128]

Even though such mechanisms do not have inherent judicial powers, the collection and preservation of evidence sets the stage for future transitional justice mechanisms.[129] Ultimately, the evidence gathered by the IIMM will aid subsequent transitional justice mechanisms for example criminal prosecution.

There was also an intervention before the International Court of Justice (ICJ). In November 2019, The Gambia filed a case against Myanmar before the ICJ, invoking the Genocide Convention.[130] A key component in the case relates to Myanmar's failure to hold its military accountable for gross violations of human rights against the Rohingya.[131] In sum, the aim of the case was to:

> establish Myanmar's responsibility for violations of the Genocide Convention, to hold it fully accountable under international law for its genocidal acts against the Rohingya group, and to have recourse to th[e] Court to ensure the fullest possible protection for those who remain at grave risk from future acts of genocide.[132]

From a transitional justice perceptive, this wording illustrates a possibility for justice for the Rohingya at the ICJ. Consequently, there is an element of transitional justice in *The Gambia v Myanmar* case.

Myanmar responded formally to the application and denied the allegations. It is also argued that Suu Kyi's act of denying genocide before the ICJ in December 2019, significantly enhanced her popular support within the country.[133] Not surprisingly, her act of defending the country at the ICJ was a further indication that transitional justice in Myanmar was still illusionary.[134] On 23 January 2020, the Court issued a ruling on provisional measures, ordering the Myanmar government to prevent the commission of further atrocities against the Rohingya.[135]

---

[128] See UNHRC, Resolution Adopted by the Human Rights Council on 27 September 2018—Situation of Human Rights of Rohingya Muslims and Other Minorities in Myanmar, UN Doc A/HRC/RES/39/2, 27 September 2018, para 22 (Resolution 39/2).

[129] Le Moli (2020, pp. 656–662).

[130] See Application of the Convention on the Prevention and Punishment of the Crime of Genocide (*The Gambia v Myanmar*), International Court of Justice, Application instituting proceedings and Request for the indication of provisional measures, 11 November 2019.

[131] *The Gambia v Myanmar*, paras 15, 73.

[132] *The Gambia v Myanmar*, para 15.

[133] Thawnghmung and Noah (2021, p. 304).

[134] Ronan (2021, p. 2).

[135] The *Gambia v Myanmar*, Request for the indication of provisional measures, International Court of Justice, Order, 23 January 2020, para 86.

As highlighted in chapter "Navigating Justice, Transitional Justice and Global North–South Dimensions" of the book, the ICC also intervened in the Rohingya situation, and the Pre-Trial Chamber determined that the Court has jurisdiction over the alleged deportation of Rohingya from Myanmar to Bangladesh.[136] As Myanmar is not a State Party to the Rome Statute of the ICC, the Prosecutor applied an innovative approach to allow the Court exercise jurisdiction in respect to crimes of deportation and forcible transfer of populations.[137] On 14 November 2019, the Pre-Trial Chamber III authorised the commencement of investigations into the situation in Bangladesh/Myanmar.[138] Just like the IIMM, the ICC investigation has the potential to collect and preserve useful evidence for the prosecution of perpetrators of crimes against the Rohingya. On 27 November 2024, ICC Prosecutor Karim Khan applied for an arrest warrant for the leader of the Tatmadaw, Senior General Min Aung Hlaing. Whilst there has not been a direct impact of the application and investigations, the Hague-based justice mechanisms are still considered as important avenues for transitional justice.[139]

As discussed in the chapter "Navigating Justice, Transitional Justice and Global North–South Dimensions" of this book, the ICC is regarded as the most influential institution of individual criminal accountability.[140] However, one should not lose sight of the challenges faced by the ICC in this complex situation. Notably, Myanmar is a non-State party to the Rome Statute and the targeted perpetrators of crimes are high-ranking government officials. These challenges certainly have an impact on the Court's legitimacy, effectiveness and efficiency in dealing with the Rohingya situation.[141]

One might argue that the international avenues do not reflect a 'localised' form of transitional justice for the Rohingya, enabling important aspects like local ownership and participation. However, as Sharp rightly argues, localised processes may not necessarily guarantee the legitimacy of the transitional justice mechanisms—with a possibility that locals may actually prefer international avenues.[142] For these reasons, it is relevant to explore the transitional justice avenues for the Rohingya at the international level. With regard to the three forms of legal action, the ICJ case, the case

---

[136] See Decision on the "Prosecution's Request for a Ruling on Jurisdiction under Article 19(3) of the Statute", ICC-RoC46(3)-01/18-37, Pre-Trial Chamber I, Decision, 06 September 2018 (Decision on the Prosecution's Request for a Ruling on Jurisdiction).

[137] For detailed analysis on the Court's interpretation of jurisdiction in the situation see Foysal (2023, pp. 73–95).

[138] *Decision Pursuant to Article 15 of the Rome Statute on the Authorisation of an Investigation into the Situation in the People's Republic of Bangladesh/Republic of the Union of Myanmar ('the situation in Bangladesh/Myanmar'), ICC-01/19, Pre-Trial Chamber III | Decision, 14 November 2019* (ICC Authorisation Decision 2019).

[139] See McIntyre and Simpson (2024).

[140] See for instance Schwöbel-Patel (2018, pp. 703–724).

[141] See generally Takemura (2023); see also Kittichaisaree (2022, pp. 186–206).

[142] Sharp (2015, p. 105).

filed in Argentina, and the ICC investigation are generally viewed as complementary strategies towards justice and accountability for the Rohingya.[143] Myanmar is certainly a unique situation as these global accountability mechanisms are working at the same time.[144] In a nutshell, whilst international justice is regarded as an important avenue for transitional justice for the Rohingya, Myanmar's domestic politics is crucial for transitional justice to become a reality in Myanmar.[145] Crucially, transnational networks need to engage with the globalised mechanisms as well as domestic avenues for reconciliation and democracy.

4 Conclusion

This chapter has shown the complexity around the Rohingya situation, revealing a wider ethno-religious context to the discussions. It has also analysed the dynamics of Myanmar's transition to democracy, showing a high level of militarisation in the country. The discussions on the process of democratisation in Myanmar have direct repercussions concerning redress mechanisms for the Rohingya, under the wider preview of transitional justice. The chapter did not set out to show Myanmar as a country under a definite form of transitional justice, but rather to set the stage for exploring prospects of transitional justice, in line with the country's history and contemporary developments. Consequently, the next chapter will seek to answer the questions of this study regarding the role of transnational networks and NGOs in transitional justice for the Rohingya. It will also show how the NGOs impact on the legitimacy of different transitional justice avenues.

References

Advisory Commission on Rakhine State (2017) Towards a peaceful, fair and prosperous future for the people of Rakhine—final report of the advisory commission on Rakhine state. Advisory Commission on Rakhine State, New York, pp 1–63

Application of the convention on the prevention and punishment of the Crime of Genocide (*The Gambia v. Myanmar*) International Court of Justice, 11 November 2019

Application of the convention on the prevention and punishment of the Crime of Genocide (*The Gambia v Myanmar*), Request for the indication of provisional measures, International Court of Justice, 23 January 2020

Aung-Thwin M (2017) The state. In: Simpson A, Farrelly N, Holliday I (eds) Routledge handbook of contemporary Myanmar. Routledge, Abingdon, pp 15–24

Badgley J, Holliday I (2017) Democracy. In: Simpson A, Farrelly N, Holliday I (eds) Routledge handbook of contemporary Myanmar. Routledge, Abingdon, pp 35–42

---

[143] See Pillai (2019) for a succinct analysis on the three interventions.

[144] For more comparative analysis on the accountability mechanism see Pillai (2023, pp. 163–185).

[145] Lee (2021, p. 4).

Burke A (2016) New political space, old tensions: history, identity and violence in Rakhine State, Myanmar. Contemporary Southeast Asia 38:258–283

Cheesman N, D'Costa B, Haberkorn T (2016) Anticipating the struggle against everyday impunity in Myanmar through accounts from Bangladesh and Thailand. Asia & the Pacific Policy Stud 3:48–61

Cho V (2017) Ethnicity and identity. In: Simpson A, Farrelly N, Holliday I (eds) Routledge handbook of contemporary Myanmar. Routledge, Abingdon, pp 43–51

Convention on the prevention and punishment of the Crime of Genocide, approved and proposed for signature and ratification or accession by General Assembly Resolution 260 A (III) of 9 December 1948 Entry into Force: 12 January 1951

Decision Pursuant to Article 15 of the Rome Statute on the Authorisation of an Investigation into the Situation in the People's Republic of Bangladesh/Republic of the Union of Myanmar ('the Situation in Bangladesh/Myanmar'), ICC-01/19, Pre-Trial Chamber III, Decision, 14 November 2019 (Authorisation Decision 2019)

Chowdhory N, Mohanty B (2020) Contextualizing citizenship, nationalism and refugeehood of Rohingya: an introduction. In: Chowdhory N, Mohanty B (eds) Citizenship, nationalism and refugeehood of Rohingyas in Southern Asia, 1st edn. Springer, Singapore, pp 1–30

Crouch M (2020) Pre-emptive constitution-making: authoritarian constitutionalism and the military in Myanmar. L Soc Rev 54:487–515

de Lang N (2012) The establishment and development of the Myanmar National Human Rights Commission and its conformity with international standards. Asia-Pacific J Hum Rights L 13:1–41

Denney L, Bennett W, San KT (2016) Making big cases small and small cases disappear: experiences of local justice in Myanmar. British Council, Overseas Development Institute and Saferworld, London pp 1–67

Dukalskis A (2015) Transitional justice in Burma/Myanmar: crossnational patterns and domestic context. Irish Stud Int Aff 26:83–97

Ganesan N (2017) Democratization and its implications for the resolution of ethnic conflict in Myanmar. Asia J Peacebuild 5:111–129

Farrelly N, Win C (2016) Inside Myanmar's turbulent transformation. Asia Pac Pol Stud 3:38–47

Foysal QO (2023) A tale of two international law principles: ensuring justice and accountability for the Rohingya. In: Hasan M, Murshed S, Pillai P(eds), The Rohingya crisis humanitarian and legal approaches. Routledge, Abingdon, pp 73–95

Global New Light of Myanmar (2017) Interim report of the investigation commission on Maungtaw. The Global New Light of Myanmar, Yangon, pp 1–9. https://www.burmalibrary.org/docs24/NLM2017-01-04-NRS.pdf

Green P, MacManus T, de la Cour VA (2015) Countdown to annihilation: Genocide in Myanmar. International State Crime Initiative, London, pp 1–107

Harding A, Oo KK (eds) (2017) Constitutionalism and legal change in Myanmar. Hart Publishing, London

Hossain M (2024) Transitional justice to address genocide denial: a case study of the Rohingya in Myanmar. Int Ann Criminol, pp 1–23

Huang RL (2017) Myanmar's way to democracy and the limits of the 2015 elections. Asian J Polit Sci 25:25–44

Human Rights Watch (2020) Myanmar: government Rohingya report falls short. Human Rights Watch, NY. https://www.hrw.org/news/2020/01/22/myanmar-government-rohingya-report-falls-short

Human Rights Watch, World Report (2015): Burma Events of 2014, https://www.hrw.org/world-report/2015/country-chapters/burma

Human Rights Watch (2022) World report 2022. Human Rights Watch, NY, pp 1–753

ICC-RoC46(3)-01/18-37 06 September 2018 | Pre-Trial Chamber I | Decision

International Crisis Group (2021) Taking aim at the Tatmadaw: the new armed resistance to Myanmar's Coup. Crisis Group Asia Briefing No. 168, International Crisis Group, Brussels, pp 1–20
Irrawaddy (2017) Govt to Implement Rakhine Commission's Recommendations. The Irrawaddy. https://www.irrawaddy.com/news/burma/govt-implement-rakhine-commissions-recommendations.html
Islam N (2017) Rohingya and Nationality Status in Myanmar. In: South A, Lall M (eds) Citizenship in Myanmar: Ways of being in and from Burma. ISEAS—Yusof Ishak Institute/Chiang Mai University Press, Singapore, pp 264–278
Kipgen N (2013) Conflict in Rakhine State in Myanmar: Rohingya Muslims' conundrum. J Muslim Minor Aff 33:298–310
Kipgen N (2016) Can Kofi Annan's commission solve the Rohingya conundrum? The Diplomat, Arlington. https://thediplomat.com/2016/09/can-kofi-annans-commission-solve-the-rohingya-conundrum/
Kipgen N (2020) Myanmar's perspective on the Rohingya crisis. Int J World Peace 3:43–70
Kirabira T (2020) Establishing accountability for gross human rights violations: An analysis of the Rohingya conflict. J Int L Peace Arm Conf 3:141–158
Kittichaisaree K (2022) The Rohingya, justice and international law, 1st edn. Routledge, Abingdon, pp 1–293
Kramer T (2011) Civil society gaining ground: opportunities for change and development. Transnational Institute, Drukkerij PrimaveraQuint, Amsterdam, pp 1–54
Le Moli G (2020) From "is" to "ought": the development of normative powers of UN investigative mechanisms. Chin J Int L 19:625–681
Lee R (2024) Islamophobia and genocide: Myanmar's Rohingya genocide. In: Aziz S, Esposito J (eds) Global islamophobia and the rise of populism. OUP, NY, pp 233–254
Lee R (2021) Myanmar's Rohingya genocide: identity, history and hate speech. Bloomsbury Publishing, London, pp 1–273
Lee Y, Drake G (2018) There can be no peace for Myanmar without justice. TIME, NY. https://time.com/5404328/myanmar-accountability-yanghee-lee/
Lee-Winter F, Kirabira T, Collins L (2021) The right to live under threat: on the armed forces (The Tatmadaw) taking power in Myanmar, *Völkerrechtsblog*
Lee-Winter F, Kirabira T (2021) Dossier: the stateless Rohingya-practical consequences of expulsion. Genocide Stud Preven 15:1–8
Leider J (2023) The Arakan Army: challenges for Rakhine State's Rising ethnonational force. In: Hoang TH, Singh D (eds) Southeast Asian Affairs 2023. Southeast Asian Affairs. ISEAS–Yusof Ishak Institute, Singapore, pp 217–232
Lowenstein A (2015) Persecution of the Rohingya Muslims: Is genocide occurring in Myanmar's Rakhine State? A legal analysis. Allard K. Lowenstein International Human Rights Clinic and Fortify Rights, Yale Law School, New Haven, pp 1–72
Manley S (2017) Transitional justice in Myanmar: Fragments of quieted voices. Inter-Asia Cult Stud 18:610–616
McIntyre J, Simpson A (2024) Legal noose tightens on Myanmar junta. East Asia Forum Quarterly: Economics, Politics and Public Policy in East Asia and the Pacific. https://eastasiaforum.org/2024/12/19/legal-noose-tightens-on-myanmar-junta/
Morada N (2020) Continuing violence and atrocities in Rakhine since 2017: Beyond the outrage, failures of the International Community. Glob Respons Prot 12:64–85
Myat MM (2019) Is politics Aung San Suu Kyi's vocation? Palgrave Communications 5: 1–8
Myanmar Digital News (2019) Committee on implementing recommendations on Rakhine State clarifies achievements, challenges at press conference. Myanmar Digital News, Yangon https://www.myanmardigitalnewspaper.com/en/committee-implementing-recommendations-rakhine-state-clarifies-achievements-challenges-press

Myint M (2017) Analysis: did advisory commission remedy Rakhine State's conflict? The Irrawaddy. https://www.irrawaddy.com/news/burma/analysis-advisory-commission-remedy-rakhine-states-conflict.html
Office of the President (2020) Executive summary of Independent Commission of enquiry, Government of Myanmar, Yangon. https://reliefweb.int/sites/reliefweb.int/files/resources/BM.pdf
Office of the United Nations High Commissioner for Human Rights (2018) Report of the detailed findings of the Independent International Fact-Finding Mission on Myanmar, A/HRC/39/64, Geneva, pp 1–21
Palmer E (2020) Adapting International Criminal Justice in Southeast Asia: beyond the International Criminal Court. CUP, Cambridge
Pillai P (2019) Three complementary legal strategies for accountability: a momentous week for the Rohingya. Opinio Juris, Geneva http://opiniojuris.org/2019/11/19/three-complimentary-legal-strategies-for-accountability-a-momentous-week-for-the-rohingya/
Pillai P (2023) A 'patchwork quilt' of fact-finding and international accountability in Myanmar. In: Hasan M, Murshed S, Pillai P (eds) The Rohingya crisis humanitarian and legal approaches, Routledge, Abingdon, pp. 163–185
Progressive Voice Myanmar (2017) Press release: Maungdaw Investigation Commission's report is not credible. Progressive Voice Myanmar. https://progressivevoicemyanmar.org/wp-content/uploads/2017/08/press-release-maungdaw-investigation-commissions-report-is-not-credible.pdf
Public International Law & Policy Group (2018) Documenting atrocity crimes committed against the Rohingya in Myanmar's Rakhine state: factual findings & legal analysis report. Public International Law & Policy Group. The Hague, pp 1–92
Renshaw C (2019a) Myanmar's transition without justice. In: Kent L, Wallis J, Cronin C (eds) Civil society and transitional justice in Asia and the Pacific. ANU Press, Canberra, pp 127–153
Renshaw C (2019b) Myanmar's transition without justice. J Curr Southeast Asia Aff 38:381–403
Renshaw C (2020) Myanmar's genocide and the legacy of forgetting. Georgia J Int Compar L 48:425–472
Roht-Arriaza N (1990) State responsibility to investigate and prosecute grave human rights violations in international. California L Rev 78:451–513
Rowen J (2018) The Transformation of legal ideas: The globalization and politicization of transitional justice in the Middle East. In: Christensen M, Levi R (eds) International practices of criminal justice, 1st edn. Routledge, Abingdon, pp 50–65
Schwöbel-Patel C (2018) The "ideal" victim of international criminal law. Eur J Int L 29:703–724
Shahabuddin M (2019) Post-colonial boundaries, International law, and the making of the Rohingya crisis in Myanmar. Asian J Int L 9:334–358
Sharp D (2014) Addressing dilemmas of the global and the local in transitional justice. Emory Int L Rev 29:71–117
Sharp D (2015) Accountability: a critical link in the security-development nexus. In: Piombo J (ed) The U.S. Military in Africa: enhancing security & development. Lynne Rienner Publishers, Boulder
Simpson A, Farrelly N (eds) (2023a) Myanmar: politics, economy and society, 2nd edn. Routledge, Abingdon
Simpson A, Farrelly N (2023b) Myanmar's complex and intersecting crises: pathways to accountability and international justice. Myanmar: Politics. Economy and Society, Routledge, Abingdon, pp 284–304
Steinberg D (2012) The problem of democracy in the Republic of the Union of Myanmar: neither nation-state nor state-nation? Southeast Asia Aff 2012:220–237
Takemura H (2023) The Rohingya crisis and the International Criminal Court, 1st edn. Springer, Singapore, pp 1–151
Thawnghmung A, Noah K (2021) Myanmar's military coup and the elevation of the minority agenda? Crit Asian Stud 53:297–309

The New Light of Myanmar (2012) Investigation Commission formed. The New Light of Myanmar, Yangon, pp 1–16 https://www.burmalibrary.org/docs14/NLM2012-08-18.pdf
UNHRC, Resolution adopted by the Human Rights Council on 27 September 2018—Situation of human rights of Rohingya Muslims and other minorities in Myanmar, UN Doc A/HRC/RES/39/2 (2018) (Resolution 39/2)
UNHCR (2022) Rohingya emergency, UNHCR, Geneva https://www.unhcr.org/uk/rohingya-emergency.html
Waters T, Panyakom S (2021) Why is peace elusive in Myanmar? an answer from the perspective of Thai Philosopher Prawase Wasi. Asian J Peacebuild 9:305–330

Mapping NGO Work in Myanmar: Impact of Transnational NGO Networks

1 Limitations of NGO Work Within Myanmar

Having discussed the different options for justice for the Rohingya, it is imperative to explore the spaces for non-State actors, in this case NGOs, in Myanmar. This is an important background when assessing the role of NGOs in transitional justice, especially within the Global South. A critical analysis of NGO work will also answer the question; how do NGOs impact on the legitimacy of the transitional justice processes? For a better understanding of NGO spaces and work in Myanmar, the analysis of their work is not limited to the field of transitional justice, but also encompasses a context of peacebuilding and conflict resolution.

Prior to 2011, both local NGOs and INGOs operated under a strict and bureaucratic environment by the military. In 2016, the government ordered the International Committee of the Red Cross (ICRC) to shut most of its operations in the country, without providing any reason.[1] As already discussed in the introduction to this chapter, the Thein Sein government initiated some political reforms in 2011 that opened up more spaces for NGOs.[2]

There was more legal clarity for the work of both local and INGOs, and they were required to register under the new Association Registration Law Myanmar (No.31/2014).[3] From a transitional justice perspective, it could be said that the legal reforms provided a platform for transnational advocacy networks. From a general overview, these reforms could be viewed as a firm foundation for justice and reconciliation in

[1] International Committee of the Red Cross (2006).

[2] Kramer (2011, pp 1–54).

[3] Dale and Samuel-Nakka (2017, p. 327).

This chapter has some overlaps with my doctoral thesis. There is also some usage of discussions from my published work-Kirabira T, Palmer E (2023) NGO roles in achieving transitional justice for crimes against the Rohingya. In: Hasan M, Murshed S, Pillai P (eds) The Rohingya crisis humanitarian and legal approaches, Routledge, Abingdon, pp 211–236.

© The Author(s), under exclusive license to Springer Nature Singapore Pte Ltd. 2025
T. R. Kirabira, *Transnational Networks and Justice in the Global South*, International Law and the Global South, https://doi.org/10.1007/978-981-95-3137-0_6

the country. Nonetheless, it is observed that local NGOs were also tied with political parties and ethnic armed groups. Scholars note that 'many ethnic CSOs have had close ties to both ethnic political parties and ethnic armed groups, as they share the goal of securing greater rights for ethnic nationalities'.[4]

Ultimately, the arena in which local NGOs operate is influenced by surrounding social and political factors like religion and ethnicity. Like in any other authoritarian regime context, there is often a blurred relationship between local NGOs and the government. NGOs in Myanmar whose policies are not aligned with the regime suffer consequences like suppression.[5] From the 1990s, NGOs in the form of Civil Society Organisations (CSOs) were formed in the diaspora in Myanmar's neighbouring countries.[6]

Most of the organisations were based on ethnic grounds, and mostly focused on humanitarian assistance, womens' rights and the environment.[7] However, they also started to document gross abuses of human rights and carried out transnational advocacy for accountability.[8] Generally, civil society in Myanmar is dominated primarily by Bamar-dominated NGOs and other ethnically orientated NGOs.[9]

Transnational networks were also vital in the work of NGOs in Myanmar, creating links between local NGOs and INGOs. Empirical studies show that most transnational networks and NGO coalitions developed as a result of increased donor presence in Myanmar's transition.[10] Notable local NGOs involved in such networks included the Forum for Democracy in Burma (FDB), Asian Forum for Human Rights and Development (Forum-Asia) and Alternative ASEAN Network on Burma (ALTSEAN-Burma).[11]

Transnational networks were further reflected in the formation of the Burma Partnership (formerly known as the Asia-Pacific Peoples' Partnership on Burma) in 2006, with NGO partnerships across Asia-Pacific region.[12] Another notable coordinating body for such networks was the Network for Human Rights Documentation—Burma (ND Burma), whose vision is to 'Achieve government recognition, redress and guarantees of non-recurrence for victims of human rights violations'.[13] ND Burma includes:

> AAPP [the Assistance Association of Political Prisoners], Burma Issues, Chin Human Rights Organisation, Human Rights Foundation of Monland, Kachin Women's Association – Thailand, Lahu Women's Organisation, Palaung Women's Organisation and Ta'ang Students and Youth Organisation ... All Arakan Students' and Youths' Congress, Pao Youth Organisation,

[4] Fink and Simpson (2017, pp. 257–267).

[5] Fink and Simpson (2017, p. 258).

[6] Fink and Simpson (2017, p. 260).

[7] Fink and Simpson (2017, p. 260).

[8] Fink and Simpson (2017, p. 260).

[9] Palmer (2020, p. 117).

[10] Simion (2019, p. 135).

[11] Dale and Samuel-Nakka (2017, p. 329).

[12] Dale and Samuel-Nakka (2017, p. 329).

[13] See ND-Burma website https://nd-burma.org/about-us/.

> Earthrights International, and Equality Myanmar (formerly the Human Rights Education Institute of Burma).[14]

From a transitional justice perspective, it is important to understand their perceptions on international accountability mechanisms. It is reported that the NGOs also informed the local communities about Myanmar's obligations under international law, and the available remedies for the victims of gross human rights violations.[15]

Due to ongoing armed conflict, the scope of NGO work and spaces varied, depending on whether the State had control over their territory.[16] What this dilemma means is that local NGOs risk getting co-opted by the state. Indeed, Stephen McCarthy argues that 'NGOs operating in government-controlled areas focused on local welfare issues and remained apolitical, partly to ensure their own survival'.[17]

Local NGOs were also vulnerable to the same ethno-social biases, like the wider populations.[18] Fink and Simpson note that:

> not all ethnic armed groups were enthusiastic about independent civil society groups emerging in their areas of control; like the regime, they did not appreciate public criticism, nor did they like having to compete with civil society groups for new recruits.[19]

The situation within the local communities was not any different from that at the national level. Even though Thein Sein's government opened up spaces for NGOs and was willing to allow them widen the scope of their activities, the military still maintained a grip on their work.[20] Examples of active NGOs at the time include Gender Equality Network, Election Education and Observation Partners and the People's Alliance for Credible Elections. More generally, the NGOs could not expand the scope of their mandates beyond aspects like the environment, to include elements like accountability.

Some NGOs also worked to promote their ethno-social agendas in the country, for example, the Association for the Protection of Race and Religion formed by Buddhist monks.[21] Similarly, the Emergency Coordination Committee was formed in 2014, comprising of government officials, international humanitarian agency representatives and local NGOs within the Rakhine State.[22] However, the association did not have legitimacy within some communities of the Buddhist Rakhine, who considered the Rohingya as immigrants.[23] This lack of wide legitimacy also has the potential to affect the work of INGOs that partner with local NGOs in the field of transitional

[14] Dale and Samuel-Nakka (2017, p. 329).

[15] Fink and Simpson (2017, p. 260).

[16] McCarthy (2015, p. 715).

[17] McCarthy (2015, p. 716).

[18] South (2008, pp. 37–38).

[19] Fink and Simpson (2017, p. 360).

[20] Fink and Simpson (2017, p. 261).

[21] Fink and Simpson (2017, p. 264).

[22] Fink and Simpson (2017, p. 264).

[23] Fink and Simpson (2017, p. 264).

justice. Nonetheless, local NGOs continue to play an intermediary function on behalf of foreign development actors working on rule of law programmes.[24]

Whilst the democratic transition to the NLD government in 2016 brought hopes for the opening up of more NGO spaces, there remained a challenge of harmonising perceptions of national reconciliation held by multiple and competing NGOs.[25] The active role of the military in the State affairs cannot be underestimated in the limited operation of local NGOs in Myanmar. Scholars researching on NGOs in authoritarian contexts are thus cautioned about the need to understand their unique challenges and limitations.[26]

Kristina Simion's socio-legal work identifies and locates a unique dimension of NGO work, in the form of intermediaries in Myanmar's democratic transition. Using qualitative methodological approaches, she traces the genesis of such actors to the emergence of rule of law programmes implemented in Myanmar by foreign development actors around 2012 and 2013.[27] For example, she highlights the opening of a country office and recruitment of an International Legal Adviser in Myanmar's capital Yangon, by the International Commission of Jurists.[28] In sum, despite the challenges faced by NGOs working within Myanmar, they remain critical actors in documenting and shaping local discourses on expressions of transitional justice.[29]

Local NGOs have a limit in terms of the scope of their work, specifically Rohingya-related justice initiatives. As the violence towards the Rohingya also draws on ethno-religious dimensions, local NGOs have to take cautious approaches. Kristina Simion's empirical study reveals that local NGOs deem Rohingya-related advocacy as too sensitive and risky.[30] Similarly, transnational coalitions are also affected, as local NGOs can be perceived as promoting the interests of foreign actors.[31]

Nickey Diamond, a Myanmar activist who worked with Fortify Rights in the country, argues that accountability mechanisms for the Rohingya are viewed by local politicians as forms of Western imperialism.[32] He also shows that prominent local NGOs were sympathetic towards Aung San Suu Kyi, arguing that; '…speaking out in favour of justice and accountability for the Rohingya has been seen as going against Suu Kyi and the NLD'.[33] Before the military coup in 2021, Fortify Rights was the organisation with local staff within Myanmar working on issues of accountability for crimes committed by the military.[34] In sum, the space for local NGOs to engage in transitional justice for the Rohingya in Myanmar is narrow.

---

[24] Simion (2019, pp. 131–133).

[25] Fink and Simpson (2017, p. 265).

[26] McCarthy (2015, p. 725).

[27] Simion (2021, p. 128) and Simion (2021).

[28] Simion (2019, p. 129).

[29] Renshaw (2019, pp. 142–146).

[30] Simion (2019, p. 134).

[31] Simion (2019, p. 135).

[32] Diamond (2021, pp. 379, 384).

[33] Diamond (2021, p. 386).

[34] Interview with Nickey Diamond, 23 May 2022.

The aim of this sub-section has been to show the context of NGO work within Myanmar, with particular reference to humanitarian work, democratisation and development. It has also shown the merits and failings of the NGOs, due to the polarised ethno-religious dimensions. The challenge of the limited NGO spaces in transitional justice is symptomatic of the incomplete democratisation process. Whilst the spaces for transitional justice-related work are narrow, transnational NGO networks provide a starting foundation to analyse the Rohingya transitional justice mechanisms.

This line of research is particularly important considering the mixed perspectives from practitioners and scholars, regarding the implementation of international justice and role of foreign actors in the Rohingya situation.[35] As such, the discussions in the next sub-section will explore the work of Rohingya activists in the diaspora and in mainly international NGOs. In order not to take transitional justice as a discursive tool with little practical meaning for contexts like that of the Rohingya, the scope of the examination is wide, to capture the work of multiple NGO actors across the globe. The idea is to show that both local and international NGOs are part and parcel of the transitional justice process. In sum, the focus and content of the book is on transnational networks and NGOs outside the territory of Myanmar, which work on justice-related initiatives for the Rohingya. Notably, diaspora networks advocate for human rights and accountability. For instance, the Global Rohingya Initiative which amplifies voices of Rohingya activists in the diaspora community led by Azeem Ibrahim.[36] Transnational networks highlighted the impact of multinational companies like Meta on the Rohingya genocide, showing how the social media platforms (Facebook) were utilised by the military government to drive hate speech against them.[37]

2 Universal Jurisdiction Case in Argentina: Diaspora NGO Network and Transitional Justice

As highlighted in the first chapter of the book, NGOs can play an important role in litigating universal jurisdiction.[38] With regard to the Rohingya situation, NGOs filed a case of universal jurisdiction in Argentina on 13 November 2019 (Argentina case). The Burmese Rohingya Organisation UK (BROUK) petitioned Argentinean courts to open criminal investigations into the crimes committed against the Rohingya by both State and non-State actors in Myanmar.[39]

BROUK is a London-based NGO, established by diaspora Rohingya, advocating for the human rights of the Rohingya in Myanmar. They also aim to achieve justice

[35] Mennecke and Stensrud (2021, pp. 111–130) and Diamond (2021, pp. 379–386).

[36] Ibrahim (2024, p. 4).

[37] For more details see Schissler (2024, pp. 1–26).

[38] Bekou (2015, pp. 219–227).

[39] Burmese Rohingya Organization UK (2019).

and accountability for the crimes and atrocities committed against the Rohingya.[40] More notably, BROUK invoked the principle of universal jurisdiction against individuals:

> criminally responsible for the crimes internationally designated as GENOCIDE and CRIMES AGAINST HUMANITY, committed against the ROHINGYA community in the territory of Myanmar, as a minimum in the period spanning from the year 2012 to the year 2018.[41]

Maung Tun Khin, the founder and President of the BROUK highlights the importance of the universal jurisdiction case:

> A case in Argentina, however, would be able to investigate to full range of crimes committed against the Rohingya. Such crimes include torture, enforced disappearances, murders, rapes and other inhuman acts of a similar nature – these have all been committed in Rakhine State, but no element of them were cross-border in nature. Our case file also includes a criminal complaint of genocide, something currently not within the scope of the ICC investigation.[42]

From a transitional justice perspective, the Argentina case aimed to address a legacy of violations against the Rohingya, including the criminal responsibility of former Presidents Htin Kyaw and Thein Sein, as well as State Counsellor Aung San Suu Kyi.[43] In the Argentina case, BROUK were legally represented by a former United Nations Special Rapporteur on the human rights situation in Myanmar, Tomás Ojea Quintana. The case was also supported by two Latin American NGOs—*Las Abuelas de Plaza de Mayo* (Grandmothers of the Plaza de Mayo) and the *Fundación Servicio Paz y Justicia* (Foundation for Justice and Peace). In a nutshell, it was not just a BROUK case, but rather a conflation of international efforts, using universal jurisdiction against Myanmar.

NGOs played a key role in the Argentina case, through the filing of *amicus curiae* opinions on legal and factual issues. The Robert F. Kennedy Human Rights organisation and Fortify Rights made a compelling case on the importance of universal jurisdiction, but also showed the jurisdictional limitations of the ICC Prosecutor's investigations into the crimes against the Rohingya.[44] Similarly, an a*micus curiae* was submitted to the Federal Criminal Appeals Court in Argentina on 23 August 2021, by six Rohingya NGOs based in Cox's Bazar District, Bangladesh: the Arakan Rohingya Society for Peace and Human Rights, Rohingya Youth for Legal Action, Rohingya Women Development Forum, Rohingya Women's Empowerment and Advocacy

[40] See Burmese Rohingya Organization UK (BROUK) website https://www.brouk.org.uk/who-we-are/.

[41] See BROUK Complaint file, 13 November 2019, available at: https://burmacampaign.org.uk/media/Complaint-File.pdf.

[42] Khin (2020).

[43] Burmese Rohingya Organization UK (2019).

[44] See *amicus curiae* by RFK Human Rights and Fortify Rights accessed at https://www.fortifyrights.org/mya-inv-stm-2021-09-30/.

Network, Rohingya Student Unity and Rights, and the Rohingya Peace Innovation Unity.[45]

It is important to note that on 12 July 2021, the Court of First Instance in Buenos Aires rejected the arguments for universal jurisdiction, on the basis that Myanmar's national transitional justice mechanisms and the ongoing ICC investigations were sufficient avenues for justice.[46] The NGOs provided legal justifications in an appeal before the Federal Criminal Appeals Court, arguing *inter alia* that:

> if the current case is discontinued, there will be no avenue for obtaining justice for survivors of sexual violence, the majority of whom stand to be excluded from both local transitional justice processes and the case at the ICC.[47]

On 26 November 2021, the Second Chamber of the Federal Criminal Court in Buenos Aires overturned the lower court ruling and opened investigations into crimes committed against the Rohingya.[48] Suffice to note, other countries could be used as forums for universal jurisdiction to provide accountability for the Rohingya, mirroring the Argentina case. However, for this to happen, the countries need to have an enabling environment for universal jurisdiction, legal and financial resources, the presence of the accused or victims, and the political will to implement transitional justice.[49]

In 2023, Fortify Rights and 16 individual complainants from Myanmar filed a complaint in Germany under the principle of universal jurisdiction, against senior Myanmar military generals and others for genocide, war crimes and crimes against humanity. The Federal Public Prosecutor General of Germany dismissed the complaint as the suspects were not within the jurisdiction, but also on the basis that there were already ongoing investigations under the Independent Investigative Mechanism on Myanmar (IIMM).[50] One thing that can be deduced from this global justice is the central importance of well-coordinated and intensive advocacy by transnational networks.

Transnational networks also draw a link between the case of universal jurisdiction in Argentina and other justice mechanisms at the ICC and ICJ. Firstly, they show that because of the jurisdictional limits of the ICC in the Bangladesh/Myanmar situation, a range of crimes like sexual violence would not be addressed—The ICC investigation is in respect to crimes related to the forced deportation of Rohingya from Rakhine State (Myanmar is not a State party to the Rome Statute of the ICC).[51] Secondly, the

---

[45] See *amicus curiae* by Arakan Rohingya Society for Peace and Human Rights and others, https://www.victimadvocatesinternational.org/wp-content/uploads/2021/08/Amicus-English-version.firma-digital-2.pdf; For a summarised analysis see Dwyer (2021).

[46] *Amicus curiae* by Arakan Rohingya Society for Peace and Human Rights and others, para 2.

[47] *Amicus curiae* by Arakan Rohingya Society for Peace and Human Rights and others, para 3.

[48] Burmese Rohingya Organization UK (2021).

[49] See Keene-McCann and Chandran (2023, pp. 132–162).

[50] See Fortify Rights (2023) for a comprehensive statement on the complaint and Prosecutor's decision.

[51] See *amicus curiae* by Arakan Rohingya Society for Peace and Human Rights and others, paras. 15–20.

NGOs posit that any findings of fact arising from the proceedings in the Argentina Courts would support the ICJ in determining Myanmar's state responsibility under the Genocide Convention.[52] What can be gathered from these arguments is that NGOs see the different Courts as avenues for transitional justice in Myanmar. This analysis links well with the subject matter of the book, as it shows the contribution of such Transnational Networks and NGOs to the legitimacy of transitional justice in Myanmar.

3 *The Gambia v Myanmar* (ICJ Case): Expanding Horizons for Intervention in International Justice

The ICJ case provides another layer for exploring transnational networks and NGO work in relation to transitional justice for the Rohingya. More specifically, there is a need to map out the transnational coalitions working with the Rohingya.

In general terms, *The Gambia v Myanmar* (ICJ case) is a contentious matter between two States, rather than one seeking an advisory opinion on a legal issue. Nonetheless, victims' lawyer Eva Buzo provides some interesting recommendations:

> the ICJ does not have outreach capabilities. Victims, however, are largely wanting information on all accountability options, and benefit from understanding more broadly how they all relate to one another. This is a gap where I/NGOs can step in and support the work of the outreach teams.[53]

The genesis of the ICJ case links to broader advocacy efforts by international NGOs. Whilst it is a contentious case before the ICJ, NGOs worked directly with The Gambia before filing the case. A representative of an international NGO asserted that:

> We [the NGO] saw the opportunity for a case at the ICJ, before The Gambia case. We were approaching States about the prospects of bringing a case, and we had generated the legal aspects of the case. As we were doing that, The Gambia emerged … [and] we travelled to The Gambia and discussed with the Minister [Abubacarr Tambadou, then Gambian Attorney General and Minister of Justice] stressing some aspects of genocide.[54]

The above discourse is similar to what is revealed by HRW's Param-Preet Singh, showing how NGOs needed to find a country to file the case at the ICJ.[55] She asserts that:

> We reached out to countries that had ratified the Genocide Convention in Europe, Africa, Asia and the Americas. Then, out of nowhere, the West African nation of Gambia made public their intention to move ahead.[56]

---

[52] See *amicus curiae* by Arakan Rohingya Society for Peace and Human Rights and others, paras. 21–25.

[53] Buzo (2021).

[54] Interview with international NGO representative, 02 April 2021.

[55] Singh and Braunschweiger (2020).

[56] Singh and Braunschweiger (2020).

Moreover, the NGOs did not stop at The Gambia's initiative, but also the lobbied other States to support case.[57]

Myanmar's legal team raised concerns about The Gambia's *prima facie* standing before the Court, arguing that country was acting as a proxy for the Organisation of Islamic Cooperation (OIC). They also seemed to suggest that The Gambia was funded by non-State actors including NGOs:

> The Gambia said nothing about funding. Yesterday, I said that it is unknown which States have donated what to the voluntary fund, or whether the donors are even confined to States. This morning might have been an opportunity for The Gambia to provide some transparency in that respect, but there was complete silence. Not only do we still not know precise amounts contributed by individual donors, we do not even know if the donors include non-State entities such as international organizations, NGOs or even private individuals. We do not even know if The Gambia is spending a single penny of its own resources on these proceedings.[58]

Much as the above allegations are unfolded in law, the explicit reference to the involvement of non-State actors before the ICJ is *inter alia* reflective of the substantial involvement of transnational networks and NGOs in the Rohingya justice mechanisms.

Legal Action Worldwide (LAW) and Global Rights Compliance (GRC) were also pivotal in advocacy around the ICJ case. LAW supports victims, including Rohingya, to access justice through advocacy, strategic litigation, legal empowerment and technical assistance.[59] GRC is equally comprised of international lawyers and experts, whose work includes a Rohingya Accountability Project.[60] In October 2019, LAW and GRC convened sessions with NGOs from Myanmar and overseas, 'to formulate an accountability strategy (both criminal and civil) for the Rohingya through utilising both domestic and international mechanisms'.[61] Such joint initiatives illustrate how global transnational advocacy can legitimise transitional justice mechanisms.

Another intervention by international NGOs relates to their support for Rohingya activists and NGOs to engage with the ICJ proceedings. LAW supported three Rohingya victims to travel from the refugee camps in Cox's Bazar to The Hague for the ICJ hearings on provisional measures, held in December 2019. The organisation considers the presence of Rohingya in the courtroom as 'an acknowledgement of great importance of these proceedings to the Rohingya community'.[62]

A more detailed legal scrutiny and advocacy around the ICJ case is illuminated in the work of the Rohingya Legal Forum (RLF), a global group of activists and jurists with a key interest in the Rohingya issues. According to the RLF, the ICJ is an

---

[57] Singh and Braunschweiger (2020).

[58] See ICJ verbatim record of public sitting of *The Gambia vs Myanmar* case, 12 December 2019.

[59] See LAW's website: https://www.legalactionworldwide.org/where-we-work/rohingya-crisis/.

[60] See GRC's website: https://globalrightscompliance.com/project/the-rohingya-accountability-project/.

[61] Global Rights Compliance (2019).

[62] See statement on LAW's website: https://www.legalactionworldwide.org/where-we-work/rohingya-crisis/.

accessible, appropriate and effective recourse for the Rohingya.[63] The RLF founding group affirms that:

> the action [The Gambia case] offers opportunities for the international community – both States and wider civil society (including, of course, the victims) – to benefit from a sober and law-based treatment of an ongoing and pre-occupying situation of current international relations.[64]

As already highlighted, the ICJ issued an order indicating provisional measures, ordering the Myanmar government to prevent the commission of further atrocities against the Rohingya.[65] LAW explained the ICJ decision to sections of Rohingya refugees in Cox's Bazar, and also translated it into Bangla language.[66] Similarly, RLF provided an informative summary, showing the significance of the order for provisional measures.[67] More notably, the use of the word 'Rohingya' is considered as an implicit push back by the Court on Myanmar government's version, which does not acknowledge the Rohingya.[68]

The International Commission of Jurists also welcomed the order for provisional measures, indicating that it is 'a significant step towards justice for the Rohingya as it imposes specific, legally binding, obligations on Myanmar to take critical steps to protect their rights under the Genocide Convention'.[69] NGOs publicised the ICJ case among the Rohingya, whilst also facilitating discourses about the merits of the ICJ ruling on provisional measures. A representative of an international NGO notes that; 'During the provisional measures hearing, we covered public events and also created space and opportunity for Rohingyas to say what they think [about the ICJ decision]'.[70]

Similarly, NGOs also facilitated the screening of television broadcasts of the events in The Hague, including the ruling on provisional measures. Abdur Rahim, a representative of the local NGO the Arakan Rohingya Society for Peace and Human Rights mentioned that the Rohingya experienced elation after watching the ICJ decision.[71] Even after the decision on provisional measures was made, legal aid NGOs made use of videos dubbed into Rohingya language, explaining the ICJ case within refugee camps in Cox's Bazar.[72] Ultimately, the Rohingya were kept aware of the international justice mechanism, thousands of miles away from them.

On 18 October 2019, an international conclave on Justice and Accountability for Rohingya was held in The Hague, organised by the Centre for Peace and Justice

---

63 See Scheffer et al. (2019).

64 Scheffer et al. (2019, p. 5).

65 *The Gambia v Myanmar*, Request for the indication of provisional measures, International Court of Justice, Order, 23 January 2020, para 86.

66 Interview with LAW representative, 02 May 2021.

67 Ashraph et al. (2020).

68 Ashraph et al. (2020, p. 4).

69 See International Commission of Jurists (2020).

70 Interview with international NGO representative, 02 April 2021.

71 See Radio Free Asia (2020).

72 Hölzl (2020).

of Brac University (CPJ), the Asia Justice Coalition (AJC) and the International Institute of Social Studies (ISS) of Erasmus University Rotterdam.[73] Both NGO and State actors brainstormed on issues of justice and accountability for the Rohingya. A notable feature in the conclave was the public announcement by The Gambian Justice Minister Abubacarr Marie Tambadou, about his country's decision to file a case against Myanmar before the ICJ, under the Genocide Convention.[74] Yasmin Ullah, a Rohingya activist who also served as president of the Rohingya Human Rights Network—an NGO based in Canada, emphasised the need for more participation by the Rohingya in justice and accountability initiatives.[75]

Besides Yasmin Ullah, other notable participants included NGO representatives from: Fortify Rights Myanmar, International Commission of Jurists, BROUK, AI, and Shireen Pervin Huq—a co-founder of womens' activist NGO, Naripokkho (NP). The CPJ is an academic institution based at Brac University in Dhaka. Besides working with academics, the organisation also collaborates with local and international NGOs on issues of accountability and justice for the Rohingya.[76] In regard to the proceedings before the ICJ, organisations like CPJ disseminate information about the case within the Rohingya camps in Bangladesh.[77]

On 6 June 2020, a live virtual conference—The ICJ and The Direction of Rohingya's Plight—was organised by the European Rohingya Council (ERC)—an umbrella organisation of Rohingya activists and NGOs. Among the speakers were Azeem Ibrahim from RLF, Phil Robertson, the Deputy Director of HRW's Asia Division, and Hla Kyaw and Amiba Perveen from the ERC. Besides revisiting the implications of the ruling, the conference also aimed to 'mobilize global coalition of actors, including civil society organisations that are working for the human rights of Rohingya to be realized'.[78]

Three important issues can be deduced from the discussions at the ERC conference. Firstly, Rohingya NGOs were called upon to write directly to the ICJ, to request that 'Myanmar's periodic reports on compliance with the Court's provisional measures order be made public…'[79] In effect, they were advocating against the keeping of Myanmar's compliance reports as confidential. As such, the NGOs were opening up avenues for more scrutiny of the State and transitional justice, using the ICJ order for provisional measures.

The second important point relates to the relationship between The Gambia and the NGOs. The conference called upon:

> The Gambia to co-ordinate closely with Rohingya civil society organizations to ensure that Rohingya voices and the pressing concerns of the Rohingya people, both within and beyond

[73] For a detailed report see Centre for Peace and Justice (2019, 1–55).
[74] Centre for Peace and Justice (2019, p. 3).
[75] Centre for Peace and Justice (2019, p. 39).
[76] Salim (2019).
[77] Interview with NGO representative, 23 March 2021.
[78] European Rohingya Council (2020).
[79] European Rohingya Council (2020).

> Myanmar's borders, are communicated to the ICJ in the course of the proceedings against Myanmar.[80]

The above text shows that the case is not simply a matter between two States, but also creates avenues for non-State actors, i.e. the Rohingya and NGOs, to be represented at the ICJ.

Thirdly, and most important, the conference affirmed the issue of transitional justice in Myanmar. Besides calling upon the intervention of the international community, the conference recognised:

> that the ICJ case and other legal actions in domestic and international courts are part of a broader political process aimed at achieving lasting reforms in Myanmar and justice for the Rohingya, and that legal solutions depend on political will and support from a wide range of actors, including governments and civil society, to succeed.[81]

A lawyer involved in an international investigation in Myanmar raises a concern about the impact of the ICJ case beyond the Rohingya communities: 'Other communities don't understand why it only the Rohingya case and not other communities ... That is going to perpetrate a certain divide between the Rohingya and other communities'.[82]

4 ICC Intervention: Navigating the Limits of International Criminal Justice

As pointed out in chapters "Navigating Justice, Transitional Justice and Global North-South Dimensions" and "Achieving Transitional Justice in Myanmar: Between Accountability and National Reconciliation" of the book, Pre-Trial Chamber III of the ICC authorised the Prosecutor to open investigations for the alleged crimes within the Court's jurisdiction in the Bangladesh/Myanmar situation. It is important to recall that the ICC investigation in the Bangladesh/Myanmar situation only covers specific crimes: crimes against humanity of deportation across the Myanmar-Bangladesh border and persecution on grounds of ethnicity and/or religion against the Rohingya population.[83] The narrow jurisdiction and scope of investigations thus created another opportunity for NGO engagement in transitional justice for the Rohingya. BROUK's president showed a need to complement the ICC investigations, through the case of Universal jurisdiction in Argentina:

> Our case file [the Argentina case] also includes a criminal complaint of genocide, something currently not within the scope of the ICC investigation. Just one specific example of a crime the ICC investigation is unable to look into is the horrific massacre in the village of Tula

[80] European Rohingya Council (2020).

[81] European Rohingya Council (2020).

[82] Interview with international lawyer and investigator, 25 March 2021.

[83] See Decision Pursuant to Article 15 of the Rome Statute on the Authorisation of an Investigation into the Situation in the People's Republic of Bangladesh/Republic of the Union of Myanmar.

Toli, when Tatmadaw soldiers killed hundreds of Rohingya women, men and children on 30 August 2017.[84]

Regardless of the narrow scope of the crimes and Court jurisdiction in the ICC intervention, NGOs have engaged directly in the case.

An important contribution of NGOs in the preliminary assessment at the ICC is illuminated in the use of the term Rohingya. The Chamber acknowledged that the use of the term 'Rohingya' was contested, and the people are often referred to as 'Bengalis'.[85] The Chamber employed the term Rohingya in its decision to refer to the victims individually and collectively, based on different NGO reports from: the Irish Centre for Human Rights (ICHR), the International Crisis Group (ICG), AI, PILPG and Fortify Rights.[86] In theory, NGO factual findings serve as useful guides for the Court's interpretation and discourse on important aspects in the Rohingya situation.

Besides the factual findings, NGOs are also involved in the ICC case by way of *amicus curiae* observations and submissions. The Thayninga Institute for Strategic Studies (TISS), a think tank of Myanmar NGOs, sought leave to file *amicus curiae* submissions to counter the narratives of the Rohingya, whilst legitimising the military's actions against them.[87] Their application was rejected as the submissions did not relate to the legal question on the Court's exercise of jurisdiction under over the deportation of the Rohingya from Myanmar to Bangladesh, and was also filed out of time.[88] Nonetheless, the action and intervention by TISS illustrates that whilst NGOs have a strong interest in the ICC case, their interests may vary, depending on whose views they seek to represent.

In specific reference to the nature and definition of the crime of deportation, detailed submissions were filed by the International Commission of Jurists and the Canadian Partnership for International Justice. A more detailed use of *amicus curiae* observations and submissions is revealed in the work of the Bangladeshi Non-Governmental Representatives (BNGR), a coalition of NGOs. In June 2018, the BNGR submitted observations in support of the Prosecution's Request for a Ruling on Jurisdiction under Article 19(3) of the Rome Statute.[89] They provided useful context in three areas: factual background to Rohingya migration to Bangladesh,

---

[84] See Khin (2020).

[85] Decision Pursuant to Article 15 of the Rome Statute on the Authorisation of an Investigation into the Situation in the People's Republic of Bangladesh/Republic of the Union of Myanmar, para. 13.

[86] Decision Pursuant to Article 15 of the Rome Statute on the Authorisation of an Investigation into the Situation in the People's Republic of Bangladesh/Republic of the Union of Myanmar, paras. 15–17.

[87] See Transmission of an Amicus Curiae Submission from the Thayninga Institute for Strategic Studies, ICC-RoC46(3)-01/18–34-AnxI, 06 August 2018, available on https://www.icc-cpi.int/RelatedRecords/CR2018_03979.PDF.

[88] See Decision on the Request of the Thayninga Institute for Strategic Studies for Leave to Submit Amicus Curiae Observations, ICC-RoC46(3)-01/18, Pre-Trial Chamber I, 10 August 2018, available on https://www.icc-cpi.int/CourtRecords/CR2018_04009.PDF.

[89] See Amicus Curiae Observations by the Bangladeshi Non-Governmental Representatives (pursuant to Rule 103 of the Rules) on the "Prosecution's Request for a Ruling on Jurisdiction

other the crimes besides deportation and Bangladeshi law on territorial jurisdiction.[90] Regarding the issue of other crimes besides deportation, they assert that:

> As will be shown, the victims of acts perpetrated against the Rohingya in Myanmar, which were known and intended to be fatal, actually resulted in the deaths of some victims in Bangladesh; the crimes of murder and extermination in relation to these victims were completed in Bangladesh.[91]

The observations make a case for the expansion of the scope of ICC investigations in the Bangladesh/Myanmar situation. For example, whilst they supported the Prosecution's Request for a Ruling on Jurisdiction under Article 19(3) of the Rome Statute, GRC argued that the approach was narrow.[92] The principal argument is that the investigations should capture crimes of 'apartheid, persecution and genocide perpetrated against the Rohingya during and related to their deportation from Myanmar to Bangladesh'.[93] GRC are the legal representatives of over 400 Rohingya victims (Shanti Mohila).

NGOs representing victims from Tula Toli made observations similar to GRC's Victims' Submissions.[94] A striking element in the observations relates to their role as intermediaries in the situation:

> These submissions are based on first-hand discussions with the victims, all of whom are former residents of the village of Tula Toli … The victims include men and women, ranging in age, and including some leaders of the community. While funding and assistance has been provided by organisations and individuals who have been working with the victims, these organisations and individuals have not sought to supplant their views for those of the victims.[95]

More notably, the observations recognise the need to distinguish individual victim needs and interests from those of NGOs, noting that:

> These views [the victims' views] are to be distinguished from positions expressed by or attributed to "civil society". While some civil society organisations may be well placed to

---

under Article 19(3) of the Statute", available on https://www.icc-cpi.int/CourtRecords/CR2018_03120.PDF.

[90] Amicus Curiae Observations by the Bangladeshi Non-Governmental Representatives (pursuant to Rule 103 of the Rules) on the "Prosecution's Request for a Ruling on Jurisdiction under Article 19(3) of the Statute".

[91] Amicus Curiae Observations by the Bangladeshi Non-Governmental Representatives (pursuant to Rule 103 of the Rules) on the "Prosecution's Request for a Ruling on Jurisdiction under Article 19(3) of the Statute", para 35.

[92] Submissions on Behalf of the Victims Pursuant to Article 19(3) of the Statute, ICC-RoC46(3)-01/18-9, 30 May 2018 (GCR Submissions).

[93] Submissions on Behalf of the Victims Pursuant to Article 19(3) of the Statute, ICC-RoC46(3)-01/18-9, 30 May 2018 (GCR Submissions), para 152.

[94] Observations on Behalf of Alleged Victims from Tula Toli, ICC-RoC46(3)-01/18-26, 18 June 2018 (Tula Toli Submissions), para. 10.

[95] Observations on Behalf of Alleged Victims from Tula Toli, ICC-RoC46(3)-01/18-26, 18 June 2018 (Tula Toli Submissions), para. 10.

provide useful input to the Court, their views plainly cannot be equated with those of the victims.[96]

In other words, the NGOs are concerned about the risk of reliance on inhouse lawyers or international NGOs in the distant justice ICC process for the Rohingya.

Another important angle relates to gender aspects and crime. Women's Initiatives for Gender Justice, the European Center for Constitutional and Human Rights and Naripokkho (NP) also submitted observations in support of the Prosecution's Request for a Ruling on Jurisdiction. They provided insights illuminating how Sexual and Gender Based Violence (SGBV) could be linked with the crime of deportation or forcible transfer of Rohingya.[97] From a more general transitional justice perspective, the NGOs show that there is little prospect for the victims to obtain justice in domestic courts.[98]

In terms of judicial impact, the Pre-Trial Chamber III referred to the observations of GRC and International Commission of Jurists, in its interpretation and commentary on the crimes of deportation and forcible transfer.[99] This commentary supports arguments on the contribution of *amicus curie* submissions to the quality of judicial decisions, including at the ICC.[100] Moving away from the direct NGO interventions in judicial proceedings at the ICC, it is also pertinent to explore how they navigate the distant sites of justice—in this case, getting the distant Hague-based institution closer to the Rohingya victims. As highlighted elsewhere, it is important that the larger INGO reports and submissions to the international justice institutions do not obscure the views of the Rohingya affected communities, hence the need for more localised approaches.[101]

Critically, a crucial first step would be to understand the ways in which NGOs localise ICC-related activities. In August 2020, a section of NGOs and victim representatives requested the Pre-Trial Chamber III to consider sitting in another country outside The Netherlands.[102] The NGOs from Cox's Bazar were the Arakan Rohingya Society for Peace and Human Rights, Rohingya Women Empowerment and Advocacy Network, Rohingya Refugee Committee, Rohingya Women for Justice and Peace, Voice of Rohingya, Rohingya Youth for Legal Action, Bangladesh Rohingya

---

[96] Observations on Behalf of Alleged Victims from Tula Toli, ICC-RoC46(3)-01/18-26, 18 June 2018 (Tula Toli Submissions), para. 11.

[97] See Decision on the "Joint Request for Leave to Submit Amicus Curiae Observations pursuant to Rule 103 of the Rules", ICC-RoC46(3)-01/18-15, Pre-Trial Chamber I, 11 June 2018; Joint Observations Pursuant to Rule 103 of the Rules, ICC-RoC46(3)-01/18-15, Pre-Trial Chamber I, 11 June 2018.

[98] See Joint Observations Pursuant to Rule 103 of the Rules, ICC-RoC46(3)-01/18-15, Pre-Trial Chamber I, 11 June 2018, para. 47.

[99] Decision on the "Prosecution's Request for a Ruling on Jurisdiction under Article 19(3) of the Statute", paras. 55, 71.

[100] See for example Williams et al. (2020) and Williams and Palmer (2016, pp. 40–65).

[101] Kirabira and Palmer (2023, p. 221).

[102] Situation in the People's Republic of Bangladesh/Republic of the Union of Myanmar (Victims' joint request concerning hearings outside the host State), ICC-01/19, Pre-Trial Chamber III, 4 August 2020.

Student Union and Rohingya Peace Innovation Unity. Even though the Bangladesh/ Myanmar situation is still in its early stages, one aspect that can be inferred is the feasibility of international court hearings in Bangladesh.

Two important issues can be drawn from this request. Firstly, the desire for NGOs to remain connected with the victims. They submit that:

> The desire to participate and be informed is at the heart of the Victims' preference for eventual ICC proceedings to be held locally. Limiting proceedings to The Hague would necessarily limit the potential for victim involvement, whether as participants or observers. Local ICC proceedings are viewed as allowing for greater participation of the victim community as a whole, and as giving more opportunity for their voices to be heard.[103]

Secondly, the NGOs make an explicit reference to the Court's limited legitimacy or illegitimacy:

> In the intervening two decades, the ICC has at times faced criticism for its delivery of "distant justice", with its remoteness being linked to a perceived illegitimacy among victim communities. Many such criticisms focus on the disadvantages of the Court's physical location, meaning that justice is neither accessible nor visible to victims. Even the Court's supporters have warned that it "runs the risk of seeming remote and of little consequence to the communities most affected".[104]

In its decision, the Chamber held that it was premature to direct the Registry to assess the potential for proceedings outside The Hague.[105] Nonetheless, it acknowledged the need to keep the process within the proximity with the conflict-affected population i.e. Rohingya living in Bangladesh, noting that 'the Chamber will keep the possibility of conducting certain procedural steps in situ under review'.[106] The application for in situ proceedings is not novel, as it also up in the ICC situation in Kenya.[107] In the Rohingya case, the request by NGOs and victims' representatives affirms the desire to keep victims as central actors in the transitional justice mechanisms, whilst maintaining NGOs as mediators.

In light of the February 2021 military coup in Myanmar, it is important to assess the prospects of the ICC investigations. As observed by coordinators within transnational

---

[103] Situation in the People's Republic of Bangladesh/Republic of the Union of Myanmar (Victims' joint request concerning hearings outside the host State), ICC-01/19, Pre-Trial Chamber III, 4 August 2020, para. 53.

[104] Situation in the People's Republic of Bangladesh/Republic of the Union of Myanmar (Victims' joint request concerning hearings outside the host State), ICC-01/19, Pre-Trial Chamber III, 4 August 2020, para.10.They use the example of Human Rights Watch, one of the notable NGOs in support of the ICC. See also Human Rights Watch (2008, pp. 1–243).

[105] Situation in the People's Republic of Bangladesh/Republic of the Union of Myanmar (Decision on Victims' joint request concerning hearings outside the host State), ICC-01/19, Pre-Trial Chamber III, 27 October 2020, para.23.

[106] Situation in the People's Republic of Bangladesh/Republic of the Union of Myanmar (Decision on Victims' joint request concerning hearings outside the host State), ICC-01/19, Pre-Trial Chamber III, 27 October 2020, para.27.

[107] See *Prosecutor v. William Samoei Ruto and Joshua Arap Sang,* Situation in the Republic of Kenya, ICC-01/09-01/11-875, Notification of the Decision of the Plenary of Judges on the "Joint Defence Application for a Change of Place where the Court Shall Sit for Trial", Presidency, Decision, 26 August 2013.

networks, the military have blocked pathways for transitional justice.[108] In August 2021, Myanmar's exile government—the National Unity Government (NUG)—announced that it had lodged a declaration with the ICC, which served to accept the Court's jurisdiction with respect to international crimes in the Myanmar territory since 2002.[109] The NUG is comprised of ousted civilian representatives of the Parliament, following the February 2021 military coup.[110] Ironically, the international NGO Fortify Rights had published a report detailing legal justifications and recommendations for the NUG to delegate jurisdiction to the ICC to investigate the legacy of crimes in Myanmar.[111] Fortify Rights sees NUG's engagement with the ICC as a way of enhancing its own political legitimacy, against that of the military.[112]

Adam Simpson, a researcher on the political economy and democratisation in Myanmar, regards NUG's engagement with the ICC as a significant step in transitional justice for the Rohingya, as it would expand the scope of the Court's investigations.[113] Antonia Mulvey, LAW's Executive Director, supports the NUG's declaration and action, noting that:

> The Rohingya clients that we represent are extremely hopeful that the ICC will accept the NUG's declaration granting jurisdiction of the Court over crimes committed in the country since 2002. This represents an important step towards justice for the community, who have suffered greatly and continue to suffer.[114]

From a more general perspective, NGOs organise outreach and training programmes in Bangladesh, on transitional justice and accountability mechanisms for the Rohingya.[115] Bangladesh is seen as a strategic place for the ICC investigations. As such, the Bangladesh government continues to engage with both NGOs and the ICC. A Representative of Bangladesh at The Hague 2019 conclave noted the enormous pressure on the country is respect to the Rohingya justice processes:

> Bangladesh is a member of the international community just like Myanmar. It should be the responsibility of all nation states and we would expect more understanding from our friends. We do not want to end up a scapegoat or held responsible for a failure that is not ours.[116]

In terms of the community outreach, there were some notable events that impact on the Court's legitimacy. In February 2022, Karim Khan, the new Prosecutor of the ICC, travelled to Bangladesh, where he also visited Cox's Bazar. Whilst meeting with Rohingya women and youth groups, Khan emphasised the need to work collaboratively; 'We are here to work with you to build the foundations of justice. The road to accountability will not be simple, but it is a goal we can only achieve by working

---

108 Gyi and Quadrini (2022).

109 Simpson (2021).

110 For details see NUG website https://www.nugmyanmar.org/en/.

111 Fortify Rights (2021a).

112 Fortify Rights (2021b).

113 Simpson (2021).

114 Legal Action Worldwide (2021).

115 For more details see Salim (2019).

116 Centre for Peace and Justice of Brac University (2019, p. 27).

together, as a partnership between us'.[117] As Emma Palmer notes, there is still a need for the ICC Registry to engage more pro-actively with the affected communities using effective communication strategies that are inclusive and context-sensitive.[118] Scholars recommend the use of victim-centred approach in order for the Rohingya to receive justice.[119]

NGO interventions in the Rohingya justice mechanisms are also negatively affected by the limitations of international justice in general. According to an NGO representative who works directly with Rohingya in the camps, the Rohingya cases show the limits of international justice mechanisms; 'These justice mechanisms move really slowly and don't have the mandate to solve the political problems … e.g. ICC can't order Myanmar to grant them [the Rohingya] citizenship'.[120] Similarly, there are perceptions of the ICC as a symbolic, and not practical avenue for justice, as expressed by an NGO representative working with the Rohingya; 'We think that international justice is important. But it does not stand alone. There is a need for security and political reforms, reconciling Rohingya with other civilians'.[121]

Having discussed the different justice mechanisms for the Rohingya, it is pertinent to address the issue of lack of proximity or distant justice; more specifically, the management of victims' expectations, and their participation in this distant justice. A lawyer involved in an international investigation in Myanmar acknowledges the relevance of NGOs in creating awareness and outreach, but reveals the challenges of multiple NGO actors in the Rohingya situation, noting that:

> NGOs create awareness that we even exist…but maybe to take a little but step back in collecting evidence, and allow the mechanisms to do their work. Myanmar is complicated because there are so many mechanisms working at the same time. Sometimes I wonder whether we are really serving justice.[122]

The narrow scope of the ICC investigation in the situation of Bangladesh/ Myanmar also triggers questions regarding justice for the Rohingya based in other regions. A lawyer involved in international investigations in Myanmar raises concerns about NGO dominance in Bangladesh, with little attention to the Rohingya in other areas like Malaysia and India; 'What about the Rohingya who did not go to Bangladesh? They are not part of the [ICC] case, so they would not qualify for participation, recognition and compensation'.[123] She thus wonders how holistic NGOs are in addressing accountability for the Rohingya.[124]

Rohingya victims' legal representative Eva Buzo provides three practical recommendations to ensure meaningful participation of victims in the various justice mechanisms: development of a long-term engagement plan, coordination among actors

---

[117] See ICC Press Release ICC (2022) on the Prosecutor's first visit to Bangladesh.

[118] Palmer (2024, pp. 355–391).

[119] Pérez-León-Acevedo and Pinto (2022, p. 479).

[120] Interview with NGO representative, 23 March 2021.

[121] Interview with NGO representative, 23 March 2021.

[122] Interview with international lawyer and investigator, 25 March 2021.

[123] Interview with international lawyer and investigator, 25 March 2021.

[124] Interview with international lawyer and investigator, 25 March 2021.

and defining participation.[125] She is equally concerned about the large number of potential victims in the ICC situation:

> The focus of the ICC investigation means there are over 800 000 people who would qualify as a victim, given that any person forcibly deported from Myanmar to Bangladesh in 2016 or 2017 would fulfil the criteria and be entitled to participatory rights.[126]

The above statement indicates a need for wider outreach by the OTP and VPRS. It also points towards a gap in the outreach and engagement with victims, which could be filled by NGOs. From a wider transitional justice perspective, the operating of multiple organisations and investigations in respect to Myanmar and the Rohingya situation raises questions about their efficiency in general.

5 Conclusion

The discussions in this chapter have illustrated that the concept of transitional justice might not seem a concept directly applicable to Myanmar in the current situation, except in the limited sense of potential in relation to atrocities committed against the Rohingya. Therefore, the focus has primarily been on the role of transnational networks and NGOs in achieving transitional justice for the Rohingya and how NGOs impact on the legitimacy of the existing Global justice mechanisms. I have mapped the different NGO actors involved in the Rohingya cases: the ICC investigation into the Bangladesh/Myanmar situation, the ICJ case, and the universal jurisdiction case in Argentina. Whilst the cases in The Hague are considered as vital in the quest for accountability and respect for rights in Myanmar, they are not in themselves the only viable alternatives for transitional justice. Kingsley Abbott, the former director of Global Accountability & International Justice at the International Commission of Jurists made an important observation that: 'It's important to not inflate victims' hopes inappropriately from the very start of the proceedings, or we will disappoint them'.[127] Consequently, in evaluating the different transitional justice mechanisms, the book highlights how the work of institutions like the ICC is legitimised before the Rohingya victims.

References

Application of the Convention on the Prevention and Punishment of the Crime of Genocide (*The Gambia v Myanmar*), Request for the Indication of Provisional Measures, International Court of Justice, 23 Jan 2020

[125] Buzo (2021).

[126] Buzo (2021).

[127] Hölzl (2020).

Ashraph S et al (2020) No place for optimism: anticipating Myanmar's first report to the International Court of Justice. Rohingya Legal Forum, Washington, DC

Bekou O (2015) Doing justice for the liberian victims of mass atrocity: NGOs in aid of universal jurisdiction. J Int Criminal Justice 13:219–227

Burmese Rohingya Organization UK (2019) Argentinean courts urged to prosecute senior Myanmar military and government officials for the Rohingya genocide. Burmese Rohingya Organization UK, London. https://www.brouk.org.uk/argentinean-courts-urged-to-prosecute-senior-myanmar-military-and-government-officials-for-the-rohingya-genocide/

Burmese Rohingya Organization UK (2021) Historic decision by Argentinian courts to take up genocide case against Myanmar. Burmese Rohingya Organization UK, London. https://www.brouk.org.uk/historic-decision-by-argentinian-courts-to-take-up-genocide-case-against-myanmar/

Buzo E (2021) Three ways to improve victim participation in the Rohingya context. Opinio Juris, Geneva. http://opiniojuris.org/2021/07/06/three-ways-to-improve-victim-participation-in-the-rohingya-context/

Centre for Peace and Justice (2019) Report on International Conclave on Justice and Accountability for Rohingya. Centre for Peace and Justice Brac University, Dhaka, pp 1–55

Dale J, Samuel-Nakka S (2017) International non-governmental organisations and advocacy. In: Simpson A, Farrelly N, Holliday I (eds) Routledge handbook of contemporary Myanmar. Routledge, Abingdon, pp 324–334

Decision Pursuant to Article 15 of the Rome Statute on the Authorisation of an Investigation into the Situation in the People's Republic of Bangladesh/Republic of the Union of Myanmar ('the Situation in Bangladesh/Myanmar'), ICC-01/19, Pre-Trial Chamber III | Decision, 14 November 2019 (Authorisation Decision 2019)

Diamond N (2021) The failure to protect in Myanmar: a reflection on national protection of Rohingya against mass atrocity crimes and prospects for the responsibility to protect. Global Responsib Prot 13:379–386

Dwyer R (2021) Rohingya groups submit amicus curiae brief. Victim Advocates International, Amsterdam. https://www.victimadvocatesinternational.org/latest/blog-post-title-four-hnd6b

European Rohingya Council (2020) The ICJ and the direction of Rohingya's plight. European Rohingya Council, Amsterdam. https://progressivevoicemyanmar.org/2020/06/07/the-icj-and-the-direction-of-rohingya-plight/

Fink C, Simpson A (2017) Civil society. In: Simpson A, Farrelly N, Holliday I (eds) Routledge handbook of contemporary Myanmar. Routledge, Abingdon, pp 257–267

Fortify Rights (2021a) Ending impunity in Myanmar: can the National Unity Government of Myanmar delegate jurisdiction to the International Criminal Court? a legal analysis. Fortify Rights, Belfast, ME

Fortify Rights (2021b) Myanmar: engage the International Criminal Court to hold military perpetrators of mass atrocity crimes accountable. Fortify Rights, Belfast, ME. https://www.fortifyrights.org/mya-inv-2021-08-19/

Fortify Rights (2023) Statement: on the dismissal of the criminal complaint filed in Germany against Myanmar generals and others for genocide, war crimes, and crimes against humanity, Fortify Rights, Belfast, ME

Global Rights Compliance (2019) Gambia argues use of forced starvation against the Rohingya in its ICJ submissions. Global Rights Compliance, London. https://starvationaccountability.org/news-and-events/gambia-argues-use-of-forced-starvation-against-the-rohingya-in-its-icj-submissions

Gyi H, Quadrini M (2022) Myanmar's junta is blocking pathways for transitional justice, Myanmar Now. https://myanmar-now.org/en/news/myanmars-junta-is-blocking-pathways-for-transitional-justice/

Hölzl V (2020) Three years after Rohingya exodus, mismatched expectations of justice. The New Humanitarian, Geneva. https://www.thenewhumanitarian.org/news-feature/2020/08/24/Bangladesh-Myanmar-Rohingya-international-justice

Human Rights Watch (2008) Courting history: the landmark international criminal court's first years. Human Rights Watch, New York, pp 1–243
Ibrahim A (2024) Introduction. In: The accountability, politics, and humanitarian toll of the Rohingya genocide. The New Lines Institute, Washington, DC
ICC (2019) ICC judges authorise opening of an investigation into the situation in Bangladesh/Myanmar. ICC Website. https://www.icc-cpi.int/Pages/item.aspx?name=pr1495
ICC (2022) ICC Prosecutor, Karim A. A. Khan QC, concludes first visit to Bangladesh, underlines commitment to advance investigations into alleged atrocity crimes against the Rohingya. ICC Website. https://www.icc-cpi.int/Pages/item.aspx?name=20220301-otp-press-release-bangladesh
ICC-RoC46(3)-01/18-37 06 September 2018 | Pre-Trial Chamber I | Decision
ICJ Verbatim Record of Public Sitting of The Gambia vs Myanmar Case, 11 Dec 2019
International Commission of Jurists (2020) Myanmar: implement "provisional measures" order of the International Court of Justice without delay. International Commission of Jurists, Geneva
International Committee of the Red Cross (2006) Myanmar: ICRC Pressed to close field offices. International Committee of the Red Cross, Geneva
Keene-McCann J, Chandran A (2023) Identifying 'other Argentinas': variables in considering universal jurisdiction forum states. In: Hasan M, Murshed S, Pillai P (eds) The Rohingya crisis humanitarian and legal approaches. Routledge, Abingdon, pp 132–162
Khin T (2020) Universal Jurisdiction, the International Criminal Court, and the Rohingya Genocide. Opinio Juris, Geneva. http://opiniojuris.org/2020/10/23/universal-jurisdiction-the-international-criminal-court-and-the-rohingya-genocide/
Kirabira T, Palmer E (2023) NGO roles in achieving transitional justice for crimes against the Rohingya. In: Hasan M, Murshed S, Pillai P (eds) The Rohingya crisis humanitarian and legal approaches. Routledge, Abingdon, pp 211–236
Kramer T (2011) Civil society gaining ground: opportunities for change and development. Transnational Institute, Drukkerij PrimaveraQuint, Amsterdam, pp 1–54
Legal Action Worldwide (2021) LAW: More than 500 Rohingya request ICC prosecutor accept NUG declaration. Legal Action Worldwide, London. https://www.legalactionworldwide.org/accountability-rule-of-law/law-icc-victim-submission-for-rohingya-clients-following-nug-declaration/
McCarthy S (2015) The limits of civil society in militarised regimes: evidence from the Asia-Pacific. Australian J Int Affairs 69:711–728
Mennecke M, Stensrud E (2021) The failure of the international community to apply R2P and atrocity prevention in Myanmar. Global Responsib Prot 13:111–130
Palmer E (2020) Adapting International Criminal Justice in Southeast Asia: beyond the International Criminal Court. Cambridge University Press, Cambridge, pp 1–327
Palmer E (2024) Disconnect: the International Criminal Court's engagement in the situation in Bangladesh/Myanmar. Int Criminal Law Rev 24:355–391
Pérez-León-Acevedo JP, Pinto TA (2022) Disentangling law and religion in the Rohingya case at the International Criminal Court. Nordic J Human Rights 39:458–480
Radio Free Asia (2020) Rohingya refugees hail world court's ruling in Myanmar genocide case. Radio Free Asia. BenarNews, Washington, DC. https://www.rfa.org/english/news/myanmar/refugees-01232020155348.html
Renshaw C (2019) Myanmar's transition without justice. In: Kent L, Wallis J, Cronin C (eds) Civil society and transitional justice in Asia and the Pacific. ANU Press, Canberra, pp 127–153
Salim R (2019) CPJ and Naripokkho organised training on 'accountability for serious human rights violations in Asia'—CPJ. Centre for Peace and Justice Brac University, Dhaka. https://cpj.bracu.ac.bd/news/cpj-and-naripokkho-organised-training-on-accountability-for-serious-human-rights-violations-in-asia/
Scheffer D et al (2019) The International Court of Justice and the duty to prevent and punish the Rohingya Genocide. Rohingya Legal Forum, Washington, DC

Schissler M (2024) Beyond hate speech and misinformation: Facebook and the Rohingya Genocide in Myanmar. J Genocide Res 27(3):445–470
Simion K (2019) Bottom-up explorations: locating rule of law intermediaries after transition in Myanmar. J Burma Stud 23:125–141
Simion K (2021) Rule of law intermediaries: brokering influence in Myanmar. Cambridge University Press, Cambridge
Simpson A (2021) Myanmar's exile government signs up to ICC prosecutions. East Asia Forum, Canberra
Singh P, Braunschweiger A (2020) Interview: landmark world court order protects Rohingya from genocide. Human Rights Watch, New York. https://www.hrw.org/news/2020/01/27/interview-landmark-world-court-order-protects-rohingya-genocide
South A (2008) Civil society in Burma: the development of democracy amidst conflict. Institute of Southeast Asian Studies, Singapore, East–West Center, Honolulu
Williams S, Palmer E (2016) Civil society and amicus curiae interventions in the International Criminal Court. Acta Juridica 1:40–65
Williams S, Woolaver H, Palmer E (2020) The Amicus Curiae in International Criminal Justice, 1st edn. Bloomsbury Publishing, London

Comparing Uganda and Myanmar Contexts: Challenges in Localising Transitional Justice

1 Introduction: Justice During Transition

The two case studies reveal interesting questions concerning variants of transitional justice: when, to whom and for what transitional justice applies. I use these variants or categories as a starting point to compare and contrast the findings in the book. When does transitional justice apply? In this case, the analysis shows the nature of transitional justice—whether transiting from authoritarianism to democracy or from armed conflict to peace. To whom does transitional justice apply? The analysis will show constructions of transitional justice and its jurisdictional limits. As to what transitional justice applies, the discussions will show the scope of transitional justice in both case studies.

A common theme in both cases is the link between transitional justice and post-conflict peacebuilding. Whilst Northern Uganda is transitioning from a two-decade war, the case of Myanmar rotates around justice following periods of armed violence in Northern Rakhine, leading to a massive exodus of Rohingya from the region. Following the periods of mass atrocities and armed conflict, a range of judicial and non-judicial mechanisms were implemented, as highlighted in the preceding chapters. The limitations of peacebuilding and transitional justice in the two countries elicit discussions on how to construct transitional justice that resonates with the contextual realities in the Global South.

Whilst peacebuilding has been observed as a crucial component to transitional justice in both cases, there are some variations regarding the actual implementation of transitional justice. Uganda implemented legalised approaches, specifically criminal prosecutions of rebel leaders in Northern Uganda, as a way of providing justice to the victims. Nonetheless, the language and practice of reconciliation are also prominent, as evidenced in the application of amnesties and traditional reconciliation mechanisms. In 2015, there were Nationwide Ceasefire Agreement (NCA) negotiations

This chapter has some overlaps with my doctoral thesis.

© The Author(s), under exclusive license to Springer Nature Singapore Pte Ltd. 2025

T. R. Kirabira, *Transnational Networks and Justice in the Global South*, International Law and the Global South, https://doi.org/10.1007/978-981-95-3137-0_7

between the Myanmar government and a section of leaders of the Ethnic Armed Organizations (EAO).[1] Just like the Juba peace talks of Uganda, the agreement in Myanmar did not take root, as evidenced by the persistence of armed conflict in the following years. In Myanmar, the process of transitional justice is thus largely dependent on the intervention of external actors. The prominent practice and discourse on transitional justice in Myanmar, as evidenced in chapters "Achieving Transitional Justice in Myanmar: Between Accountability and National Reconciliation" and "Mapping NGO Work in Myanmar: Impact of Transnational NGO Networks", is mostly centred on formal accountability mechanisms at The Hague. The case of Myanmar is consistent with a liberal ideology of transitional justice, largely comprised of legalised and atrocity justice approaches.[2] This dominance is not surprising, considering the contemporary challenges in the democratisation process in Myanmar, as shown in the above discussions.

The two case studies show a close connection between political transition and post-conflict peacebuilding and justice. As was shown in chapters "The Case of Uganda: A Fusion of Domestic Transitional Justice and International Criminal Law" and "Actor-Oriented Analysis of Accountability Mechanisms in Uganda", transitional justice in Uganda was largely construed as post-conflict peacebuilding and justice following the LRA war in Northern Uganda. However, the findings show that the country is still grappling with the legacy of the conflict, and the government maintained a particular narrative of the conflict. I posited that the process of transitional justice in Uganda is both contested and incomplete, which has complicated the (de)legitimisation process of the different mechanisms. Turning to the case of Myanmar, the element of transition in largely considered as a movement from oppressive military rule. Many of the NGO reports detail the need for urgent restoration of democratic rule in Myanmar. Similarly, a majority of the elites interviewed expressed little hope in achieving transitional justice for the Rohingya, without a comprehensive democratic transition in Myanmar. Yet, it appears from the same data set, that transitional justice would not be possible without integration of peacebuilding initiatives for the rebuilding of the conflict-affected communities in Northern Uganda and Northern Rakhine in Myanmar.

Another important point of comparison relates to the timeframes employed for transitional justice. This line of comparison is helpful in understanding how transitional justice links with peacebuilding, but also useful when planning for transformative or socio-economic justice approaches. Transitional justice in Uganda has greatly evolved since the Juba Peace talks in 2006–2008. The immediate goal at the time was the restoration of peace in Northern Uganda, at the height of the LRA war. However, there were also long-term plans for justice, as evidenced in the decision to create a domestic war crimes court to deal with the legacies. In terms of policy, it was not until 2019 that Uganda adopted a formal Transitional Justice Policy to

---

[1] See Agreement via https://www.refworld.org/legal/agreements/natlegbod/2015/en/147771 The NCA was signed between the civilian government of President Thein Sein, the military and eight ethnic armed organizations (EAO).

[2] For more details see Sharp (2015, pp. 159–160).

guide the implementation of a range of issues, including reparations. The divergence in the timeframes has complicated the (de)legitimisation process of the different mechanisms.

Whilst the case of Uganda demonstrates a shift from the urgency of peace-building to long-term transformation, the findings in Myanmar show a bleak picture of transitional justice. The urgency of the addressing ethnic tensions and violence necessitated the adoption of short-term strategies in Myanmar. As highlighted in chapter "Actor-Oriented Analysis of Accountability Mechanisms in Uganda", the Annan-led commission provided recommendations within five thematic areas: 'conflict prevention, humanitarian assistance, reconciliation, institution building and development'.[3] More notably, it acknowledged the need for long-term conflict transformation in the regions, with inter-communal dialogue among the ethnic groups in Northern Rakhine State.[4] The empirical findings in this book lend credence to such recommendations. For example, an NGO representative working with Rohingya refugees in Bangladesh noted that: 'We think that international justice is important. But it does not stand alone. There is need for security and political reforms … There is also social reform … reconciling the Rohingya with other civilians'.[5]

Both case studies show a nexus between mass displacement and transitional justice. In Uganda, a lot of focus was placed on addressing the needs of formerly displaced persons. One of the primary areas of focus for the International Criminal Court (ICC) case was on attacks by the LRA on IDP camps. Ongwen was also charged for crimes committed during attacks on IDP camps. For the case of Myanmar, a lot of focus was placed on the Rohingya refugees in Bangladesh, including the ICC investigations into the deportation and forcible transfer of people. Juxtaposing the two cases shows the complexity of adopting transitional justice during contexts of displacement. Overall, the findings in the two case studies raise interesting questions concerning transitional justice within the context of mass displacement. For instance, how do the different justice mechanisms contribute to the resettlement of the conflict-affected communities? How do the experiences of displaced victims inform their perceptions on transitional justice? As was shown in the Rohingya case, victims of gross human rights violations and international crimes may not appreciate the justice strategies, unless they can lead to their long-term goals—in this case repossession of land.

Looking at the timeframes for transitional justice in these two cases reminds us on the need to address the socio-economic needs of the conflict-affected communities, which is framed as transformative justice.[6] What this means, in Pádraig McAuliffe's words, is that the approaches might have to shift 'from "Urgent" Justice to "Late Justice"'.[7] Against this backdrop, a view of transitional justice in Myanmar entirely

[3] See Final Report of the Advisory Commission on Rakhine State (2017, p. 12).

[4] Final Report of the Advisory Commission on Rakhine State (2017, p. 50).

[5] Interview with NGO representative, 23 March 2021.

[6] See for generally Lai and Bonora (2019), Baines and Oliveira (2020, pp. 341–361) and Gready and Robins (2014, pp. 339–361).

[7] McAuliffe (2021, p. 819).

along the line of democratic change would make transformative or socio-economic justice irrelevant within the context of the Rohingya. Similarly, the ability of transitional justice to redress structural injustice against the Rohingya and other ethnic minorities would need to be embedded in the wider national transitional justice policies and projects for economic and social transformation in the country.

The findings thus reinvigorate scholarly suggestions for long-term plans by all stakeholders in order to achieve social-economic justice and implement structural changes.[8] Uganda is therefore a classic example on how long-term transitional justice can be achieved, beyond the narrow purview of immediate post-conflict interventions. As was shown in chapter "Actor-Oriented Analysis of Accountability Mechanisms in Uganda", there has been increased institutional strength for domestic prosecution of war crimes and crimes against humanity in Uganda, following the domestication of the Rome Statute. However, in terms of transformative justice, there is still a lot of work to be done to rehabilitate the post-war-affected communities in Northern Uganda.

As the analysis for both case studies has demonstrated, the element of transition, in itself, hinges on interdependent relations among all key stakeholders—victims, conflict-affected communities, NGOs, State actors, etc. Uganda only adopted a national Transitional Justice Policy in 2019, and is yet to adopt a formal law to support its implementation. In Myanmar, the legal exclusion of the Rohingya from citizenship remains a key stumbling block to reconciliation. As such, we cannot consider transitional justice in isolation from this dilemma. Moreover, the country is still far from being a paradigmatic transition to democracy, due to the military coup of February 2021. Crucially, the dynamics of institutional reform necessitate long-term considerations, if structural changes are to be achieved. As such, transition is not simply a linear notion of time where the past is wiped out in a few years. This observation somewhat lends credence to scholarly calls for transformative approaches to transitional justice, with long-term commitments to reform.[9]

2 Ethno-Cultural and Religious Dynamics in Transitional Justice

Besides aspects of time and temporality in transitional justice, it is interesting to see how local and cultural particularities affect the process of transitional justice. The more pertinent question is how local and cultural particularities affect the perceived legitimacy of the mechanisms. The Ugandan case demonstrated a delicate balance between reconciliation based on local traditions on one hand, and achieving justice on the other. Like Uganda, the case study of Myanmar also shows that armed conflict has links to ethnic cleavages. An exploration of Myanmar's political history showed deeply entrenched ethno-religious divides between the Rohingya and other ethnic

[8] McAuliffe (2021, p. 838).

[9] McAuliffe (2021, pp. 817–847).

groups in the Rakhine region. Whilst some NGOs inside Myanmar promote their ethno-social agendas,[10] the analysis also showed that there is limited involvement of other ethnic groups in the justice initiatives for the Rohingya.

The transitional justice context of Northern Uganda, as discussed in chapter "The Case of Uganda: A Fusion of Domestic Transitional Justice and International Criminal Law", is predominantly focused on the Acholi ethnic group. The traditional justice mechanisms that were implemented, such as *Mato Oput*, were also based on the Acholi cultures and traditions. The four crime scenes in Dominic Ongwen's case at the ICC are also located in the Acholi sub-region of Uganda. Another angle can be drawn from the choice of stakeholders that work with transitional justice institutions. An NGO founder interviewed noted that: 'Most organisations that got funding were from Lira [another district in Northern Uganda], because they were not hostile to the ICC'.[11] It is important to note that Dominic Ongwen, the rebel commander tried and convicted by the ICC, hails from the Acholi region, whose main city is Gulu. Similarly, a lot of the transitional justice-related work was implemented in the Acholi region. Going by the concerns of the NGO leader interviewed, it would appear illogical for actors from other ethnic groups to get involved in the transitional justice activities in the Acholi region.

The discourse and practice on transitional justice for the Rohingya are not an exception from the ethnic paradigms. An international criminal lawyer and investigator involved in the Myanmar case raised important concerns when asked about the relevance of The Hague-based justice mechanisms, saying that 'Other communities [ethnic minorities] do not understand why it is only the Rohingya case and not other communities'.[12] What is more critical in her view is the potential for more ethnic divides as a result of these targeted transitional justice approaches.[13] A comparative reference by the international criminal lawyer to another context of Kenya also serves as a useful illustration on the fusion of cultural and transitional justice. According to her, 'the Kenyan cases [ICC intervention] were embarrassing because the Prosecution did not know about Kenyan culture'.[14] The example used here is relevant for the Rohingya context, since the transitional justice in Kenya was meant to address post-election violence that hinged on ethnic divisions.[15]

The focus by The Hague-based justice mechanisms on the Rohingya ethnic group can be attributed to the massive influx of refugees into neighbouring Bangladesh in the past years, but also the reports suggesting genocide committed by the State officials. Against this background, the concerns about the prioritisation of the Rohingya by the international community seem far-fetched. A founder of an NGO representing Rohingya victims in Bangladesh, who was also involved in The Hague-based justice

[10] Fink and Simpson (2017, p. 264).

[11] Interview, 3 May 2021.

[12] Interview, 2 May 2021.

[13] Interview, 2 May 2021.

[14] Interview, 2 May 2021.

[15] A number of scholars have written about the ICC backlash in Kenya. See De Vos (2020, pp 147–194), Bosire and Lynch (2014, pp. 256–276), and Oloka-Onyango (2020, pp. 41–68).

mechanisms, was optimistic about inter-communal reconciliation following the International Court of Justice (ICJ) ruling on preliminary measures in January 2020.[16] She asserted that 'the immediate outcome was that the other ethnic groups, when they saw that the Rohingya went to the ICJ, they came out in solidarity, e.g. the Karen'.[17] This observation affirms earlier statements issued by the Karen Grassroots Women's Network (KGWN) welcoming the legal action against Myanmar in The Hague, as a way for transitional justice in the country.[18] Along these lines, the findings in both case studies reveal the cultural underpinnings of transitional justice, and more broadly, the impact of NGOs on its legitimacy.

Besides ethnicity, religion is a key feature of transitional justice in both contexts. The findings in the preceding chapters illustrate a common pattern in respect to the fusion of religion in transitional justice. The case of Uganda exemplifies a great involvement of religious actors and leaders in transitional justice, with a strong focus on forgiveness and reconciliation, in line with peacebuilding efforts. Religious leaders were critical actors in the 2008 Juba peace talks. In chapter "The Case of Uganda: A Fusion of Domestic Transitional Justice and International Criminal Law", anthropological literature showed a close link between the ARLPI—a collation of religious denominations in Northern Uganda—and the traditional conflict resolution mechanisms in the region.[19] In doing so, the religious leaders maintained a strong discourse against the ICC intervention, which they viewed as a barrier to peacebuilding. Nonetheless, the religious leaders also recognised the role of the ICC as a means for achieving accountability. Little wonder that religious leaders were among the delegations that travelled from Uganda to The Hague to attend the trial of Dominic Ongwen. The attendance by religious leaders of an international criminal trial which doesn't ascribe to reconciliation is not surprising, when closely linked to the experiences of local NGOs that shifted their focus from reconciliation to support the ICC intervention.

Religious leaders, just like local NGO actors, had to negotiate the boundaries between local reconciliatory practices on one hand and the ICC on the other. When juxtaposed with the analytical question of this book regarding legitimacy of transitional justice, it is safe to say that by attending the Ongwen trials, the religious leaders lent legitimacy to the ICC before the conflict-affected communities where they serve. Based on the findings in the Uganda context, I agree with prior scholarly findings and arguments in regard to the crucial role of faith-based actors in transitional justice, including the legitimisation of international criminal accountability norms.[20]

In a similar way, the case of Myanmar illuminates strong religious discourses and practices, which help in our understanding of the Rohingya justice approaches.

---

[16] Interview, 1 April 2021.

[17] Interview, 1 April 2021.

[18] See Media Statement by the Karen Grassroots Women's Network, via Burma Campaign UK (2019) https://burmacampaign.org.uk/the-karen-grassroots-womens-network-welcomes-cases-against-burma-for-genocide/.

[19] Apuuli (2011, pp. 116–129).

[20] See for instance Boesenecker and Vinjamuri (2011, p. 364) and Cismas (2017, pp. 303–304).

Fractious Buddhist-Muslim relations in the region are a central barrier to peace-building efforts in the Rakhine State. In chapter "Achieving Transitional Justice in Myanmar: Between Accountability and National Reconciliation", ethnographic fieldwork by genocide scholars showed ethno-religious tensions and anti-Muslim discourses, which contribute to the contemporary problems facing the Rohingya.[21] As such, in addition to NGOs, the religious actors and faith-based institutions will have a significant influence on the form of transitional justice and its implementation in Myanmar.

As the discussions in the book have shown, an understanding of the historical contexts is crucial for the adoption and implantation of transitional justice. Whilst the war in Northern Uganda was originally embedded in spiritualism by the LRA leader Kony, the conflict in itself did not have any religious dimensions. On the other hand, the violence against the Rohingya in Myanmar is deeply entrenched in the fractious Buddhist-Muslim relations. As such, a point of divergence between the two case studies relates to the depth of the connection which religion has on the conflicts. Against this background, one cannot ignore the ethno-religious dimensions of transitional justice. This line of enquiry in transitional justice brings us to another issue, reminding us about the genesis of the ICJ case against Myanmar. The fact that The Gambia filed the ICJ case with the support of 57 nations in the Organization of Islamic Cooperation (OIC) speaks to the religious geo-politics within South Asia. Generally, the two cases demonstrate an embedment of ethno-cultural and religious dimensions and actors within transitional justice.

3 The Promises and Pitfalls of International Criminal Justice

An important distinction between the two case studies relates to the trajectory of the ICC intervention and proceedings. In the Ugandan case, one person—Dominic Ongwen—was successfully tried and convicted for war crimes and crimes against humanity, in 2021 and is serving 25 years imprisonment sentence. As I have mentioned elsewhere, the Ongwen judgement represents a significant step forward in ICL, being:

> the first time a Chamber has considered the offence of forced pregnancy as a crime against humanity and war crime, the first time it has considered forced marriage, and the first time that a Chamber dealt with a former victim turned perpetrator.[22]

It can thus be suggested that by considering a wide range of victims' harm, for example SGBV, the ICC implicitly enhanced its sociological legitimacy.

On the other hand, the ICC intervention in the Bangladesh/Myanmar situation was still at the investigation stage, at the time of this writing. As already highlighted

[21] For a detailed study see Green et al. (2015, pp. 1–107).

[22] Kirabira (2021, pp. 1–5).

in chapter "Actor-Oriented Analysis of Accountability Mechanisms in Uganda", in November 2019, the Court authorised the Prosecutor to investigate crimes against humanity of deportation and persecution of Rohingya, following the preliminary examination. In November 2024, the Prosecutor filed a request with the Court for an arrest warrant for Senior General Min Aung Hlaing, the Commander-in-Chief of the Myanmar military for the crimes against humanity of deportation and persecution of Rohingya. Since January 2020, the Prosecutor and the Registry have established outreach and communication channels with the affected communities living in Bangladesh. Just like in the Ugandan situation, local NGOs were supportive in these activities.

With a striking difference between the two countries in regard to the trajectory and stage of ICC intervention, a question could be; how does the investigation stage in the Bangladesh/Myanmar situation affect the legitimacy of the ICC? The findings in the book showed that the ICC intervention, even in its infancy, elicited significant discourse about getting Rohingya involved in the process. The Court had to make a ruling on whether to move the current ICC processes away from The Hague, to get justice closer to the Rohingya.[23]

More notably, the involvement of Rohingya activists and representatives by way of *amicus curiae* submissions also works to enhance the legitimacy of the ICC intervention, as gathered from the interviews. Even though these interventions are at the preliminary level, they also impact on the Court's legitimacy. In addition to the high degree of Prosecutorial discretion in the investigations akin to what Carsten Stahn terms 'soft power', these early stages express the Court's important role in addressing situations of mass atrocities.[24] As also revealed in chapter "Actor-Oriented Analysis of Accountability Mechanisms in Uganda", the OTP's investigation in the Uganda situation and the outreach programmes by the VPRS also enhanced the ICC as a legitimate avenue for transitional justice. Succinctly, both case studies are reflective of the legitimation power of the ICC as a key institution for justice and accountability.

Another important distinction in the ICC interventions in the two case studies relates to the levels of political support and cooperation for the ICC. As the first State to refer a situation to the ICC, the Ugandan government placed itself at the centre of the intervention and supported the Prosecutor's investigations. As has been shown in the empirical analysis, the government used the ICC intervention as a tool to legitimise its own narrative of the situation.

The situation in Myanmar is different, as the country is not a State party to the Rome Statute, and also does not accept the Court's jurisdiction. Even at the Preliminary investigation stage, Myanmar's government did not cooperate with the Prosecutor. As shown in chapter "Achieving Transitional Justice in Myanmar: Between Accountability and National Reconciliation", a section of leaders in the diaspora under the NUG declared their support for the ICC and its jurisdiction over crimes

---

[23] See Situation in the People's Republic of Bangladesh/Republic of the Union of Myanmar (Decision on Victims' joint request concerning hearings outside the host State), ICC-01/19, Pre-Trial Chamber III, 27 October 2020.

[24] Stahn (2017, p. 416).

in Myanmar.[25] Whether the NUG's declaration would have a legal impact on the current ICC investigations is a troubling question, as it has not been considered as an accession to the Rome Statute.[26]

Generally, Myanmar's military government remains opposed to the ICC and other international justice mechanisms.[27] Whilst Uganda's president has maintained a critical discourse against the ICC over the past years,[28] the Court's staff in the country, including those involved in the Ongwen case, have not been adversely affected. In contrast to the case of Myanmar, the ICC intervention in Uganda was largely premised on State cooperation and political support. This distinction is important when exploring the impact of the ICC in terms of transitional justice.

The political dimensions of the ICC also influenced the outcomes—in this case, the choice of who to prosecute. In the Ugandan case, emphasis is placed on the responsibility of non-State actors, i.e. LRA rebel leaders. As shown in chapter "The Case of Uganda: A Fusion of Domestic Transitional Justice and International Criminal Law", members of the Uganda's armed forces were excluded from the ICC investigations, despite evidence that they committed a range of crimes like torture, wilful killing, murder and rape. A lot of such crimes were also committed as the government soldiers contained the Acholi civilian population in IDP camps.[29] A few soldiers were prosecuted within the jurisdiction of military courts, under the category of service offences, for example, disobedience of lawful orders.[30] A jurisdictional uncertainty would arise, if the soldiers were tried for war crimes and crimes against humanity under both the Rome Statute and the Uganda Peoples' Defence Forces (UPDF) Act. The legitimacy of the ICC was generally also enhanced by the NGOs that worked directly with the victims before the ICC.

One interesting angle is that of Emma Lubaale, who makes a strong case for Uganda's military Courts' jurisdiction over international crimes under the Rome Statute as well, based on the liberal wording of the UPDF Act and ICC Act.[31] However, there has not been any explicit mention of war crimes or crimes against humanity by the military in respect to the conduct of its forces during the counter LRA operations in Northern Uganda. Similarly, the domestic prosecution at the ICD did not provide any link with the actions of the State forces in Northern Uganda. As such, the Ugandan case can be described as a one-sided transitional justice approach, at least, from the formal justice processes implemented over the years. On the other hand, the Myanmar case describes and shows transitional justice as primarily aimed at addressing State actor oppression and atrocities committed by the military against the Rohingya.

---

[25] Simpson (2021) and Legal Action Worldwide (2021).

[26] See Article 12(3) of the Rome Statute allows non-States Parties to grant jurisdiction to the ICC, by lodging a declaration with the Court's Registrar. See also Stahn et al. (2005, pp. 421–431).

[27] Strangio (2021).

[28] Oloka-Onyango (2020, p. 47).

[29] For more details see Wegner (2012).

[30] See Lubaale (2017, pp. 709–747).

[31] Lubaale (2017, p. 747).

A common feature in both case studies relates to the way in which crimes of SGBV are addressed. The *Ongwen case* at the ICC encompassed novel aspects of SGBV in the form of forced pregnancy. As I have indicated elsewhere, it was the first case where the ICC considered the offences of forced pregnancy and marriage specifically as war crimes.[32] This ICC case was used by NGOs to legitimise transitional justice in Uganda. Considerable attention was equally placed on providing redress to victims of SGBV in Myanmar, as was shown in the discussions on the case of universal jurisdiction in Argentina. Besides NGO reports detailing a prevalence of sexual violence in the military operations in Rakhine State of Myanmar, against the Rohingya, there were NGO observations in support of the Prosecution's Request for a Ruling on Jurisdiction.[33] The analysis showed that such observations provided crucial insights, illuminating how SGBV crimes could be linked with the crime of deportation or forcible transfer of Rohingya.[34] Generally, the analysis supports scholarly findings that show an instrumentalised and persistent nature of SGBV crimes by Myanmar's military in the region.[35]

From a normative perspective, there are different levels of jurisdictional certainty in the two case studies. Uganda is a unique case study in terms of jurisdiction-Application of both the ICC and its complementarity regime under the auspices of a hybrid tribunal at the domestic level. As such, chapter "Actor-Oriented Analysis of Accountability Mechanisms in Uganda" of the book revealed an evolution of NGO practice and discourse that emphasises the role of the domestic court in prosecuting war crimes and international crimes in Uganda. The normative foundations were largely supported by both technical and financial support by international donors and NGOs. These interventions included the establishment of the Court (ICD), training of judges, drafting of relevant legislation, outreach and supporting victim participation.

In contrast, the case study of Myanmar showed jurisdictional dilemmas in the accountability mechanisms. The case of universal jurisdiction filed in Argentina is a starting point to illustrate this challenge. The discussions showed how the Court of First Instance dismissed the petition, on the basis of lack of jurisdiction. The key rationale was that the ongoing ICC investigations were sufficient avenues for justice.[36] An important question in this case is whether ICC interventions take precedence over domestic Courts using universal jurisdiction? An exploration of the Court submissions showed that transnational networks and NGOs played a significant role, by way of *amici curiae*, before the Federal Criminal Appeals Court, in the interpretation of universal jurisdiction. More specifically, the NGOs showed that because of the jurisdictional limits of the ICC in the Bangladesh/Myanmar situation, a range of

[32] For detailed analysis see Kirabira (2021, pp. 1–5) and Kirabira and Choukroune (2021).

[33] See Decision on the "Joint Request for Leave to Submit Amicus Curiae Observations pursuant to Rule 103 of the Rules," ICC-RoC46(3)-01/18–15, Pre-Trial Chamber I, 11 June 2018.

[34] Decision on the "Joint Request for Leave to Submit Amicus Curiae Observations pursuant to Rule 103 of the Rules," ICC-RoC46(3)-01/18–15, Pre-Trial Chamber I, 11 June 2018.

[35] Ryan (2020, p. 62).

[36] See *amicus curiae* by Arakan Rohingya Society for Peace and Human Rights and others, para 2. https://www.victimadvocatesinternational.org/wp-content/uploads/2021/08/Amicus-English-version.firma-digital-2.pdf; For a summarised analysis see Dwyer (2021).

crimes like sexual violence would not be addressed. As such, the NGOs legitimised the accountability mechanism in Argentina as a viable form of transitional justice for the Rohingya.

Besides the case of universal jurisdiction in Argentina, the ICC intervention in Myanmar also encountered jurisdictional challenges and uncertainty. As shown in chapter "Achieving Transitional Justice in Myanmar: Between Accountability and National Reconciliation", the ICC intervention in Myanmar posed normative difficulties, as the country is not a signatory to the Rome Statute of the ICC and did not accept the Court's jurisdiction. Under Article 13(b) of the Rome Statute, the ICC can exercise jurisdiction over a situation based on a referral by the UNSC, pursuant to the latter's powers under Chapter VII of the UN Charter (Chapter VII referral).[37] Such a referral would afford the ICC jurisdiction over all crimes under the Rome Statute committed by the military since 2002. As highlighted in chapter "Actor-Oriented Analysis of Accountability Mechanisms in Uganda", the UNSC was not able to refer the Rohingya situation to the ICC, despite calls from NGOs.[38]

The use of domestic judicial organs as transitional justice mechanisms also differs, depending on the country's engagement with the international community. It is important to note that even though the issue of the ICC jurisdiction was not contested in Uganda, there has been strong discourse supporting the use of complementary justice at the ICD—the domestic ICT. This assertion is supported by the findings in chapter "Actor-Oriented Analysis of Accountability Mechanisms in Uganda", in regard to NGO engagement with the ICD. In summary, the two case studies reveal that the adjudication of international crimes is not always a linear process in terms of jurisdiction, as there is room for innovation.

4 Legitimacy of Transitional Justice Mechanisms: NGOs as Local Norm Entrepreneurs

The findings in both cases underscore the relevance of transnational networks and NGOs in transitional justice. Empirically, they have contributed to the dominance of legalism in transitional justice, working along the lines of mechanisms like the ICC. In Uganda, the international organisations like International Center for Transitional Justice and REDRESS are linked directly with national actors and local NGOs dealing with issues like amnesty, accountability and peace-building. For the case of Myanmar, a plethora of NGOs deal directly or indirectly through local intermediaries, with Rohingya refugees residing in Bangladesh.

Across both the Ugandan and Rohingya conflict-affected communities, the analysis shows how ICC programmes impacted on victims' perceptions on transitional justice. More specifically, the outreach of the NGOs generated interest in victims' participation in the ICC processes. It can thus be argued that by generating such

[37] See Rome Statute; The Charter of the United Nations, June 26, 1945, 1 UNTS XVI.

[38] See NGO reports Fortify Rights (2021) and Human Rights Watch (2018).

interest among victims, there is limited room for the conflict-affected communities to challenge these normative conceptions of transitional justice, or the work of the ICC.

However, the presence of multiple NGOs and the ICC outreach teams also risks creating disillusionment among the locals, especially if they create overly high expectations in respect to aspects like victims' participation and relations. Phil Clark draws on such local and communal discourses in Uganda and DRC to support his arguments against a distanced ICC.[39] With such findings in mind, we should not lose sight of the NGO work which filled the gaps in the Court's outreach programmes. Nonetheless, what can be gathered from the two case studies is that it really matters how the conflict-affected communities interpret justice. Furthermore, NGOs remain a key factor in these discourses, as they engage directly with the institutions and their constituents.

Unlike in Myanmar, the Ugandan case demonstrates how the ICC relates with national jurisdictions and the impact on domestic accountability. As was observed in chapter "Actor-Oriented Analysis of Accountability Mechanisms in Uganda", central to NGOs work in Uganda has been the domestic implementation of the Rome Statute and ICC complementarity framework. The prosecution and trial of Thomas Kwoyelo at the ICD illuminated these narratives and practice. As the ICC intervention in Myanmar is premised on limited jurisdiction and the country is not a State party to the Rome Statute, it would be illogical to expect a national implementation of the Rome Regime. Nonetheless, the Ugandan case shows that the ICC is not simply a physical site of justice in The Hague, as different NGOs implemented its complementarity framework in Uganda.

The findings in Uganda mirror similar observations regarding the impact of ICL on domestic reforms. The International Criminal Tribunal for the former Yugoslavia (ICTY) had a significant domestic influence, framed as a catalyst for the State Court of Bosnia & Herzegovina.[40] Empirical work that assesses the ICTY's impact in Bosnia and Serbia shows how the Tribunal catalysed domestic war crimes trials.[41] Besides the ICTY, the International Criminal Tribunal for Rwanda and the Special Court for Sierra Leone (SCSL) engaged in national capacity-building initiatives, akin to the positive complementarity framework at the ICC.[42] The relatively limited impact of the SCSL on Sierra Leone's domestic judicial system-partly attributed to application of the amnesty regime,[43] also helps to explain the complex interactions between NGOs and the ICC in Uganda. As was shown in chapter "Actor-Oriented Analysis of Accountability Mechanisms in Uganda", the ICC intervention in Uganda initially faced resistance from local NGOs, that prioritised peace over justice. It will be interesting to see whether the ICC will use a hands-off approach towards the domestic prosecution of international crimes in Bangladesh, in case the country prosecutes

[39] Clark (2018).

[40] For more details see Burke-White (2008, p. 282).

[41] Orentlicher (2018, p. 323).

[42] Horovitz (2013, pp. 339–367).

[43] Horovitz (2013, p. 365).

crimes in relation to the Rohingya situation. In sum, such mechanisms require legitimacy in the eyes of conflict-affected communities, in order to be successful within the dimension of transitional justice.

One can't overlook Christian M. De Vos's arguments in respect to the ICC interventions in Uganda, Kenya and DRC, lending credence to the view of the Court as a 'Catalyst' for domestic implementation of international criminal law.[44] In particular, this can be seen in the role of non-State actors including NGOs in the ICC's complementarity regimes as a potential to achieve transitional justice. The Myanmar case findings also revealed some strategies by NGOs geared towards moving the ICC processes in the Bangladesh/Myanmar situation from The Hague to Bangladesh. Whilst such strategies and advocacy have not yielded fruit, it remains clear from such discourse and practice that the ICC is a key institution, with the potential to stimulate transitional justice across boundaries. I argue that the Court is therefore a beneficiary of the legitimation work of NGOs, working on transitional justice-related work in Uganda, Myanmar and beyond.

The Myanmar case is unique, due to the invocation of two Hague-based justice mechanisms—the ICC and the ICJ. The book has shown how transnational NGO networks collaborated with States to file a case against Myanmar at the ICJ. Whilst there is significant discourse relating to criminal accountability as a form of transitional justice for the Rohingya, the findings also showed that the ICJ case is viewed as an important step towards justice and accountability for the Rohingya. As such, the case study is suitable for analysing the prospects and limitations of the ICJ during periods of democratic transition.

It will be interesting to see how scholars analyse the impact of the ICJ case against Myanmar in the coming years. Martin Mennecke views the ICJ case from a Responsibility to Protect context, suggesting that the ICJ can contribute to the accountability framework, even though it is a State-centred Court.[45] Similarly, the majority of NGO elites interviewed were equally interested in the impact of the ICJ case and how the Myanmar government would engage with it in the coming years. As such, the ICJ case cannot be looked at in isolation from the other forms of transitional justice for the Rohingya. As the findings in both case studies suggest, the transitional justice framework including NGO practice and discourse is comprised of interrelated and sometimes overlapping mechanisms.

What exactly makes NGOs local norm entrepreneurs? The landscape of transitional justice rotates on three dimensions—local, national and global. However, it is also referred to as a 'global project', due to the emergence of customary international law and the globalisation of transitional justice norms.[46] Similarly, transitional justice is largely based on external donor funding and international NGOs, as has been revealed in the book. The empirical findings help in our understanding on how NGOs localise global transitional justice norms through decision-making, participation funding and priorities. In both case studies, NGOs contributed to the

[44] De Vos (2020, pp 147–194).

[45] Mennecke (2021, pp. 324–348).

[46] See Nagy (2008, p. 276).

localisation of transitional justice in two ways. Firstly, by engaging with transnational networks, NGOs localise the work of global justice mechanisms, adapting their practices and statements for the conflict-affected communities. Secondly, NGOs engaged in victim-oriented work, which is a central aspect of transitional justice.

The pragmatic approaches by NGOs to the ICC are not unique to these two case studies. Empirical assessment of the work of hybrid criminal tribunals in Sierra Leone and Cambodia shows how local and international NGO work enhanced their legitimacy.[47] The close intersection of the ICC and NGOs in the Myanmar and Uganda cases is akin to the Cambodian situation, where local NGOs engaged but also legitimised transitional justice mechanisms.[48] Local NGOs equally played a significant role in the work of the ECCC, framing the Court's intervention within public discourse on transitional justice in the country.[49] Hence, the legitimation of international justice mechanisms by NGOs is not entirely new in transitional justice. What makes a difference is how the mechanisms stimulate transformations in the different contexts.

How are the internationalised transitional justice processes diffused at the local levels? The findings in the book reinvigorate claims that diffusion of transitional justice norms of ICL by transnational networks and NGOs is a non-linear process of the diffusion-there is potential for adaptability and reframing of these mechanisms, depending on the specific context.[50] The book showed how advocates for the ICC intervention in the Rohingya situation sought for a more localised approach, where the Court would sit outside The Hague. If this request is successful in the future, it would significantly enhance the Court before the conflict-affected people in Cox's Bazar refugee camps. The book also revealed how NGOs contributed to the domestication of the Rome Statute in Uganda, which further shows the localisation of international norms of accountability.

Whilst transnational networks and NGOs are important actors in transitional justice, there are also some pertinent issues worth considering. Firstly, the tensions between different NGOs across national and international spaces. As was highlighted in the empirical analysis, there is a high level of competition among local NGOs because of donor funding. As such, local NGOs are torn between specific mandates and donor-driven projects in transitional justice. Nonetheless, the findings also remind us of the precarious situation of local NGOs, where transitional justice is underpinned by socio-political dimensions. Some local NGOs are side-lined because of the particular stands they have on the nature of transitional justice, which does not resonate with popular international positions. As such, NGOs (de)legitimise the work of transitional justice mechanisms, depending on the sort of issues they prioritise. Similarly, local NGOs risk appraisal from their governments—as also revealed from an interview with a journalist from Myanmar, who noted that: 'If a big local NGO was to make a statement about the Rohingya, they would face reprisal. However,

47 Stensrud (2009, pp. 5–15).

48 Sperfeldt (2012, pp. 149–160).

49 See Palmer (2016, p. 116).

50 Palmer (2016, p. 101).

an NGO like Human Rights Watch would not worry about it'.[51] This statement can be supported by the analysis on the Rohingya cases, showing a significant role of Rohingya diaspora NGOs in transitional justice.

In adapting certain practices of institutions like the ICC at the local levels, NGOs also turn into intermediaries. However, as was revealed in the findings, NGOs also have the potential to obscure the procedural work of institutions like the ICC. They may not always agree with the strategies employed by the Court and the OTP, for example, on aspects like victim categorisation. An ICC staff interviewed raised a concern about the masking of victims, saying 'I can see many NGOs speaking on behalf of victims, but it is important to hear the voices of the victims themselves'.[52] Similarly an international criminal lawyer and investigator was worried about the negative impact of NGOs on victims and investigations in general, noting that; 'The procedures of NGOs' documentation sometimes falls below basic standards e.g. whilst interviewing vulnerable victims, they [NGOs] don't employ support staff'.[53] Whilst implicitly acknowledging that NGOs legitimise international criminal justice mechanisms, she recommends for a lesser engagement of NGOs in fact-finding; 'NGOs create awareness that we even exist…But maybe to take a little bit step back in collecting evidence and allow the mechanisms to do their work'.[54] In sum, these observations remind us about the complexities surrounding the implementation of transitional justice in general, due to fragmented approaches and interests by the different stakeholders.

An exploration of two very different contexts with very different experiences of transitional justice, with very different opportunities for NGOs shows some specific lessons about how NGOs affect legitimacy—it depends on their engagements with other partners. Generally, the analysis is in line with earlier scholarly perspectives on the primacy of legitimacy as a necessary tool for transitional justice mechanisms.[55] The two case studies have explored the empirical dimensions of sociological legitimacy, through the practice and discourse of transnational networks and NGOs. In constructing the transitional justice norms, significant attention has been given to the relationships between NGOs and conflict-affected communities. However, as the book has shown, there are also other social elites, for example, local leaders and victim representatives that need to work with the 'international justice proponents', as Jaya Ramji-Nogales calls them.[56]

[51] Interview, 8 May 2021.

[52] Interview, 1 May 2021.

[53] Interview, 8 May 2021.

[54] Interview, 8 May 2021.

[55] Ramji-Nogales (2010, p. 13, 2015, pp. 106–121).

[56] Ramji-Nogales (2010, p. 19).

5 Conclusion

Taken together, these two cases demonstrate that transitional justice is a non-linear process which is open to contestations depending on the context. The nature of transition in the country also influences the legal landscapes of transitional justice. Important distinctions have been made between the two case studies in respect to the ICC intervention. In answering the question on how transnational networks and NGOs (de)legitimise transitional justice, the chapter has identified common patterns and divergences between the two case studies. These include dependence on external donor funding for their engagements with internationalised justice mechanisms, victim-oriented strategies and different approaches towards State actor atrocities.

The chapter then connected the work of NGOs to the localisation of transitional justice norms in two ways: firstly, by showing how transnational networks localise the work of global justice mechanisms through adapting their practices and statements for the conflict-affected communities; and secondly, by showing the victim-oriented work of NGOs, which is a central tenet of institutions like the ICC. Together, these two case studies presented a nuanced picture of a dynamic and fragmented process of localisation. The chapter has shown that understanding the role of NGOs in transitional justice cannot fully occur without such empirical data. For NGOs working on Myanmar, the Ugandan case provides illuminating practices regarding the fusion of reconciliation and formal accountability approaches in transitional justice.

References

Advisory Commission on Rakhine State (2017) Towards a peaceful, fair and prosperous future for the people of Rakhine—Final Report of the Advisory Commission on Rakhine State. Advisory Commission on Rakhine State, New York, pp 1–63

Apuuli KP (2011) Peace over justice: the Acholi Religious Leaders Peace Initiative (ARLPI) vs. The International Criminal Court (ICC) in Northern Uganda. Stud Ethn Nationalism 11:116–129

Baines E, Oliveira C (2020) Securing the future: transformative justice and children 'Born of War.' Social Legal Stud 30:341–361

Boesenecker AP, Vinjamuri L (2011) Lost in translation? civil society, faith-based organizations and the negotiation of international norms. Int J Transitional Justice 5:345–365

Bosire LK, Lynch G (2014) Kenya's search for truth and justice: the role of civil society. Int J Transitional Justice 8:256–276

Burke-White W (2008) The domestic influence of International Criminal Tribunals: the International Criminal Tribunal for the former Yugoslavia and the creation of the State Court of Bosnia & Herzegovina. Columbia J Transnational Law 46:279

Cismas I (2017) Reflections on the presence and absence of religious actors in transitional justice processes: on legitimacy and accountability. In: Duthie R, Seils P (eds) Justice mosaics: how context shapes transitional justice in fractured societies. International Center for Transitional Justice, New York, pp 302–343

Clark P (2018) Distant justice the impact of the International Criminal Court on African politics. Cambridge University Press, Cambridge

De Vos C (2020) The ICC in Uganda, Kenya and the Democratic Republic of Congo. In: De Vos C (ed) Complementarity, catalysts, compliance: The International Criminal Court in Uganda,

Kenya, and the Democratic Republic of Congo. Cambridge University Press, Cambridge, pp 147–194
Fink C, Simpson A (2017) Civil Society. In: Simpson A, Farrelly N, Holliday I (eds) Routledge handbook of contemporary Myanmar. Routledge, Abingdon, pp 257–267
Fortify Rights (2021) U.N. Security Council: refer myanmar to the ICC, impose a global arms embargo. Fortify Rights, Belfast, ME. https://www.fortifyrights.org/mya-inv-2021-02-02/
Gready P, Robins S (2014) From transitional to transformative justice: a new agenda for practice. Int J Transitional Justice 8:339–361
Green P, MacManus T, de la Cour Venning A (2015) Countdown to annihilation: genocide in Myanmar. International State Crime Initiative, Queen Mary University of London, London, pp. 1–107
Horovitz S (2013) How international courts shape domestic justice: lessons from Rwanda and Sierra Leone. Israel Law Rev 46:339–367
Human Rights Watch (2018) UN Security Council: refer Myanmar to ICC. Human Rights Watch, New York. https://www.hrw.org/news/2018/05/08/un-security-council-refer-myanmar-icc
Kirabira T (2021) Ongwen at the International Criminal Court. ASIL Insights 25:1–5
Kirabira T, Choukroune L (2021) Dominic Ongwen: ICC conviction of former child soldier establishes 'forced pregnancy' as a war crime. The Conversation. https://theconversation.com/dominic-ongwen-icc-conviction-of-former-child-soldier-establishes-forced-pregnancy-as-a-war-crime-154671
Lai D, Bonora C (2019) The transformative potential of post-war justice initiatives in Bosnia and Herzegovina. In: Matthew Evans (ed) Transitional and transformative justice, 1st edn. Routledge, Abingdon
Legal Action Worldwide (2021) LAW: More than 500 Rohingya request ICC Prosecutor accept NUG declaration. Legal Action Worldwide, Geneva
Lubaale E (2017) Military courts and prosecution of offences by National Defense Forces in the dawn of the complementarity regime: the case of Uganda. Crim Law Forum 28:709–747
Lubaale E (2025) The conviction and sentencing of ex-rebel, Thomas Kwoyelo, 15 years on. Opinio Juris, Geneva. https://opiniojuris.org/2025/02/12/the-conviction-and-sentencing-of-ex-rebel-thomas-kwoyelo-15-years-on/
McAuliffe P (2021) Transitional justice, institutions and temporality: towards a dynamic understanding. Int Criminal Law Rev 21:817–847
Mennecke M (2021) The International Court of Justice and the responsibility to protect: learning from the case of The Gambia v Myanmar. Global Responsibility to Protect 13(2–3):324–348
Nagy R (2008) Transitional justice as global project: critical reflections. Third World Q 29:275–289
Oloka-Onyango J (2020) Unpacking the African backlash to the International Criminal Court (ICC): the case of Uganda and Kenya. Strathmore Law J 4:41–68
Orentlicher D (2018) Some kind of justice: the ICTY's impact in Bosnia and Serbia. Oxford University Press, Oxford
Palmer E (2016) Localizing international criminal accountability in Cambodia. Int Relat Asia Pac 16:97–135
Ramji-Nogales J (2010) Designing bespoke transitional justice: a pluralist process approach. Michigan J Int Law 32:1–72
Ramji-Nogales J (2015) Bespoke transitional justice at the International Criminal Court. In: De Vos C, Kendall S, Stahn C (eds) Contested justice the politics and practice of International Criminal Court interventions. Cambridge University Press, Cambridge, pp 106–121
Rome Statute of the International Criminal Court, U.N. Doc. No. A/ CONF.183/9 (1998), Article 126
Ruhweza D (2022) Wild goose chase, or a quest for genuine prosecution? lessons from Uganda's ongoing trial of Thomas Kwoyelo. In: Lubaale E, Dyani-Mhango N (eds) National accountability for international crimes in Africa. Palgrave Macmillan, Cham, London, pp 427–468
Ryan S (2020) When women become the war zone: the use of sexual violence in Myanmar's military operations. Glob Responsib Prot 12:37–63

Sharp D (2015) Emancipating transitional justice from the bonds of the paradigmatic transition. Int J Transitional Justice 9:150–169

Simpson A (2021) Myanmar's exile government signs up to ICC prosecutions. East Asia Forum, Canberra

Sperfeldt C (2012) Cambodian Civil Society and the Khmer Rouge Tribunal. Int J Transitional Justice 6:149–160

Stahn C (2017) Damned if you do, damned if you don't: challenges and critiques of preliminary examinations at the ICC. J Int Criminal Justice 15:413–434

Stahn C, El Zeidy M, Olásolo H (2005) The International Criminal Court's Ad Hoc jurisdiction revisited. American J Int Law 99:421–431

Stensrud E (2009) New dilemmas in transitional justice: lessons from the mixed courts in Sierra Leone and Cambodia. J Peace Res 46:5–15

Strangio S (2021) Myanmar Junta orders judges to ignore correspondence from international courts. The Diplomat. https://thediplomat.com/2021/12/myanmar-junta-orders-judges-to-ignore-correspondence-from-international-courts/

The Charter of the United Nations, June 26, 1945, 1 UNTS XVI

Wegner P (2012) A genocide in northern Uganda?—The 'protected camps' policy of 1999 to 2006. Justice in Conflict. https://justiceinconflict.org/2012/04/09/a-genocide-in-northern-uganda-the-protected-camps-policy-of-1999-to-2006/

Concluding Remarks

1 Introduction—Recap on Objectives and Structure

The book has shown how transnational networks influence justice in the Global South, particularly their impact on transitional justice in different contexts. The first chapter explained the aims and objectives of the book, including the choice of research methodology, design and data collection process. Chapter "Navigating Justice, Transitional Justice and Global North- South Dimensions" explored the conceptual framework of the book, including the critical discourse and practice within transitional justice. It also discussed the normative boundaries of ICL, making a case for examining transnational networks and NGO engagement with global mechanisms like the ICC. More importantly, the chapter introduced the analytical framework of the book-theory of legitimacy, in order to understand how transnational networks and NGOs enhance or undermine the legitimacy of transitional justice mechanisms.

Chapter "The Case of Uganda: A Fusion of Domestic Transitional Justice and International Criminal Law" began the shift from doctrine to practice, introducing the first country case study—Uganda—where I argued that the country is still under transition. Chapter "Actor-Oriented Analysis of Accountability Mechanisms in Uganda" delved into core analysis, revealing key dimensions of transnational NGO work and engagement with international criminal justice through their victim-oriented work, and technical and capacity-building initiatives around the Courts. Chapter "Achieving Transitional Justice in Myanmar: Between Accountability and National Reconciliation" introduced the case study of Myanmar, analysing the dynamics of its transition to democracy and the Rohingya Question. In the next chapter, I examined the role of NGOs in achieving transitional justice for the Rohingya, showing

This chapter has some overlaps with my doctoral thesis. Additionally, there are major overlaps with my published work- Kirabira TR (2021) NGO influence in global governance: Achieving transitional justice in Uganda and beyond. Cambridge Int Law J 10: 280–299, for which permission to re-use content was obtained.

© The Author(s), under exclusive license to Springer Nature Singapore Pte Ltd. 2025

T. R. Kirabira, *Transnational Networks and Justice in the Global South*, International Law and the Global South, https://doi.org/10.1007/978-981-95-3137-0_8

how transnational networks have steered pathways at the Global level. Chapter "Comparing Uganda and Myanmar Contexts: Challenges in localising Transitional Justice" made a comparative and systematic analysis of the findings from the two case studies, showing the similarities and divergencies in transitional justice and NGO work in both contexts.

The final chapter of this book connects transitional justice and the work of NGOs to the wider context of global governance, inviting deeper reflections on the nuances of global justice making in general. I will draw attention to the dual dimension of transnational networks and NGO work across global spaces—legitimisation of transitional justice and enhancing of global governance. This examination is largely based on the findings in both case studies of the book which confirmed scholarly concerns about the articulation of a global transitional justice discourse by powerful elites, using a global human rights discourse.[1] In light of the hegemonic forms of global justice exemplified in the book, in this last chapter, I will show a need for further inquiry into the implications of NGO work in global governance. In doing so, I also pave the way for more research on how non-State actors could counter-hegemonic structures of global governance under the purview of transitional justice.

2 Global Governance in Contested Spaces

The conclusion of the book draws upon a critical reflection following my presentation at the 10th Annual Cambridge International Law Conference, held in March 2021.[2] I made a case for the consideration of the work of NGOs, as part of any assessment of global governance structures, but also more broadly on solving the contemporary challenges facing the international legal order. The feedback I received from a diversity of stakeholders during and after the conference further led me to refine my study and critically assess how transnational networks and NGO work connect with global governance, albeit within the purview of transitional justice. The people I engaged with were not only from within the legal field and academia, but also included NGOs, private practice and government.[3] Against this background, these closing remarks on NGOs are equally helpful for future studies and research on the legitimacy of global governance institutions in general.

---

[1] See for example Robins (2012, pp. 3–30).

[2] The theme 'National Sovereignty and International Cooperation: The Challenges of Navigating Global Crises', invites broader reflections on the work of both State and Non-State actors in general.

[3] This engagement forms the crux on which I wrote an article on the role of NGOs in transitional justice, which was published in the Cambridge International Law Journal- Kirabira (2021c, pp. 280–299).

2.1 *Global Governance Through International Criminal Justice*

Global governance has had significant influences in the doctrinal areas of international law, due to interactions between different legal orders and disciplines. The evolving normative shift from State-centric to the individual represents what Teitel calls 'humanity law'.[4] Thus, the growing focus on individual criminal responsibility has expanded the global legal order.[5] It is also linked to the growing demands for accountability for gross violations of human rights across national jurisdictions.[6] Transitional justice initiatives, mostly those linked with ICL, are also viewed as tools or avenues of global governance.[7] At this point, it is important to recall that the expansion of transitional justice is linked with the post-Cold War political developments that occurred in Eastern Europe and the 'third wave' of democratic transitions in Latin America between 1980 and 1990.[8] The concerns about the imagery of Western liberal democracy in this field are important for our understanding of the practices and discourse of NGOs.[9] The practice of transitional justice as shown in the book's findings is undoubtedly globalised but also politicised. Therefore, scholarly suggestions for the rethinking of this globalisation should not be underestimated.[10]

As a starting point, an understanding of the concept of global governance is relevant. Global governance relates to 'the entirety of regulations put forward with reference to solving specific denationalized and deregionalized problems or providing transnational common goods'.[11] Next is to identify how global governance links with transitional justice norms and global justice norms in general. What are the global governance norms in transitional justice and why should particular understandings of justice be considered or implemented in different local contexts? More generally, what do the findings in the book suggest about the adoption of global governance norms?

Evaluating the impact of actors in contested spaces also leads us to question the normalisation of Western conceptions of justice in the Global South, infused within discourse and practice on transitional justice, akin to what can be termed as 'Global Projects for Global Governance'.[12] However, having a legal framework that supports the prosecution of international crimes may not always imply the acceptance of global governance norms of international criminal accountability. As was shown

---

[4] Teitel (2008, pp. 667–668).

[5] Teitel (2008, p. 668).

[6] Interview with David M. Crane, Founding Chief Prosecutor of the Special Court for Sierra Leone, 1 March 2021.

[7] Sharp (2015b, p. 162).

[8] Teitel (2003, pp. 69–94); Sharp (2013, p. 175).

[9] For deeper critique of both local and internationalised practices in transitional justice see Sharp (2013, p. 184).

[10] See for example Rowen (2018, p. 60).

[11] Zürn (2012, p. 730).

[12] Sharp (2015a, pp. 517–526).

in the Uganda case study, there was strong discourse and practice on the use of local norms of justice embedded in reconciliation and the amnesty laws. I posit that global governance is a contested space that requires legitimisation. The basis of this assertion is equally premised on the pluralist conceptions of justice and perceptions about roles of global institutions at local, domestic and international levels.[13] This assertion will be unpacked by analysing global governance through the prism of international criminal courts and NGOs.

Critical perspectives on ICL remind us of the hegemony in global governance and the marginalisation of the Global South.[14] A notable site of influence within the sphere of global justice is the ICC. As the previous discussions in the book have shown, a wide range of actors have interests in the structure of the Court, its operations and outcomes. The ICC is viewed as an instrument of global governance of human rights under a liberal democratic order.[15] With the fragmentation of human rights norms across the Global North and Global South, the implementation of liberal norms of human rights under the auspices of ICC interventions can be viewed as a propagation of Western hegemony. Not forgetting that critical voices in ICL acknowledge the anti-colonial struggles within the field, characterising it as a double-edged sword for Western hegemony, but also a means to resist it.[16]

Theoretically, global governance is also associated with 'the turn to anti-impunity' and the pursuit of global polices to fight impunity within the field of International Human Rights Law.[17] It is argued that the turn to anti-impunity contributed to the normalisation of individual accountability under the Rome Statute.[18] Additionally, it triggered transformations in the practices of other regional and international institutions and NGOs.[19] Karen Engle further attributes the global fight against impunity to the rise of neoliberalism following the end of the Cold War, leading to more international criminal justice-focused remedial approaches.[20] This assertion is not without merit, considering the historical evolution of transitional justice in the early 1990s and the prosecutions that followed.

Global governance can also be linked with international criminal justice. Mégret's definition of international criminal justice is instructive; 'the operation of a pluralist international legal system based on liberal values that entail the peaceful coexistence of sovereign entities'.[21] How could such a definition be exemplified in practice? The obvious example that comes into mind relates to the establishment of *ad hoc* International Criminal Trials (ICTs) for the Former Yugoslavia and Rwanda in the early 1990s. Similarly, international criminal justice is linked to the proliferation

---

[13] See Nouwen and Werner (2015, p. 164).

[14] See for instance Klamberg (2020, pp. 623–646); Kotiswaran and Palmer (2015, pp. 55–88).

[15] Nesiah (2016, pp. 985–1009); Birdsall (2010, p. 465).

[16] Burgis-Kasthala and Sander (2024, pp. 127–150); Jeßberger et al. (2023, p. 4).

[17] For details see Sayed (2019, pp. 1–26).

[18] See Sayed (2019, p. 4).

[19] Engle (2015, p. 1072).

[20] Engle (2015, p. 1072).

[21] Mégret (2016, p. 199).

of hybrid tribunals. Beyond the classical role of courts as legal actors, international criminal courts also act as social agents, in what Carsten Stahn describes as 'the construction of legacies'.[22] In essence, this description suggests that international criminal justice institutions are concerned with much more than juridical work, but also long-lasting legacies within the affected communities. Considering the long-term nature of transitional justice, the legacy of ICL institutions cannot be detached from the wider structural reforms, including adoption of global norms of governance.

From a normative perspective, global governance can also be seen through the prism of the notion of universal jurisdiction, derived from the prosecution of grave breaches under international instruments like the four Geneva Conventions of 1949.[23] Nonetheless, the notion of universal jurisdiction is also problematic among many States, because of the exercise of sovereignty. As an ICC judge interviewed pointed out, 'It is quite a hard sale to get a country to engage in universal jurisdiction'.[24] However, the way in which domestic and global institutions interact raises instrumental questions regarding implementation of transitional justice, for instance, in the legal interpretation of UN agreements with States for domestic prosecution of war crimes. Interpretation of agreements within the ambit of transitional justice requires careful thought on the texts. For example, Nouwen and Werner note an ambiguity with the use of the notion 'mandate from the "international community"' in hybrid tribunals, suggesting a need for a more concrete interpretation of the customary law on immunities.[25] Here, we see crucial concerns about the globalisation of transitional justice embedded within the work of ICL institutions.

Crucially, there is a need to keep track of international law scholars' concerns about the growing use of ICL as a path for global justice, in what is referred to as the 'Justice Cascade' and 'monopolization of justice'.[26] A key argument is that Tribunals created to serve such justice do not necessarily further the aims of ICL,[27] thus the need for more nuanced and contextual approaches. In addition, there are different conceptions of justice at both regional and international levels.[28] As was illustrated in the findings, transitional justice is not simply an issue of criminal accountability, especially in ethnically diverse contexts.

The application of universal jurisdiction has a direct impact on global governance, specifically the extension of Western liberal norms across States. Critics of universal jurisdiction argue for more differentiated degrees of criminal responsibility for mass atrocities like in Uganda, and the application of what is termed 'non-Western perspectives of accountability'.[29] From criminological and sociological perspectives,

[22] Stahn (2018, p. 278).

[23] For a more detailed analysis see Cassese (2004, p. 3).

[24] Interview with ICC judge, 4 March 2021.

[25] Nouwen (2019, p. 604).

[26] McAuliffe (2013, pp. 106–123 and Nouwen and Werner (2015, pp. 157–176).

[27] Nouwen and Werner (2015, p. 160).

[28] See Slye (2016, p. 234) for critical reflections on Africa and International Criminal Law, including a response to African proposals for a regional international criminal court.

[29] See Minkova (2021, p. 229 and Branch (2017, p. 40).

Lohne raises concerns regarding the orthodox emphasis on individual retribution for mass atrocity crimes, with an assertion that penalty is a global justice project.[30] This is also observed in Clarke's legal anthropology, in where she links the growth of ICL to anti-impunity movements.[31] In general, legal anthropology is not just critical of the global justice-making process, but also reminds us about the need for more counter-hegemonic work within the field of ICL.

Whilst he recognises the limitations of national courts in rendering justice following large scale violations of human rights by State agents, Antonio Cassese asserts that they are the most appropriate mechanisms for the prosecution of international crimes.[32] Regarding the notion of universal jurisdiction, Cassese is critical of the establishment of ICTs by the UNSC, as they are highly politicised.[33] What emerges clearly from Cassese's criticism is the need for in-depth examination of the institutional interests of international justice institutions like the ICC, in order to understand how global governance works. For instance, Barrie Sander illustrates the work of the ICC using a theory that he terms 'strategic expressivism' in the broader field of international criminal justice. He presents a plausible argument that expressive avenues like victim-oriented discourses improve the sociological legitimacy of international criminal courts.[34] Considering the nature of the ICC's engagement in the Ugandan and Bangladesh/Myanmar contexts, one would be inclined to agree with views that the Court is an expressive avenue for global justice. At the same time, we cannot neglect the dimensions of power from the Global North, to which the Court looks for funding and other crucial strategies like compliance.

As I have shown in the book, most States in the Global South where the ICC intervenes, tend to be highly politicised, with contestations about the mode of justice to be implemented. The analysis in the book reveals interrelated influences between the ICC and the target situations of Myanmar/Bangladesh and Uganda—The Court is seen as an instrument of State and non-State actors in terms of documentation and trial of international crimes. As such, we should not only focus on the legal outcomes of the investigations or trials, but also the political interactions the ICC creates across its spectrum of constituents, from victims to State actors. This kind of approach helps in understanding of the multi-level global governance structures, where the Court plays a central role. William Burke-White's view on this relationship is instructive in this regard:

> If the Court's [ICC] broader role is used wisely, it may well promote domestic reform, good governance, and accountability. If ignored, however, the Court's position in a system of multilevel global governance may well invite dangerous political manipulation.[35]

---

[30] Lohne (2021, pp. 3–23).

[31] Clarke (2015, pp. 592–614 and Clarke (2019b, p. 253).

[32] Cassese (2004, p. 4).

[33] Cassese (2004, p. 5).

[34] Sander (2019, p. 867).

[35] Burke-White (2005, p. 559).

Crucially, legitimising the instrumentalisation and institutionalised use of the ICC in the Global South could be perceived as a way of bolstering the hegemonic power structures inherent in global governance.

Moreover, the influence of global governance in ICL extends beyond the ICC, and can be observed in the work of internationalised and hybrid tribunals. Such institutions need to maintain the support of powerful actors in order to operate, as was observed with the ICD in Uganda. Like Frédéric Mégret has argued, this lack of autonomy by the Tribunals is a source of anxiety for international criminal justice in general.[36] So, what do we make of the relationship between powerful actors like the UNSC and the operations of internationalised tribunals?

The UN Mission in Kosovo (UNMIK) represents another example of the nuanced relationship between domestic and global governance, under the rubric of international justice. One would wonder whether such a *sui generis* global governance approach is a useful model for achieving transitional justice in the Global South? Whilst scholarly evaluations of the UNMIK show the relevance of international justice following gross violations of human rights, inter-ethnic violence and war crimes, they reveal a need for complementarity through building the local capacities of judges and lawyers.[37] Conversely, these concerns suggest that 'internationalised' justice is not always a one size fit all, but rather, requires the careful consideration of unique domestic contexts.

Similarly, the ECCC exemplifies the nuanced relationships between global and domestic institutions regarding accountability. The UN and the Cambodian government agreed on the legal procedures, including the definition of international crimes and recognition of amnesty.[38] More generally, the agreement was regarded as a difficult compromise due to the parties' initial disagreements about the composition of the court.[39] The above challenge is an indication of the limitations of global governance structures in such complex contexts. Moreover, States are increasingly drawn towards the implementation of ICL norms through enactment of national implementing legislation.[40]

Aside from Cambodia, studies on other hybrid tribunals in East Timor and Sierra Leone reveal that this 'internationalised justice' is a viable, yet problematic form of transitional justice.[41] It is important to note that there were two parallel transitional justice institutions Sierra Leone: the Truth and Reconciliation Commission and the SCSL. This context thus begs a question of how to evaluate global governance and the responses to domestic transitional justice processes when hybrid mechanisms are employed. As in Cambodia, the SCSL was created following an international

[36] Mégret (2016, pp.197–221).

[37] See for instance Cady and Booth (2004, p. 77).

[38] For details see Meijer (2004, p. 214).

[39] Meijer (2004, p. 213).

[40] For detailed analysis see Birkett (2019, p. 355).

[41] See generally Sriram (2005, p. 80).

agreement between Sierra Leone and the UN. Procedural aspects of the Tribunal were derived from those of the ICTR.[42]

Theoretical debates and criticisms on the practices of globalised justice institutions provide sightlines for more counter-hegemonic work within international criminal justice in general. A good illustration of the political economy of international criminal justice is revealed in Christine Schwöbel-Patel's work.[43] She presents an intriguing critique of the manner in which the global justice project sells itself in this political economy.[44] I find her analysis intriguing in so far as it relates to the position of global elites that benefit from marketised global justice.[45] In essence, there are direct beneficiaries of global governance embedded in international criminal justice.

Implementing the principle of universal jurisdiction is one unique way in which global governance is exemplified in practice, within the preview of international criminal justice. As shown in the discussions on the Rohingya situation in this book, the prosecution of a country's leaders in other States far away from the sites of atrocities is a toll order. Most important, however, is the challenge of getting States to trigger universal jurisdiction, due to the global power dynamics. The controversy around the practice of universal jurisdiction based on the global power dynamics and State-centrism leads us to think twice about the future of transitional justice in post-colonial settings, especially where neocolonial powers remain influential. As such, one would be inclined to agree with critical legal scholarship in ICL which recommends for the reformulation of the practice in the Global South.[46]

2.2 *The Future of NGOs in the New Era of Global Governance*

As posited throughout this book, a comprehensive analysis of the local impact of global institutions like the ICC requires one to unpack how they engage with transnational networks and NGOs actors. The nuances of interactions between NGOs and globalised justice mechanisms invite broader discussions beyond the parameters of transitional justice, which help in our understanding of the global governance system. As the book has shown, the State and Non-State actors are not completely detached from each other, but work in a structure akin to a global multi-level governance system. This kind of relationship entails interconnected governance practices where the actors cross-influence and reshape their activities.[47] Specifically, I argue that transnational networks and NGOs confer legitimacy to global institutions operated

[42] Schabas (2004, p. 174).

[43] Schwöbel-Patel (2016, pp. 247–274, Schwöbel-Patel (2018, pp. 703–724 and Schwöbel-Patel (2021).

[44] See generally Schwöbel-Patel (2021).

[45] Kirabira and Sehmi (2022, pp. 725–729).

[46] Ramji-Nogales (2015, pp. 106–121 and Canefe (2021).

[47] Burke-White (2005, p. 558).

by States, for example, the ICC, ICJ and UN investigative mechanisms, in line with the strategic goals of States.

A good starting point is to recall Antonio Gramsci's writings which also inform many scholarly views on the nexus between State-civil society relationships and the concept of hegemony.[48] In other words, civil society, including NGO actors, is an integral element in the global hegemonic structures. Applying Gramsci's ideas to contemporary issues elicits more questions about the role of NGOs in global governance. To start with, we can ponder the question posed by Peter van Tuijl, Executive Director of the Global Partnership for the Prevention of Armed Conflict (GPPAC): 'do the increasing numbers of NGOs and NGO networks represent hope and building blocks for a system of global governance that will enforce human rights more effectively?'[49] His answer is affirmative, based on the quality of the relationships and networks that they have across local, domestic and international fora. More direct questions could be; what should we think of NGOs working within the often-contested spaces of Global South-North global governance? How do they impact on the imbalances in the global governance structures? Are there avenues for countering hegemony within transnational networks and NGO work in international criminal justice?

Often, lawyers view NGOs in terms of their specific contribution to the dimensions of global justice, i.e. as advocates or partners in the field. An ICC judge I interviewed asserted that 'NGOs may be the principal force in pushing for universal jurisdiction'.[50] To David Crane, the founding Chief Prosecutor of the SCSL, the rise of grassroots efforts by NGOs is a key element in the age of accountability.[51] This Special Tribunal had a very good relationship with NGOs and needed their support, particularly the Office of the Prosecutor.[52] Not forgetting that NGOs were influential in the interpretation of the Special Court Agreement (Ratification) Act of 2002, with regard to the contested legal relationship between the Tribunal and the Truth and Reconciliation.[53] If we are to go by these assertions, it would seem logical to suggest that NGOs are indirectly tailored towards the promotion of norms of global governance in different contexts and countries.

The donor-driven and often top-down dimensions of international criminal justice leave NGOs with little room to navigate the political economy. As also observed by Dustin Sharp, technical assistance and funding provided by international NGOs and donors contribute to global–local dilemmas and imbalances in the field, mostly in the relation to the work of international criminal courts and tribunals.[54] Internationalised tribunals in countries like Uganda, Cambodia and Sierra Leone were largely funded by powerful external actors, who also extended support to NGOs. From a

---

48 Buckel and Fischer-Lescano (2009, pp. 437–454 and Chakraborty (2016, p. 24).

49 Van Tuijl (1999, p. 511).

50 Interview with ICC judge, 4 March 2021.

51 Interview with David M. Crane, Founding Chief Prosecutor, 1 March 2021.

52 Interview with David M. Crane, Founding Chief Prosecutor, 1 March 2021.

53 For more details see Schabas (2004, p. 166, 174,175).

54 Sharp (2014, pp. 97–99).

law and development point of view, one could argue that such interventions are part and parcel of foreign-policy strategies of donor States like the US. However, these donor aid dimensions are closely linked with the push towards adoption of norms of international criminal justice, as evidenced in this book, but also in other contexts like Sierra Leone.[55]

Besides the tribunals, global governance also manifests in the work of Commissions of Inquiry. As is revealed by empirical work on the practices of International Commissions of Inquiry, proponents of these models may have more goals that simply achieving transitional justice.[56] The recommendations that such commissions make also add important dimensions to the Global South-North power dynamics. For example, the International Commission of Inquiry on Darfur strongly recommended that the UNSC refers the situation to the ICC.[57] As was also noted by scholars, the resultant UNSC action triggered hostility by the government against local NGOs in Sudan.[58]

I add my voice to interdisciplinary scholarship on NGO participation in global governance, alive to the fact that their work is usually shaped by 'incentives and pressures at global and national levels' involving domestic politics and overseas aid.[59] The UN Fact-Finding Mission on the Gaza Conflict (Goldstone Commission) is a classic example of the way in which global power dynamics impact on the implementation of norms of international law. Aside from Israel's refusal to cooperate with the mechanisms, the mixed responses from States remind us about the politicised nature of global governance, where States and Non-State actors comply with recommendations if they resonate with their own geopolitical interests.[60] These power dynamics ultimately shape the ways in which NGOs are perceived by both States and the conflict-affected people. It is not surprising that the Goldstone Commission report triggered a backlash on local NGOs in Israel and the Occupied Palestinian Territory, that were perceived as biased against Israel.[61] Likewise, in Kenya, NGO interventions in transitional justice were largely influenced by local political actors and international pressure.[62]

A notable observation from the book relates to the high level of competition among some NGOs working on particular aspects of transitional justice, for example, victims' reparations. As also acknowledged by the International Center for Transitional Justice (ICTJ), there is increasing competition within NGOs for funding towards their transitional justice activities:

---

[55] Kendall (2011, pp. 585–606).

[56] Becker and Nouwen (2019, p. 841).

[57] See Report of the International Commission of Inquiry on Darfur to the United Nations Secretary-General, Pursuant to Security Council Resolution 1564 of 18 September 2004, Geneva, 25 January 2005, available at https://www.un.org/ruleoflaw/files/com_inq_darfur.pdf.

[58] Becker and Nouwen (2019, p. 837).

[59] Henry et al. (2019, pp. 291–332).

[60] Farer (2010, pp. 139–143), Schabas (2010, pp. 307–312).

[61] Khoury-Bisharat (2019, p. 887).

[62] Hansen and Sriram (2015, p. 462).

> [T]he current global environment is one of increasing competition among nonprofit organizations for financial support, and funders increasingly demand evidence of what works (and what works where) in order to inform their funding decisions. Actors in the transitional justice sector face the challenge of producing this evidence while there is little agreement among practitioners, donors, and stakeholders on the right approach and means to do so.[63]

The above statement is important for two reasons: Firstly, it reminds us that NGOs do not operate in a vacuum, at least in the field of transitional justice. They need to meet the expectations of several stakeholders, besides the victims and conflict-affected communities that they represent or advocate for. Secondly, they are faced with a challenge of having to justify their actions or strategies, to their donors or funders. What can be inferred from these multifaceted interactions is that the work of NGOs in this era of global governance remains largely tilted towards the interests of the Global North.

Against this background, investigating the legitimacy of institutions like the ICC will remain an important dimension, especially for scholars examining the influence of global governance on conflict resolution and accountability. The legitimation of the work of institutions like the ICC by NGOs is not entirely motivated by their own missions or ideas, but also their ability to maintain funding for their activities. Similarly, transnational networks and NGOs also need to work with influential State actors, in order to push the envelope of universal jurisdiction across the global spaces. We are thus reminded that the work of NGOs amidst global justice making is not always a bed of roses, especially for those operating in the Global South.

A pertinent issue relates to the ways in which NGOs could localise global norms of accountability in ways that fit with the realities of the conflict-affected people in the Global South. One salient observation that I make in the nook pertains to the element of diffusing transitional justice norms within the Rohingya population and conflict-affected communities in Northern Uganda. I posited that the discourse and practice of NGOs explain why particular transitional justice norms are adopted within the local contexts. For international relation scholars, a key point of concern is why these ideas and norms are accepted in some societies, yet rejected in others.[64]

Where this concept might link with the empirical observations in this book is on the relationship between local and international NGOs, and how they engage with global justice. I have shown how International NGOs (INGOs) with transnational networks engage directly with the ICC and ICJ. In some cases, they obscure the roles of local NGOs, as they act as direct interlocutors with the institutions. In situations where there are divergent local discourses on transitional justice, local NGOs are placed in a difficult situation where they need to satisfy different stakeholders—victims, conflict-affected communities, states and the international community. As such, some local NGOs often clash in their ideological discourse with INGOs, as they work to implement transitional justice. This brings me to the question on how to achieve global governance without relegating the voices of local NGOs and other actors in the Global South. This is an issue that requires further scholarly attention.

---

[63] Porciuncula (2021, p. 2).

[64] Acharya (2004, p. 240).

Proponents of global justice will have to deal with the moderate voices in the field, as more NGOs consider alternatives to institutions like the ICC. As I showed in the book, NGOs are not entirely dependent on ICC-related work. Whilst they tend to strategise around the Court's intervention within the situations, they also maintain spaces for dialogues in respect to other alternative judicial avenues, for example, hybrid courts or specialised tribunals. In this book, I have not conceptualised NGOs as intermediaries—a conceptual departure from emerging scholarship in International Criminal Justice which perceives NGOs as intermediaries of the ICC within the situations.[65]

Whilst I acknowledge that NGO work is akin to that of intermediaries in some instances, I see a wider scope for engaging with transitional justice in general, beyond the work of globalised institutions of justice. I agree with transitional justice scholars and practitioners who recommend for broader engagement of NGOs in transitional justice-formulating and implementing polices, promoting reconciliation following armed conflict, promoting victims' and womens' participation and regional networking.[66] One thing that comes out clearly is that more structured networking is key for the promotion of global governance.

The future of global governance within the auspices of international criminal justice will largely depend on the activities of global NGO networks like the Asia Justice Coalition and the Coalition for the CICC. The ways in which these networks enhance the legitimacy of institutions like the ICC have been explicated in depth in the book findings. The CICC is regarded as an important turn in achieving global governance reform, evidenced from its role in the establishment of the ICC.[67] The Report of the Commission on Global Security, Justice and Governance further illustrates the benefit of this kind of multi-stakeholder networking:

> Such an approach [international public dialogues] to diffusing norms, reframing issues, and building transnational coalitions will allow for international actors with specific interests and expertise to identify linkages and undertake specific campaigns within the overall, broad reform effort.[68]

For the future, we need to pay closer attention to decision-making dimensions of transnational networks and NGO networks in global governance. Policy implementation forms the bulk of the analysis on NGO work in international criminal justice. However, there is a shift in dynamics of their engagement with global governance, beyond the usual consultative and implementation roles. In fact, some commentators are already contemplating what they call a 'Third and Fourth United Nations', encompassing NGOs and other intergovernmental organisations.[69] If we are to achieve what David Crane calls the 'Third Wave' of accountability, we need to pay closer attention

---

65 Haslam and Edmunds (2013, pp. 49–85, Ullrich (2016, pp. 543–568 and De Silva 2017, pp. 170–188).

66 See for instance Amenya and Mpaayei (2015, p. 14).

67 See Report of the Commission on Global Security, Justice & Governance (2015, p. 106).

68 Report of the Commission on Global Security, Justice & Governance (2015, p. 108).

69 Report of the Commission on Global Security, Justice & Governance (2015, p. 97).

to the emerging NGOs and grassroots movements.[70] Their ability to make important decisions, informed by local expertise and knowledge, would have a bearing on the hegemonic parameters within international criminal justice.

3 Limitations and Opportunities for Further Research and Engagement

Empirical research on the legitimacy of institutions of global governance is of valuable benefit to the ICC, in addition to other stakeholders in international law. As different commentators have argued, the understandings of the ICC's mission and work within different audiences-local and global, also determine the type of strategies that decision makers make.[71] As also noted from Phil Clark's research, the ICC also utilises research findings on local perceptions to legitimise its work.[72] Justifications for the focus on the ICC are based on emerging views of the Court as a mechanism for transitional justice, premised on its local justice narratives and centralisation of victims as key constituents.[73] The political economy of global governance extends the ICC's area of influence, through the work of transnational networks and NGOs. Such interfaces show that global justice making is a lot more than the orthodox black letter law in the Statutes. Lawyers engaged in ICL ought to understand the dynamics of the institutions and the constituencies which they serve.

Assessing the future of NGOs within the contested spaces of global governance requires careful methodological and theoretical choices. The analytical theory of legitimacy has proved handy in this book, as it has shown a link between the work of global institutions and the audiences they seek to serve. However, one could also consider exploring in detail the 'global–local divide' as another relevant frame that can be used to assess the work of NGOs in global governance. Whereas a depth of literature in transitional justice refers to concepts of 'local' and 'global', there is need for empirical or socio-legal studies on how NGOs influence or impact on global governance, and how they link with the (counter) hegemonic practices. Like I have argued elsewhere, local NGOs can counter-hegemonic global governance through the choice of transitional justice—reconciliatory approaches relegate the position and viability of international criminal justice.[74]

On the flipside, using the global–local frame requires one to be cautious about the nature of the context in which they seek to research. Empirical findings show that the global–local discourses are not entirely reflective of the actual sites of justice. As I revealed in Chapter "Mapping NGO work in Myanmar: Impact of Transnational Networks", there are influential Bangladesh and diaspora-based NGOs working on

[70] Crane (2020, p. 415).

[71] deGuzman (2020, p. 389); Ullrich (2016, p. 547).

[72] Clark (2018, p. 101).

[73] deGuzman (2020, p. 392).

[74] See Kirabira (2023, pp. 153–174).

Rohingya justice. For the Ugandan case, some NGOs examined are based outside the sites of justice in Northern Uganda. In essence, I lend credence to prior findings by Leila Ullrich, who suggests that the global–local frame is not always self-evident, 'but claims that different actors make to particular forms of legitimacy'.[75]

As I argued elsewhere in respect to the backlash against the ICC in Africa, international law scholars will need to do more examination of the African engagement with the emerging regional justice systems.[76] The backlash against global institutions like the ICC reflects a crisis in global governance, in the last decade. A critical analysis of victim-oriented discourses in African countries, like I have done previously, illustrates that the ICC is still a relevant institution in Africa.[77] Nonetheless, the global power dynamics embedded in processes like UNSC referrals have dire impacts on the national sovereignty of African states. The hugely debated issues on the ICC's relevance in Africa certainly have an implication on the strategies that NGOs make, within the field of transitional justice.

As I posited on the backlash, besides the aspect of sovereignty, there is an alternate ideology that can be understood and perhaps negotiated with the broader goals of universal jurisdiction.[78] The alternative ideology can be reflected in the discourse on using regional mechanisms to respond to atrocities. At the same time, there are key gaps in the use of such mechanisms, ranging from limited ratification of key instruments and clauses that accord immunity to leaders accused of crimes. NGO actors will need to navigate the normative gaps and challenges related to the global governance system, by engaging more at national and regional levels. Much as one might argue that the African regional systems are constrained by power dynamics, the same thing can be noted from the ICC interventions (referrals) under the auspices of a highly politicised UNSC. As such, I reiterate the importance of exploring the alternatives to the hegemonic global order.

One way for scholars to explore new alternatives to the polarised global justice order is to explore how to implement the African Union Transitional Justice (AUTJ) Policy Framework. No doubt, there are Global North–South gaps in the understandings and beliefs about transitional justice aspects like reconciliation and retribution. As I have argued elsewhere, NGOs have a key role to play in the domestic implementation of the AUTJ Policy Framework.[79] However, the dimensions of justice and accountability are also evident within the African transitional justice framework. What this means for proponents of international criminal justice is that there is still an explicit avenue to provide judicial redress for victims of gross human rights violations. The drawback is that regional and sub-regional bodies would take priority over the orthodox forms of universal jurisdiction. As also acknowledged by practitioners and researchers on global justice, the rise of such institutions can either contribute

---

[75] Ullrich (2016, p. 550).

[76] Kirabira (2021a, pp. 23–33).

[77] Kirabira (2021a, pp. 23–33).

[78] Kirabira (2021b, pp. 340–343).

[79] Kirabira (2021d, pp. 180–201).

to or detract from the global justice infrastructure.[80] As such, proponents of international criminal justice should make efforts to integrate these key actors in the adoption and implementation of their programmes.

On the African continent, scholars should look deeper into the genealogy of the new African Court of Justice—a reconceptualisation of the AU and African States engagement with global justice. A key normative development to think about is the Malabo Protocol for the African Court (Malabo Protocol), which extended the jurisdiction of the African Court of Justice and Human Rights, to include international criminal accountability based on international law.[81] This regional mechanism has the potential to shift the attention of States in Africa away from The Hague. Of particular importance is the discourse around the formulation of this African mechanism. As revealed in legal anthropology, the reconceptualisation of accountability in Africa is largely motivated by States' desires to break away from the deep inequalities embedded in the global justice system.[82] Proponents of global justice will equally have to deal with the Pan-African campaigns in a way that supports the new regional initiatives. The critical narratives of global justice making as a means to enforce liberal Western norms of justice would be better overtaken by shifting the focus to the regionalised accountability approaches.

How should NGOs engage with the new African accountability mechanisms? Whilst transnational networks and NGOs played a key role in the formulation of the Malabo Protocol, the institutions maintain a restrictive approach towards the actual participation of NGOs in their work- there is a narrow window for NGO observer status.[83] This restriction has negative implications for any counter-hegemonic strategists. In essence, NGOs might engage more with the Hague-based system. As also noted by key NGO representatives in Africa, the organisations should keep pushing for the universal ratification of the necessary legal instruments like the African Protocol on the Establishment of an African Court on Human and Peoples' Rights.[84] In this regard, more NGOs could engage with the existing networks like the Coalition for an Effective African Court (ACC). Like I showed in the book, ratification of the normative instruments provides a solid foundation for transitional justice in general.

The findings of this book call for careful reflection on the implementation of global accountability in a polarised environment. An important issue for international lawyers to think about is how to respond to both colonial and post-colonial legacies which have a bearing on contemporary conflicts like that of the Rohingya in Myanmar. By examining the historical dimensions of the Rohingya conflict, the book lends credence to international lawyers' concerns on the inherent relationship between colonialism and accountability, and the adverse impacts of post-colonial statehood.[85]

---

[80] See Report of the Commission on Global Security, Justice & Governance (2015, p. 95).

[81] For more details see Nsereko (2011, pp. 337–354).

[82] Clarke (2019a, pp. 177–216).

[83] For a more detailed analysis see Belay and Biegon (2019, p. 1108).

[84] Belay and Biegon (2019, p. 1123).

[85] See in particular Shahabuddin (2019, pp. 334–358).

This is where the broader field of transitional justice becomes relevant, in so far as it transcends formal judicial accountability, allowing for a range of approaches depending on the context. For example, achieving transitional justice in respect to colonial legacies of violence and gross violations of human rights is an uphill task. As much an international lawyers grapple with questions of how to address such crimes, non-judicial transitional justice is best suited to address these legacies, through the establishment of official historical records, shaping of narratives about the past, and social transformations. Little wonder, there have been normative shifts in the scope of transitional justice in the past years, to include transformative elements like social and economic rights and forms of political engagement.[86]

Just like Obiora Okafor, I posit that global power matrices—ranging from military, political, economic and social relations—have a huge impact on how international norms are implemented.[87] Here, we can pose a question; to what extent do these global power dynamics affect the way in which NGOs approach transitional justice? To this end, scholars need to re-evaluate the relationships of key stakeholders in global justice, in a manner that challenges the hegemonic international legal order. Some attempts have been made by international lawyers to explore how to respond to colonial and post-colonial wrongs. For Myanmar, Morten Bergsmo provides a nuanced understanding of Rakhine's demography in light of the transfer of civilians into colonial Burma by the British.[88] As such, ICL could expand to incorporate broader technical definitions of crimes like transfer of civilians into occupied territory and deportation out of a territory. Otherwise, as argued by Ryan Mitchell, ICL runs the risk of de-legitimisation, for its failure to address colonial crimes like those in Myanmar.[89]

As a final note, scholars would need to deal with the double standards in international law, including the implementation of accountability mechanisms. Addressing this dilemma is important because of the growing involvement of the international community, including NGOs, in situations where there is active armed conflict or mass atrocities—examples include Sudan, Ukraine and Palestine.

At the peak of the armed conflicts in Ukraine and Gaza, the language of international law and global governance form a great part of public and State discourses-notably the potential impact from interventions at The Hague-based institutions.[90] Of particular concern are the inconsistencies in how both States and non-State actors relate with these interventions- either support or push pack against the measures. With the evolving international legal order that places strong emphasis on accountability, scholars should not overlook the imperial power of the United States and other Western based countries.[91] Specifically, seeking accountability for the unlawful use of force by powerful countries in contexts like Ukraine, Iraq and Afghanistan would

[86] Van der Merwe and Moyo (2020, p. 52).

[87] Okafor (2017, pp. 179–194).

[88] Bergsmo (2020, p. 234).

[89] Mitchell (2020, pp. 285–315).

[90] See also Krever et al. (2024, pp. 217–301).

[91] See generally Sadat (2018, pp. 851–872).

start from the sort of narratives that are created by equally powerful transnational networks and NGOs.

A report by Amnesty International on the Russia-Ukraine war detailed how 'Ukrainian fighting tactics endanger civilians'.[92] However, the executive director of the Ukrainian office of Amnesty International resigned following the publication of the report, questioning the credibility of the allegations, noting that:

> Of course, no one can be expected to understand the local context and languages of every conflict. But instead of trusting and relying on local staff, some international organizations like Amnesty fail to be inclusive and centralize decision-making, which was the case with this report.[93]

Amnesty International's report elicited widespread criticism from key observers including Gerald Steinberg, the founder and president of NGO Monitor.[94] The criticism and backlash suffered by Amnesty International are a perfect illustration of the precarious positions of NGOs, especially where they report on violations of IHRL or war crimes during active conflicts.[95] As such, global governance and its dynamics are equally embedded in other contexts, besides Africa and the Global South. Exploring these debates would help challenge the notions that global justice and accountability are primarily targeted for States in the Global South. The questions that come to mind are; why do NGOs approve the creation of hybrid tribunals or ICC interventions in some situations, and not others? As such, the practice and discourse of key actors in respect to the contemporary global issues remain crucial. I will close this chapter with a quote from Professor Tim Murithi on the need to reform the current system of global governance; 'the era of globalisation is here to stay, and the challenge is to create institutions to be able to respond to international issues before they threaten the survival of humanity'.[96]

References

Abrams E (2022) Amnesty international's attack on Ukraine. Council on Foreign Relations. New York. https://www.cfr.org/blog/amnesty-internationals-attack-ukraine

Acharya A (2004) How ideas spread: whose norms matter? norm localization and institutional change in Asian regionalism. Int Organ 54:239–275

Amenya C, Mpaayei F (2015) International conference on transitional justice in post-conflict societies in Africa. Hekima Institute of Peace Studies and International Relations, Nairobi

Amnesty International (2022) Ukraine: Ukrainian fighting tactics endanger civilians. Amnesty International. New York. https://www.amnesty.org/en/latest/news/2022/08/ukraine-ukrainian-fighting-tactics-endanger-civilians/

---

[92] Amnesty International (2022).

[93] Pokalchuk (2022).

[94] See Abrams (2022); Steinberg (2022).

[95] Langrand (2022).

[96] Murithi (2018).

Becker M, Nouwen SM (2019) International commissions of inquiry: what difference do they make? taking an empirical approach. Eur J Int Law 30:819–841
Belay N, Biegon J (2019) Civil society and international criminal justice in Africa: perspectives on the proposed African court of justice and human rights. In: Jalloh C, Clarke KM, Nmehielle V (eds) The African court of justice and human and peoples' rights in context: development and challenges. CUP, Cambridge, pp 1101–1124
Bergsmo M (2020) Myanmar, colonial aftermath, and access to international law. In: Bergsmo M, Kaleck W, Hlaing KY (eds) Colonial wrongs and access to international law. Torkel Opsahl Academic EPublisher, Brussels, pp 229–252
Birdsall A (2010) The 'monster that we need to slay'? global governance, the United States, and the international criminal court. Glob Gov 16:451–469
Birkett D (2019) Twenty years of the Rome Statute of the international criminal court: appraising the state of national implementing legislation in Asia. Chin J Int Law 18:353–392
Branch A (2017) Dominic Ongwen on trial: the ICC's African dilemmas. Int J TransitAl Justice 11:30–49
Buckel S, Fischer-Lescano A (2009) Gramsci reconsidered: hegemony in global law. Leiden J Int Law 22:437–454
Burgis-Kasthala M, Sander B (2024) Contemporary international criminal law after critique: towards decolonial and abolitionist (dis-)engagement in an era of anti-impunity. J Int Crim Justice 22:127–150
Burke-White W (2005) Complementarity in practice: the international criminal court as part of a system of multi-level global governance in the democratic republic of Congo. Leiden J Int Law 18:557–590
Cady J, Booth N (2004) Internationalized courts in Kosovo: An UNMIK perspective. In: Romano C, Nollkaemper A, Kleffner J (eds) Internationalized criminal courts: Sierra Leone, East Timor, Kosovo, and Cambodia. OUP, New York, pp 59–78
Canefe N (2021) Crimes against humanity: limits of universal jurisdiction in the global south. University of Wales Press, Cardiff
Cassese A (2004) The role of internationalized courts and tribunals in the fight against international criminality. In: Romano C, Nollkaemper A, Kleffner J (eds) Internationalized criminal courts: Sierra Leone, East Timor, Kosovo, and Cambodia. OUP, New York, pp 3–14
Chakraborty SL (2016) Gramsci's idea of civil society. Int J Res Humlties Soc Stud 3:19–27
Clarke KM (2015) Refiguring the perpetrator: Culpability, history and international criminal law's impunity gap. Int J Hum Rights 19:592–614
Clarke KM (2019a) Affective justice: the international criminal court and the Pan-Africanist pushback. Duke University Press, Durham, North Carolina
Clarke KM (2019b) Affective justice: the racialized imaginaries of international justice. Polit Leg Anthropol Rev 42:244–267
Clark P (2018) Distant justice the impact of the international criminal court on African politics. CUP, Cambridge
Commission on Global Security, Justice & Governance (2015) Report of the commission on global security, justice and governance. The Hague Institute for Global Justice and the Stimson Center, The Hague and Washington, DC, pp 1–136
Crane D (2020) The third wave-accountability for international crimes in an age of extremes. Case West Reserv J Int Law 52:407–416
deGuzman M (2020) Mission uncertain: what communities does the ICC serve? In: deGuzman M, Oosterveld V (eds) The Elgar companion to the international criminal court. Edward Elgar Publishing, Cheltenham, pp 387–407
De Silva N (2017) Intermediary complexity in regulatory governance: the international criminal court's use of NGOs in regulating international crimes. Ann Am Acad Pol Soc Sci 670:170–188
Engle K (2015) Anti-Impunity and the turn to criminal law in human rights. Cornell Law Rev 100:1070–1127
Farer T (2010) Introduction. Glob Gov 16:139–143

Hansen TO, Sriram CL (2015) Fighting for justice (and survival): Kenyan civil society accountability strategies and their enemies. Int J TransitAl Justice 9:407–427
Haslam E, Edmunds R (2013) Managing a new 'partnership': 'professionalization', intermediaries and the international criminal court. Crim Law Forum 24:49–85
Henry L, Sundstrom L, Winston C, Bala-Miller P (2019) NGO participation in global governance institutions: International and domestic drivers of engagement. Interes Groups Advocacy 8:291–332
Jeßberger F, Mehta K, Steinl L (2023) Hegemony and international criminal law—an introduction. In: Jeßberger F, Mehta K, Steinl L (eds) International criminal law—a counter hegemonic project? Asser Press, The Hague, T.M.C, pp 1–9
Kendall S (2011) Donors' justice: recasting international criminal accountability. Leiden J Int Law 24:585–606
Khoury-Bisharat H (2019) The unintended consequences of the goldstone commission of inquiry on human rights organizations in Israel. Eur J Int Law 30:877–901
Kirabira TR (2021a) Surrender of Ali Kushayb and Paul Gicheru: new perspectives in Africa's relationship with the ICC. NY Univ J Int Law Polit 54:23–33
Kirabira TR (2021b) Book review: Africa and the backlash against international courts by Peter Brett and Line Engbo Gissel. Soc Leg Stud 31:340–343
Kirabira TR (2021c) NGO influence in global governance: Achieving transitional justice in Uganda and beyond. Cambridge Int Law J 10:280–299
Kirabira TR (2021d) The role of NGOs in the domestic implementation of the African Union transitional justice policy framework: perspectives from Uganda. Afr Hum Rights Yearb 5:180–201
Kirabira TR (2023) NGOs and legitimacy of international criminal justice in Uganda. In: Jeßberger F, Mehta K, Steinl L (eds) International criminal law—a counter hegemonic project? Asser Press, The Hague, T.M.C, pp 153–174
Kirabira TR, Sehmi A (2022) C. Schwöbel-Patel, marketing global justice: the political economy of international criminal law.Leiden J Int Law 35:725–729
Klamberg M (2020) Rebels, the Vanquished, Rogue states and scapegoats in the crosshairs: hegemony in international criminal justice. In: Bergsmo M, Klamberg M, Lohne K, Mahony C (eds) Power in international criminal justice. Torkel Opsahl Academic EPublisher, Brussels, pp 623–646
Kotiswaran P, Palmer N (2015) Rethinking the 'international law of crime': provocations from transnational legal studies. Transnatl Leg Theory 6:55–88
Krever T et al (2024) On international law and Gaza: critical reflections. Lond Rev Int Law 12:217–301
Langrand M (2022) Amnesty report on Ukraine: Do the rules of war apply to everyone? Geneva Solutions, Geneva. https://genevasolutions.news/peace-humanitarian/amnesty-report-on-ukraine-do-rules-of-war-apply-to-everyone
Lohne K (2021) Penal welfarism 'gone global'? Comparing international criminal justice to the culture of control. Punishment Soc 23:3–23
McAuliffe P (2013) The roots of transitional accountability: interrogating the justice cascade. Int J Law Context 9:106–123
Mégret F (2016) The anxieties of international criminal justice.Leiden J Int Law 29:197–221
Meijer E (2004) The extraordinary chambers in the courts of Cambodia for prosecuting crimes committed by the Khmer Rouge: jurisdiction, organization, and procedure of an internationalized national tribunal. In: Romano C, Nollkaemper A, Kleffner J (eds) Internationalized criminal courts: Sierra Leone, East Timor, Kosovo, and Cambodia. OUP, New York, pp 207–232
Minkova L (2021) Expressing what? The stigmatization of the defendant and the ICC's institutional interests in the Ongwen case. Leiden J Int Law 34:223–245
Mitchell R (2020) Myanmar and the hegemonic discourse of international criminal law. In: Bergsmo M, Kaleck W, Hlaing KY (eds) Myanmar, colonial aftermath, and access to international law. Torkel Opsahl Academic EPublisher, Brussels, pp 285–315

Murithi T (2018) GUEST BLOG: Towards a Revised UN Architecture for Peace. Global Vision Institute, Exeter. https://globalvisioninstitute.org/guest-blog-towards-revised-un-architecture-peace/2229

Nesiah V (2016) Local ownership of global governance. J Int Crim Justice 14:985–1009

Nouwen SM (2019) Return to sender: let the international court of justice justify or qualify international-criminal-court exceptionalism regarding personal immunities. Cambridge Law J 78:596–611

Nouwen SM, Werner W (2015) Monopolizing global justice. J Int Crim Justice 13:157–176

Nsereko DN (2011) The international criminal court and Africa. In: Ssenyonjo M (ed) The African regional human rights system: 30 years after the African charter on human and peoples' rights. Brill | Nijhoff, Leiden, pp 337–354

Okafor OC (2017) Between tunnel vision and a sliding scale: power, normativity and justice in the praxis of the international criminal court. Temple Int Comp Law J 13:179–194

Pokalchuk O (2022) What Amnesty got wrong in Ukraine and why I had to resign. The Washington Post, Washington DC. https://www.washingtonpost.com/opinions/2022/08/13/amnesty-ukraine-civilians-at-risk-why-i-quit/

Porciuncula M (2021) Measuring results and monitoring progress of transitional justice processes. International Center for Transitional Justice, New York, pp 1–32

Ramji-Nogales J (2015) Bespoke transitional justice at the international criminal court. In: De Vos C, Kendall S, Stahn C (eds) Contested justice the politics and practice of international criminal court interventions. CUP, Cambridge, pp 106–121

Robins S (2012) Transitional justice as an elite discourse. CritAl Asian Stud 44:3–30

Rowen J (2018) The transformation of legal ideas: the globalization and politicization of transitional justice in the Middle East. In: Christensen MJ, Levi R (eds) International practices of criminal justice, 1st edn. Routledge, Abingdon, pp 50–65

Sadat LN (2018) Seeking accountability for the unlawful use of force. CUP, Cambridge

Sander B (2019) The expressive turn of international criminal justice: a field in search of meaning. Leiden J Int Law 32:851–872

Sayed H (2019) The regulatory function of the turn to anti-impunity in the practice of international human rights law. Stanf J Int Law 55:1–26

Schabas W (2004) Internationalized courts and their relationship with alternative accountability mechanisms: the case of Sierra Leone. In: Romano C, Nollkaemper A, Kleffner J (eds) Internationalized criminal courts: Sierra Leone, East Timor, Kosovo, and Cambodia. OUP, New York, pp 157–180

Schabas W (2010) Gaza, goldstone, and lawfare. Case West Reserv J Int Law 43:307–312

Schwöbel-Patel C (2016) Spectacle in international criminal law: the fundraising image of victimhood. London Rev of Int Law 4:247–274

Schwöbel-Patel C (2018) The "Ideal" victim of international criminal law. Eur J Int Law 29:703–724

Schwöbel-Patel C (2021) Marketing global justice: the political economy of int criminal law. CUP, Cambridge

Shahabuddin M (2019) Post-colonial Boundaries, International Law, and the Making of the Rohingya Crisis in Myanmar. Asian J Int Law 9: 334–358

Sharp D (2013) Beyond the post-conflict checklist: linking peacebuilding and transitional justice through the lens of critique. Chic J Int Law 14:165–196

Sharp D (2014) Addressing dilemmas of the global and the local in transitional justice. Emory Int Law Rev 29:71–117

Sharp D (2015a) Development, human rights and transitional justice: global projects for global governance. Int J TransitAl Justice 9:517–526

Sharp D (2015b) Emancipating transitional justice from the bonds of the paradigmatic transition. Int J TransitAl Justice 9:150–169

Sriram CL (2005) Globalizing justice for mass atrocities a revolution in accountability, 1st edn. Routledge, Abingdon

Stahn C (2018) Legacy in international criminal justice. In: deGuzman M, Amann D (eds) Arcs of global justice: essays in honour of William A. Schabas. OUP, Oxford, pp 271–287
Steinberg G (2022) False accusations and ideological bias: amnesty international, Ukraine, and the illusion of NGO fact-finding expertise. Quillette, Sydney https://quillette.com/2022/08/11/false-accusations-and-ideological-bias/
Slye RC (2016) Reflections on Africa and international criminal law. In: Slye RC (ed) The Nuremberg principles in non-western societies: a reflection on their universality, legitimacy and application. International Nuremberg Principles Academy, Nuremberg, pp 230–242
Teitel R (2003) Transitional justice genealogy. Harv Hum Rights J 16:69–94
Teitel R (2008) Humanity law: a new interpretive lens on the international sphere. Fordham Law Rev 77:667–702
Ullrich L (2016) Beyond the 'global–local divide': local intermediaries, victims and the justice contestations of the international criminal court. J Int Crim Justice 14:543–568
van Tuijl P (1999) NGOs and human rights: sources of justice and democracy. J Int Aff Ed Board 52:493–512
van der Merwe H, Moyo A (2020) Transitional justice for colonial era abuses and legacies: African versus European policy priorities. In: Bergsmo M, Kaleck W, Hlaing KY (eds) Colonial wrongs and access to international law. Torkel Opsahl Academic EPublisher, Brussels, pp 41–67
Zürn M (2012) Global governance as multi-level governance. Levi-Faur D(ed) The oxford handbook of governance. OUP, Oxford, pp 730–741

MIX
Papier aus verantwortungsvollen Quellen
Paper from responsible sources
FSC® C105338

If you have any concerns about our products,
you can contact us on
ProductSafety@springernature.com

In case Publisher is established outside the EU,
the EU authorized representative is:
Springer Nature Customer Service Center GmbH
Europaplatz 3, 69115 Heidelberg, Germany

Printed by Libri Plureos GmbH
in Hamburg, Germany